The Best of Patsy Clairmont

The Best of
Patsy
Clairmont

Three Bestselling Books
Complete in One Volume

God Uses Cracked Pots

Normal is Just
a Setting on Your Dryer

Sportin' a 'Tude

Inspirational Press . New York

First Inspirational Press edition published in 1999.

Inspirational Press
A division of BBS Publishing Corporation
386 Park Avenue South
New York, NY 10016

Inspirational Press is a registered trademark of BBS Publishing Corporation.

Published by arrangement with Focus on the Family.

Library of Congress Catalog Card Number: 99-71869

ISBN: 0-88486-250-X

Printed in the United States of America.

Contents

God Uses Cracked Pots

To the men in my life

My husband

Les, without your constant nudging and your willingness to help me carve out time in my jammed schedule and your vigilance to guard that time, this book would not have been completed. Your confidence in this project was a constant source of encouragement. Thank you, too, for adding your spunky and mischievous humor to my life, our marriage and our home.

Our sons

Marty and Jason, I take delight in both of you. Thank you for all the ways you lace my life with laughter and fill my heart with joy.

Contents

Acknowledgments

Thanks to all of you who supported this effort through your friendship and words of encouragement. I feel fortunate to have so many cheerleaders in my life.

I have often been aware of my mom's (Rebecca McEuen) prayers and am grateful for her love for Him and for me.

A big thank you to the Pauls for the loan of paradise during the countdown on my manuscript.

Thank you, Bob and Sarah, for helping to "prop" me up.

Mary-Lou, thanks for your willingness to put the manuscript into the computer. What a tedious task, which you did with such grace.

Ginny, your calls and notes of love and confidence were often the gentle nudge I needed.

I had tried to write previous to this book without success. I believe the key that unlocked my words was two-fold: the Lord's timing and my gifted editor, Janet Kobobel.

Janet, your expertise and wonderful gift of encouragement helped me to realize a lifetime dream. Thank you for being both firm and funny and knowing when to do which. Thank you for your editorial nurturing, for laughing at my stories and at times being counselor as well as my friend.

For the past ten years, I have had the life- and ministry-expanding opportunity to work and travel with Florence Littauer on her C.L.A.S.S. staff. I would be amiss if I did not say a neon-sign thank-you to Florence for believing in me and for years of guidance.

Thanks also to Edith, Lana, Barbara, Jan, Lauren, Betty, Nancy, Joyce, Will, Rose, Jo Ann and Carol for listening and laughing.

1

All We, Like Cracked Pots

WOULD YOU SAY you are a person given to bursts of babble? Do you just *love* to talk?

Imagine your family's reaction if you suddenly became a quiet person. Perhaps they would say, "Praise the Lord; He lives!" Because they know it would take the power of God to make that adjustment in your personality.

Likewise those of you who are quiet and sweet . . . oh, so *sweet*. If you were to speak up loud and clear, your family might say, "Praise the Lord; He lives, and so does she!" They have been waiting to hear from you.

Such changes are examples of God working in our cracked lives. Picture an empty pitcher with a network of cracks down the front. Now imagine that pitcher filled with light and a lid put on the top. Where does the light shine through? The cracks.

That is the same way the Lord's light shines through our lives. Not so much by what we do well naturally, but by what He must do in us supernaturally for it to be so. Like going from talkative to tranquil and from cringing to courageous.

The stories in this book will validate that I am a cracked pot in need of divine repair. My prayer for myself is that His light shines through my cracks. And my prayer for you is that within these pages you will find reprieve from life's pressures, which add stress to your "pot," and that you might continue to shine brightly for Him.

2

Lookin' Good

I REMEMBER THE day well. It was one of those times when everything goes right. I took a shower and fixed my hair. It went just the way I wanted it to, as it so seldom does. I pulled on my new pink sweater, giving me added color, since I need all the help I can get. I pulled on my gray slacks and my taupe heels.

I checked the mirror and thought, *Lookin' good!*

Since it was a cool Michigan day, I slipped on my gray trench coat with pink on the lapels. I was color-coded from head to toe.

When I arrived in downtown Brighton, where I intended to take care of some errands, I was surprised to find heavy traffic. Brighton is a small town, but it has a large health food store. Usually, I can park right in front and run in.

But today business was so brisk I had to park two blocks away. When your attitude is right, and it's a great day, however, inconveniences and inter-ruptions are no big deal.

I thought, *I'll just bounce down the street in time to the sunshine.*

I got out of the car, bounced down the street, crossed the road and entered the store.

As I headed toward the back of the store, I caught my reflection in the glass doors of the refrigeration system. It reaffirmed I was lookin' good. While enjoying my mirrored self, I noticed something was following me. I turned and realized it was my panty hose!

I remembered the night before when I had done a little Wonder Woman act and taken panty hose and slacks off in one fell swoop. This morning I put on new panty hose and must have pushed the old hose through when I pulled on my slacks.

I believe they made their emergence as I bounced down the street in time to the sunshine. I remem-bered the truck driver who stopped his truck to let me cross. As I looked up, he was laughing, and I thought, *Oh, look! The whole world is happy today.*

So I waved. Little did I realize how much I was waving.

I assumed I had reached some amount of matu-rity by this time in my life, but I can honestly say that when I looked back and saw that . . . that . . . dangling participle, the thought that crossed my mind was *I am going to die!*

I knew they were my panty hose because the right foot was securely wrapped around my right ankle. I knew it was secure because I tried to shake the thing off and pretend I had picked it up in the street.

It's amazing to me that we gals buy these things in flat little packages, we wear them once, and they grow. Now I had a mammoth handful of panty hose and no place to pitch them. The shelves were crowded with groceries, and my purse was too small and full, so I stuffed them in my coat pocket. They became a protruding hump on my right hip.

I decided to never leave that store. I knew all the store owners in town, and I figured that by now they would have all their employees at the windows waiting for a return parade.

I glanced cautiously around the store and noticed it was Senior Citizens' Day. They were having their blood pressures read, so I got in line to avoid having to leave the store.

The bad news was no one noticed I didn't belong in line. The good news was I had an elevated blood pressure reading. Usually nurses take mine and say, "I'm sorry but you died two days ago." Today I registered well up the scale.

Finally I realized I'd have to leave. I slipped out the door, down the street, into my car and off for home.

All the way home I said, "I'll never tell anyone I did this, I'll never tell anyone I did this, I'LL NEVER TELL ANYONE I DID THIS!"

I made it home and got out of the car. My husband was in the yard raking.

I screamed, "Do you know what I did?!"

He was so proud to know his wife had gone through town dragging her underwear. I told him I thought we should move—to another state—in the night. He thought that was extreme and suggested instead that for a while I could walk ten feet behind him. After thinking that through, we decided it should be ten feet in front of him so he could check me out.

If you have ever done anything to embarrass yourself, you know that the more you try not to think about it, the more it comes to you in living color. As I walked through my house, the replay of what I did came to me again and again.

At last I cried out to the Lord, "You take ashes and create beauty, but can You do anything with panty hose?"

Almost immediately I realized that I had dragged a lot worse things through my life than panty hose. I dragged guilt, anger, fear and shame. I was reminded by the Lord that those were far more unattractive and distracting than my hose, for they prevented others from seeing His presence and His power in my life. I needed to resolve the pain in my past that I might live more fully today and look forward to my tomorrows.

Excuse me, but what is that you're dragging?

3

Guest Appearance

I HAD JUST finished doing a seminar with speaker Florence Littauer in Texas. She had made a special point of reminding the audience, "Be alert to the people the Lord places around you, especially on airplanes."

This was a new thought for me. When I get on an airplane, I have two people in mind—the pilot and me. I am in deep prayer for both of us.

As I headed for the airport, I reminded myself to be alert.

The first leg of my flight was uneventful. Then we changed planes in Chicago, and I noticed an airline attendant helping to board an older woman in a wheelchair.

When my row was called, I found I was seated in front of the older woman. We each had an empty seat next to us. A few minutes later a young couple came down the aisle. They stopped at the row of the older woman.

The young woman looked at her ticket, looked at the number on the overhead panel, then leaned into the woman and said with contempt, "You're in my seat."

I turned around at this abruptness and saw the older lady shake her head and shrug her shoulders in an attempt to say, "I don't understand."

When the woman shrugged, the younger gal announced for all to hear, "You're in my seat!"

I tried to defuse the situation by saying, "Excuse me, but I don't think she speaks English."

The young woman turned on me and hissed, "I don't care what she speaks, I want her out of my seat." With that she called, "Stewardess."

Good, let the airlines handle her, I thought. I didn't want to deal with this traveling time bomb.

Usually flight personnel are trained to handle people problems. I think this attendant missed that class. She was almost as crude as the tactless traveler.

She looked down at the confused woman and demanded, "Let me see your tickets."

The older passenger realized this must be serious when she saw the attendant's uniform. Not understanding what they wanted, she gave her entire purse to the stewardess.

After rifling through her belongings, the flight gal found the ticket that verified the woman was in the wrong seat.

"Excuse me," I called to the attendant, "did you realize they boarded her in a wheelchair?"

"Really?" she whined, obviously annoyed. "This is going to make it harder to move her."

"Listen, why don't I move back there with her, and this . . . this . . . this couple can sit here," I said, pointing to my seat and the empty one beside me.

As I changed rows and took my new seat, I wanted this woman to know that all was well. I looked at her and smiled. She didn't respond.

Then I noticed she didn't have her seat belt on. I decided to help. It was a bigger job than I thought. I extended that belt as far as it would go, and it was prayer that closed it.

With that accomplished, I put on my belt, leaned back and closed my eyes. As the plane was taxiing for takeoff, I felt a hand on my hand. I turned and looked.

The older woman leaned over to me and slowly spoke the first words she had said, "You . . . first . . . Amer-i-can . . . be nice . . . to me."

Then taking her bracelet off her wrist, she pressed it into my hand and said, "I give you, you keep . . . okay?"

For a moment I couldn't respond. Then I swallowed the growing lump in my throat, slipped on the friendship bracelet and patted her hand. Her eyes filled with tears. My heart filled with gratitude.

Any room in your schedule for an unexpected guest?

4

Wiped Out

Mom, mom, come quick! You've got to see what's on TV," Jason insisted.

Certain it would be something to make housework easier, I raced to the living room. Much to my surprise, the young girl on the screen leaned forward and announced, "I've got a zit right here," pointing to her nose. "But it's okay," she encouraged, "because I have a stick of Erase."

Confused (and unamused) I stared at Jason, who sheepishly confessed, "Well, I just thought maybe you could use it on those . . . those . . . wrinkles." He gestured toward my well-deserved grooves of maturity.

"These are not wrinkles," I stated clearly.

Jason surveyed my face again, as if he was reading a well-worn map. "They look just like wrin—" he stammered, losing confidence as I moved toward him.

"Jason," I interrupted, "this is depth! The good Lord has just entrusted some of us with more depth than others."

I marched off, feeling insulted or at least slightly defaced. I thought about the girl on TV and remembered her remedy. I began to picture a stick of Erase, in fact a great big stick. Then I mentally erased Jason.

That was such fun I began to think of others who had said or done something I didn't appreciate. I thought of our eldest son, Marty.

Each day I would meet him at the door with a melodic greeting as he returned from work. His typical response was to grunt. I erased him.

Then my husband came to mind. Now he never actually says it, but at times his attitude seems to shout, "Is this all you've done today?" Erase.

I was really getting into this game. I thought of other family members, neighbors, checkout clerks, co-workers, bank tellers, beauticians. . . .

Now, the only drawback to this mental game was that everyone at one time or another had said or done something I didn't appreciate. By the time I erased them, it left me all alone. Somehow I didn't like the company.

I began to think of some things I've said or done I wished I could erase—like the last hasty word I felt "led" to say, or my unloving attitude with the clerk who was too slow, or the years I lost to agoraphobia, house-bound in fear. This game wasn't much fun after all.

Then I remembered that God provided a stick of Erase—a permanent eraser, the shed blood of Jesus. Our sins and iniquities He remembers no more—erase!

What a relief. What a release.

Pardon me, is that a stick of erase in your ha—

5

Hair-Raising

I CAN HARDLY believe that French braids are popular again. I was certain that type of braiding was leftover torture tactics from World War II and had worn out its welcome.

I certainly didn't welcome the times when Mom would call me into the living room where she had the weapons of warfare laid out before her: a brush and comb, a glass of water to help catch any stray ends, rubber bands and some ribbons. Sounds harmless enough . . . unless you're on the receiving end.

When Mom would plait my hair, it stayed in for a week. Those braids would not have dared move once she had placed them, nor did I while the braiding procedure was taking place.

I knew, from past experience, that the brush had a duo purpose of smoothing or rapping. She used quick staccato raps as reminders not to move. It worked.

The constant surprised look on my face in childhood pictures was actually caused by my coiffure. To implement this technique, Mom would first firmly grip three hanks of hair at the top of my head. It was imperative at this point to place one's knee in the middle of the braidee's back to secure one's hair hold, then pull until the victim's eyebrows arc and touch the first notch in the design of the braid. Come to think of it, I saw Hulk Hogan use that same tactic on one of his opponents . . . and win!

My mom always won, too. When she finished, my hair and I were enmeshed. Once Mom secured the lacing of hair and scalp with a rubber band, she then finished off the end with a ribbon, disguising this maiming updo with an innocent look.

People always commented on what a high forehead I had as a child. Actually that was my neck. It had been pulled up over my face in Mother's zeal to make the braids stay in. Had I continued to wear them that might not have mattered, but when the braids were finally released, my neck slid back down to my shoulders, leaving my face looking like a venetian blind.

The braiding did keep me from falling asleep in school. My lids were pulled so taut there wasn't enough skin left to cover my eyes.

Braids gave the boys a definite advantage, serving as handles to tug and jerk. Any girl with French braids would become hostile with the behind-the-back attack. Not only was it disconcerting, but we also knew if one of those braids was dislodged, our moms would redo the process.

Les and I have sons, but I've always wondered if we had had a daughter, would I have passed on this part of my heritage?

What painful part of your past are you passing on?

6

Forget It

I AM THE type of person who can walk from one room to another and not know why I've gone there. I know I had a reason when I began my trek, but I lost it on the way. Sometimes I try backing up in hopes it might come to me.

My family can usually tell this is the problem by the bewildered look on my face. Walking in reverse also seems to be a giveaway. Sometimes they try to help and other times they just let me wander aimlessly, figuring I'll wise up or wear out.

I try to blame this forgetfulness on age. But those who have known me for years remind me that my wires have never all been touching,

Just as I loomed over him, his eyes the size of saucers, he held up one hand and yelled, "Let's pray!"

Marty had learned a valuable lesson in life: "When Mommy talks to Jesus, we're all a lot better off."

Who lights your lava?

8

Half-Pint

MY DAD WAS a milkman when I was growing up, which might explain his nickname for me, "Half-Pint." His route was in the area where I attended school. I would sometimes see his truck from the window of my classroom as he delivered to his customers. One delivery stands out in my mind . . .

The girls' gym class was playing baseball on one end of the school field, and the boys were playing at the farthest opposite point. I guess that was supposed to help us stay focused on the game and not the guys. Actually, the boys were so far from us we didn't know they were there until . . . The Big Spill.

I was playing shortstop. I think I was given that spot because I was five feet tall (maybe that was why Dad called me Half-Pint).

I certainly wasn't put in the infield because I was good at catching the ball. Any hopes of that skill developing came to an abrupt halt when I stopped a line drive with my throat. That game forever drove home the term "hard ball." Ever since, when a baseball would head in my direction, I'd sidestep it or duck.

This particular day, my team was heading for our field positions after I had made the third out. I turned to face home plate when I spotted my dad's milk truck coming down a side road toward the field.

"Dad, Dad, hi Dad!" I shouted enthusiastically and repeatedly, while jumping up and down, waving my baseball mitt.

My dad spotted me and leaned out his truck's open door to return my greeting. His truck was the kind you drive standing up. As he waved, he veered too close to the edge of an incline, and the truck slid and tipped sideways. As the truck fell to the right, my dad jumped out the door to the left just as the load of milk shifted to the front. In those days most of the milk was in glass bottles, which we could hear shattering as the cases collided.

I couldn't move. I realized my dad was safe and unhurt, but there was still the ditched truck and damaged cargo. Tears began to run down my face. I felt responsible because I had distracted him.

As I stood staring at my dad while he surveyed his "milk shake," something else began to shake. It was the earth beneath my feet. I turned to see the boys' gym class stampeding across the field toward the girls' now halted game. They ran through and around us, out to the road, and over to my dad's dairy disaster. With the strength of young men motivated by the squeals of the girls, they were able to upright the milk "cart."

My dad was so relieved he didn't have to call a tow and the inside damage sounded worse than it was, he rewarded the boys by throwing boxes of ice cream bars into their midst.

The boys, equally thrilled with themselves, began to run down the road (now affectionately called the Milky Way) with their reward, laughing, with the rest of the group in hot pursuit. The poor coach was winded from blowing his whistle in attempts to regroup his "milk men."

I still had not moved. I was peeking through the webbing of my mitt. My gym suit was wet with tears.

Which just goes to prove . . .

It's not worth crying over spilled milk.

9

Kin

FROM MY EARLIEST years Aunt Pearl was my favorite kinfolk. Her Southern-country upbringing spiced her conversation with unexpected surprises that delighted the heart and often startled you into laughter.

Her wit was quick, but so was her temper. Even though she was my favorite, I knew better than to sass her. When I stayed at her house, which was every chance I could, you can bet your shoofly pie I obeyed her.

She was short and round and twirled her long brown hair into a tight little circle on the top of her head, capped by a hairnet. She moved fast, worked hard and relaxed fully. Aunt Pearl deeply loved the

Lord, her family and a good meal, especially if it was served with laughter.

On one of her visits to Michigan, I remember her sitting at my kitchen table sharing life lessons with me.

She looked up and said, "Child, there ain't nothin' worse than a whuppin' from the Lord."

"A whuppin' from the Lord?" I puzzled.

"Yes, child, ain't you never had no whuppin'?" she questioned.

"I guess I have. My mom used to send me out to get a switch off the tree. The worst part of that whuppin' was picking the weapon to be used on you."

"That ain't nothin' like a whuppin' from the Lord," she insisted.

"I was at this here hospital a-waitin' in the hall to visit my friend," she continued, "when they come abringin' a woman down the hall on a gurney. The Spirit of the Lord said to me, 'Take that woman's hand.'"

She resisted, "Lord, I can't be a-takin' that woman's hand. I don't know her."

Again she heard Him state, "Take that woman's hand."

Aunt Pearl said at this point she began to "ar-gee" with the Lord, "afeard" someone "would be a-lockin' her up if she wusta be takin' that woman's hand."

The woman was rolled past her, and for one moment their eyes met. Then she was gone down that long hall and through the double doors. Word came out a short time later that the woman had died.

With tears in her eyes, Aunt Pearl said, "Child, there ain't nothin' worse than a whuppin' from the Lord."

She believed the Lord had given her the opportunity to be the last person on this earth to touch that woman with His love, and she had failed to respond.

Then, with new determination in her voice, she announced, "Now when the Lord tells me to take someone's hand, I take her hand, her arm, I hug her neck, and I don't wanna let her go. 'Cause I don't want no more whoopin's from the Lord."

Have you been to the woodshed lately?

10

Leaning

WHY, OH WHY did I ever say I would do this?

Fear was bobsledding through my body, creating havoc in my breathing apparatus and digestive tract. My tummy was gurgling so loud people were turning around, trying to decide who was guilty of such distracting sounds. When they looked in my direction, I'd roll my eyes toward the lady on my right, then I'd give a slight smile, as if we shared a secret about her noisy anatomy.

I was speaking for a ladies' retreat day to 250 women. I was only doing the book reviews, but I knew I was incompetent and would probably be incoherent by the time I crawled my way up on stage. I wasn't sure of my name much less what was in the six books I was to review.

I had notes, but they seemed so small now. My eyes didn't seem capable of focusing.

Maybe I needed a doctor. Yes, that's it . . . a doctor. I was way overdue for a physical. This seemed like a good time, so I stood to leave.

My friend Joyce had been observing my twitchy behavior and sensed I was bolting to run. She grabbed my arm, stuck a postcard in my face and said with authority, "Read this."

I wasn't in a reading mood, but something in her voice made me do it anyway. Still struggling with my eyes and concentration, the only thing I could make out was the title of what appeared to be a poem. It was called, "Lean Hard on Me."

The title was enough. I made an about-face and headed for the platform.

I kept repeating, "Lean hard on Him, lean hard on Him."

And I was. Had you been standing in the back watching me walk to the front, I'm sure I would have been at a thirty-degree angle I was leaning so hard.

I was now at the front row, and my friend Rose was announcing the book reviews. She introduced me as Klutzy Paramount. Well, the audience got almost hysterical over the slip.

Being inexperienced on stage, I didn't know what one should do when the audience was in gales of laughter at your name. I walked up the steps and started across the stage.

When they saw me they laughed harder. I'm not sure if they were agreeing the name fit my appearance or what.

As the hilarity began to subside, I leaned into the microphone and said, "My name is—" but before I could set the record straight, they were off in riotous laughter once again.

When they took a breath, I rattled off my reviews and retreated . . . relieved and rejoicing.

Are you leaving or leaning?

11

Main Attraction

I HAVE A theory about why opposites attract. I think it's because we have a deep desire to get on each other's nerves.

My husband loves TV nature specials. I personally have never been that interested in the brain cells of a bumblebee or the anatomy of an anteater. He, in turn, does not understand my elation as I watch my video collection of "Winnie the Pooh" cartoons.

Les believes to be on time means to arrive a half hour early. I believe to enter as the big hand strikes the appointed hour is soon enough. Besides, if you arrive too early, you end up as part of the work crew.

Les loves his air conditioner . . . on high . . . while I have been accused of having a fixation for my electric blanket (which I wouldn't need so often if he'd turn off his air).

My husband longs to travel, but his job keeps him home. I enjoy being home, but my job keeps me on the road.

Country-and-western music is what Les sings along with, while I can lose myself in classical.

Les is your basic get-it-over-with shopper, while I'm a detailed investigative researcher.

I love books. Les looks forward to the newspaper.

My husband is a trivia buff. The only thing I retain is water.

He is a meat-and-potatoes man. I am a salad-and-veggie-plate gal.

Sometimes I think Les likes things just the opposite of me to agitate me, but then I remember . . . these are the things that drew me to him in the first place.

Do you let differences divide or
define your relationships?

12

Hungry Heart

AS A CHILD, my favorite pastime was a board game covered with colorful pictures of scrumptious sweets. Today, as an adult, I'm still following a tantalizing trail of tempting treats.

I've noticed that thin people don't have to work as hard as us hefties to make it down the trail. After all, we have to hold in our tummies. Tummy tucking (T.T.) takes stamina. I discovered a rich source of stamina can be found in French silk pie covered in mounds of shaved chocolate and also in goblets of tapioca smothered with dollops of fresh whipped cream.

Did you ever notice what happens to your anatomy when you hold in your tummy? First, T.T. punches your stomach into your diaphragm, which then catapults your esophagus into your tonsils. Your propelled tonsils, in turn, spiral your sinuses into your brain, causing you to blow your top!

If you release your tummy tuck position too quickly, because of the acceleration of gravity, you could bottom out. No wonder weight is such a heavy issue.

Speaking of heavy issues, try this appet-teaser test. It will help you weigh your eating choices. You might want to grab an eclair before beginning; tests can be strenuous.

Check appropriate boxes:

  I eat because,
    ❏ I'm mad
    ❏ I'm glad
    ❏ I'm sad
    ❏ I've been bad
    ❏ I'm bored
    ❏ It's there
    ❏ Everyone else is eating
    ❏ I need it to sustain life

Depending on the results of your test, you, like me, may want to go on a diet . . . again.

I've learned from experience at times it is best not to diet. For instance, if you are on a business trip, vacation, expecting guests, eating out, holidays, stressful times, when you're moving, potlucks, picnics, in the evening or during daylight.

Sometimes I get miffed with a modified menu lifestyle. Tonight I rebelled and ate two pieces of homemade pumpkin pie and filled up—with regret. Usually I can bury my guilt, temporarily, under an avalanche of chocolate chip cookie crumbs. I have no room left this time, not even for Jell-O.

I wonder which weighs more: my groceries or my guilt? One makes my scale heavy, the other my heart.

*Are you eating because you're hungry . . .
or hurting?*

13

Viewpoint

W HEN YOUR FULL stature measures five foot, you find yourself drawn to Scripture like "You shall say to this mountain, 'Move from here to there,' and it shall move" (Matt. 17:20, NAS).

I, believe it or not, was captain of a girls' basketball team in high school. I loved this position because I enjoy telling other people what to do.

But I had this problem, for me a mountainous problem, that I kept running into. Her name was Mount Kathy. She stood five feet eleven inches.

In those days, when giants walked the land, girls played half-court basketball. That meant you either shot the baskets or you guarded your opponents. I was a guard by choice. First, because I did not want to purposely embarrass myself attempting to get that big heavy ball into that exceedingly high hoop.

Second, I enjoyed being a guard and was pretty good at it. My height, or lack thereof, was at times to my advantage since I could move quickly around the half court. I was aggressive and as aggravating as a swarm of mosquitoes to the opposing forwards.

Then into my life lumbered Mount Kathy, who began to rob me of my reputation and my confidence. I just couldn't seem to get past her. I certainly couldn't go over her. The best I could do was get us into a jump ball situation.

Now that was a joke. I would jump my little heart out, and she didn't even have to move to her tiptoes. She'd stand flat-footed, looming over me, smiling down, braces and all, and then with a flick of her wrist direct the ball anywhere she wanted it to go. She certainly had no interference from me. Try as I might, I could not attain her altitude.

Probably just as well. I understand the higher you go, the harder it is to breathe.

I don't think Kathy read the same Bible verses I did, because no matter how often I said, "Move from here to there," she didn't budge.

Gratefully the basketball season ended, and now volleyball season was upon us. I once again was captain.

At our first game, after my serve I rotated to the front. I crouched, ready for serious play when I realized I was staring into a familiar pair of knee caps. Sure enough, it was Kathy.

I wonder if there are some mountains
He doesn't move . . . to keep us humble?

14

Musical Pews

I LOVE TO sing. I have yet to find anyone who loves to hear me. I don't sound that bad to myself, but I've had a number of people who have encouraged me in the art of humming.

I remember in junior high school my music teacher turned pale when she realized I had taken her class again. That semester she put me in the bass section with the boys. Her strategy worked; I was so embarrassed I switched to Home Ec.

Evidently voices don't improve with age. I remember singing a favorite of mine, "He Touched Me," at church one Sunday morning.

My friend Shirley was in the pew in front of me. I was really projecting on the chorus when she turned around, motioned me toward her, and whispered, "Trust me on this; He hasn't touched you yet, Patsy. Just mouth the words."

One good thing about a person's bathtub, there's no pew in front of you. Besides, I enjoy the acoustical benefit of the tiles when I shower.

I was into the bouncing chorus of "Zippity Doodah," as I lathered up, when my husband's panicked voice yelled through the door, "What's the matter?"

"Nothing, I was just singing," I called out melodically.

"Singing?" he asked incredulously. "I thought you were in pain!"

Even the shower isn't sacred anymore.

Invariably when I speak for a retreat, they seat me beside the soloist. That used to make me uncomfortable.

Sometimes I try what Shirley suggested: I mouth the words and hope people nearby think the singer's voice is coming out of me.

Why is it that those of us who can't sing marry those who can? Punishment maybe, for some past crime we forgot to confess.

Les has a delightful voice and knows a thousand songs. Except, I notice when I try to join him, he changes the words.

I've asked to join the church choir several times; but our director, Bill, always walks away laughing.

"That's a good one, Patsy," he says. "That's a good one."

Do the people around you seem uncomfortable with your singing? Take my advice—change pews.

15

Imprints

ISN'T IT FUNNY what we remember about people?

In elementary school, my friend Diane had us call her Fred. Her hero was Fred Mertz of "I Love Lucy," and she wanted to grow up to be just like him.

I thought this was an unusual goal.

She called me Fatsy instead of Patsy.

Diane made us laugh a lot.

When I was in high school, a girl named Eva was in my gym class. She was the only girl I knew who shaved off her eyebrows and drew in new ones— very artistic, long, curved, full brows that were coal black.

When we had swimming class, her carefully applied artwork would wash away. I had never seen naked eyebrows before. I was fascinated. I tried not to stare, but sometimes I just couldn't help it.

Another unique feature about Eva was her honesty. When she found out I had a private scoop on a mutual friend, she said, "Well, whatever you do, don't tell me! I can't keep a secret."

I had never heard anyone admit that aloud, especially before she even heard the tantalizing tidbit. Eva impressed me with her bare brows and her heroic honesty.

I was from a good-sized high school, but when we got a new shorthand teacher, the school was abuzz. One reason was her unusual appearance. She must have been a trendsetter, because she was back-combing her hair long before anyone else. She had it so voluminous you could have hid a basketball in there, and no one would have known.

When I saw her I was certain I wouldn't like her. Who could like someone who looked like her hair had been inflated with a tire pump? She ended up being the best teacher I ever had.

For a while, as a young married couple, Les and I lived in a mobile home. Next door to us was a lot that was used for short-term travel trailers.

A couple in their thirties from Texas pulled into that spot on April 3, 1966. I remember the date because it was my twenty-first birthday. That was significant for two reasons: one, in that era it meant you had attained maturity; two, not one member in my family remembered this was my day!

To prove my grown-up status, I had been pouting all evening.

When I spotted our new neighbors backing into the lot, I invited them in for coffee in an attempt to cheer myself up.

The woman was unique-looking. She wore her hair in braids that were in a circle on the side of her head, and she had filled the circle with hibiscus. I hadn't seen anything like that since the movie *South Pacific.*

As we were getting acquainted, I mentioned it was my (sniff) birthday, and Les almost fell off the couch. He went from realization to repentance. He knew he had goofed.

Our guests, feeling the awkwardness of the situation, quickly departed. I felt they feared a family feud might follow, so they fled.

About an hour later there was a knock at our door. I opened it to find my new neighbor holding up a cake. She had gone home, baked, decorated and even swirled my name and all-important age in frosting on this creation.

Even though they were next door for only a couple of days, I've never forgotten her.

What kind of imprint are you leaving?

16

Night Life

WHEN MY PARENTS called in the middle of the night because their furnace broke, Les went to help them. I felt a little pang of discomfort at being left alone. Well, to say I was alone isn't accurate—both our young boys were upstairs asleep. Also, our fearless cockapoo, Tuesday, was snoozing outside.

Tuesday was a lovable dog, but she had no discernment. She greeted beggar and thief, as well as doctor and chief, with sloppy enthusiasm.

She also had what I thought was a strange defect for a dog. Her barker was broken. Seldom if ever did she gr-r-r or arf. That was until . . . The Night of the Broken Furnace.

Les was gone about an hour when the barking began. I was startled at the unfamiliar sound and thought it must be a stray. I peeked out cautiously. Tuesday was on our porch, arfing in the direction of the woods.

Oh, yes, did I mention we were living on a Boy Scout reservation containing six hundred acres of woods, swamps, lakes and assorted monsters? The latter was my immediate concern.

Stop and think about it. What else would cause a bow-wow's broken barker to suddenly kick in?

Tuesday began to run from the front door, to the back door, to the front again. I knew what this meant. Whatever was out there was closing in.

I crept out of bed and began to look for a weapon. I had always believed investing in the Kirby vacuum cleaner would one day pay off. This was the day.

I took the long nozzled tube section to bed with me for protection. I placed the telephone beside me with the phone book open to emergency numbers. My heart was thumping as I strained to hear sounds of the approaching monster.

With Kirby in hand, I rotated my vision from watching the window to the door, to the window to the door, when suddenly I turned my head too far and caught my reflection in the mirror.

You want to talk about frightening . . . no . . . make that ridiculous.

I said to myself, "What's wrong with this picture?"

I've known the Lord well enough and long enough to realize He wants to be my refuge and hiding place. Here I was, trying in my anemic strength to handle this imagined invasion.

I laid down my Kirby sword and picked up the sword of the Spirit, which is the Word of God. I reviewed every peace and power promise I'd ever read. I'm not sure how long I'd been reading when fear started to drain out and quietness began to seep in, and I nodded off.

Soon I was sound asleep. I never heard my husband when he pulled up in front. I didn't hear him when he came in the door. I didn't even hear him when he entered our room. I didn't hear him until he shook my foot and asked, "What's the vacuum cleaner doing in bed with you?"

Caught with my sword down.

Are you armed or alarmed?

17

Feathered
Friends

IF ANYONE HAD told me I would become a bird-watcher, I would never have believed it . . . nor would anyone else. Did you know that the different species have unique personalities?

Ms. Hummingbird is our flitter. She has so much nervous energy her wings seem to hum her theme song, "Much to do, much to do, much to do."

She actually could conserve a lot of her strength if she didn't worry about what the other humming-birds were doing. We have three feeders for them, but let even one of her own kind get near the feeders, and she gets herself in an uproar. Ms. Flit dive-bombs anyone who attempts to drink the sweet water, preventing others from getting the nurturing they need.

Then there's Mr. Woodpecker. What a guy—seems to always be beating his head against a dead tree. He's a handsome bird—a classy dresser with every feather in place. He taps his message repeatedly, "Picky, Picky, Picky." It seems kind of sad to see him knock himself out over the tiniest matter.

Watch out, here come the Jays. Boy, what squawkers. When they fly in, everybody knows it. A flash of blue, and then they start bossing. They think they should be in charge of the whole seed scene. The Jay family has a lot to offer, if they just weren't so pushy and demanding.

Mr. and Mrs. Cardinal are a real study. She's a dear and is content to share the feeder with all who are hungry. But that husband of hers is so brazen. Many times he won't even allow her to eat until he's done. A real chauvinist, if you ask me. They make such a good-looking couple. I just wish he were more thoughtful of her.

My friend Margret raises peacocks—beautiful but obviously arrogant birds that strut around so everyone can see their newest attire. With beaks in the air, they ruffle and fan, and if they don't get enough attention, they repeatedly cry, "Help! Help!" I guess they've done it too many times though, because no one seems to take them seriously anymore.

Let's see now, is this a list of our fowl . . .
or our friends?

18

Oba . . . Who?

I'M NOT INTO heights, closed places, or riding in vehicles where I can't make suggestions on the maneuvering of it. Therefore, flying has never interested me—until I received an invitation I couldn't resist.

My friend Florence Littauer invited me to a leadership seminar in California. I was excited about everything except the flight. I made plans, purchased my tickets and packed my suitcase.

Flight day arrived, and my husband escorted me through the airport toward my gate. Actually, he was shoving me as my resistance grew. I remember passing a large plate glass window and seeing the ominous aircraft with a big AA tattooed on its side.

Fear can do funny things. This time, it grew feet and scampered up my arm, jumped onto my shoulder, leaned into my ear and screamed, "Run!"

My husband, using a linebacker's lunge, prevented my escape. Reluctantly, I trudged onto the plane.

My friend Rose, who was also attending the seminar, was my seat partner. That should have helped, but several minutes after we took our seats she reached into her bag and came up with a camera.

Puzzled, I asked, "Why are you taking that out now?"

"I want to capture fear in color when they start the engines," she informed me, aiming the camera in my direction.

"Oh, great, I'm shaking in my seat belt, and I've got Ms. Candid Camera sitting next to me," I fumed as the flash illuminated our row.

The day was cold, slushy and gray. I still remember the contrast as we moved up through the murky clouds and into the brilliant sunlight. As I watched out the window, there, arched in the heavens, from one cloud to another, was a rainbow.

I knew it was mine. It was a telegram from the Lord that read, "You're going to make it."

The lady beside me responded with, "Oh, look, a rainbow!"

"It's mine," I stated too abruptly. Realizing my overreaction, I softened it with, "Excuse me," and then under my breath whispered, "but it is mine." I needed that rainbow-gram too bad to share it with her.

After reaching our cruising altitude, the ride was smooth and uneventful.

Then the pilot, a man who obviously needed counseling, began to share information he should have kept to himself. "Strong Santa Ana winds are being reported ahead. We are running lower on fuel than we had anticipated. We'd like everyone to stay in their seats for the remainder of the flight."

His voice was unemotional. He didn't need to have any emotions because I had enough for both of us. I began to scan the heavens for another rainbow of promise.

Rose was reading her Bible. I think she thought it was the yellow pages as she let her fingers do the walking. She would let her Bible fall open, read a passage and then move to another.

On one portion she nudged me and said with a giggle, "Look."

I nervously glanced down and began to read. "Give that to me!" I said. "It's my other rainbow."

Listen to what it says in Obadiah (who really reads Obadiah?): ". . . Who says in his heart, Who can bring me down to the ground? Though you mount on high as the eagle, and though you set your nest among the stars, I will bring you down from there, says the Lord."

Thank You, Lord, and thank you, Obadiah! Now, I know Obadiah didn't pen that one with me in mind, but it sure helped this trembling traveler until we touched down.

After sharing this story at a retreat, a lady came up and said, "My version reads differently than yours. Where yours says, '"I will bring you down," declares the Lord,' mine reads, '"I will plummet you to the earth," saith the Lord.'"

Somehow I wasn't interested in her version. One plummet, and it would have been all over for me.

That plane flight gave me a new appreciation for terms like "landlubber," "westward ho," and "good old terra firma." Nevertheless, there is an upcoming flight I don't want to miss. I understand flight time is minimal, ". . . in the twinkling of an eye." We won't even have a chance to buckle our seat belt, although in-flight music will be provided—trumpets, I believe.

Yes, one glad morning with fearless abandon, I'll fly away.

Are you booked?

19

Messages

WHEN OUR BIG twenty-fifth anniversary arrived, Les bought me nothing. Of course that's what I had asked for, but what does that have to do with anything? Mates are supposed to be able to decipher mixed messages. Les is supposed to discern when I mean "absolutely no" from when I mean "sort of no."

Here's the thing. Wives don't want to shoulder the responsibility of giving husbands permission to be extravagant. It frees us from guilt if we say no and our husbands don't listen to us, which of course is what we're hoping will happen. That way we can say to others, "I told him not to do this, but he did it anyway."

Les and I agreed to take a trip south as a shared gift, but I was hoping for something a little more personal. I must have been too convincing when I said, "If you get me anything I'll be mad." Maybe I should have said, "If you get me anything I might, in a minute way, be temporarily displeased."

Most of us gals secretly hope for a good "show and tell" kind of gift, especially for our twenty-fifth. It's difficult to flaunt—I mean show—a trip to your friends.

I decided to subtly retract my giftless declaration at the first appropriate moment.

A week later Les dropped me off for a speaking engagement and announced he was going to the area mall for his morning coffee. The word "mall" flashed like a neon opportunity.

With more zeal and clarity than I meant to display, I blurted out, "Why don't you buy me something!"

Oops, I probably confused him by being that . . . that . . . honest. Not that I'm not always honest . . . sort of.

When Les came back to pick me up, he had heard the message, for there, on the front seat, was a beautifully wrapped gift. I admired it for a moment and then began to remove the floral paper. Inside were layers of soft white tissue secured with a gold seal that read "lingerie."

Well, this was proof that honesty did pay; I was getting what I deserved. So what if it was a week late.

I gently pulled back the last layer of tissue and lifted out my . . . my . . . prehistoric gift. What unfolded was a long white cotton nightshirt sporting a gregarious dinosaur, which wore a lopsided hat.

This truth thing, girls, . . . you'll need
to be more specific!

20

Pricey

I HAVE ALWAYS wanted to play an instrument. Well, not any instrument. Mostly I dreamed of playing a piano. I pictured myself moving my fingers across the ivories without looking, as I threw back my head and sang with throaty gusto. It didn't take me long to find out I couldn't sing. But piano . . . that took a little longer.

I was in my thirties when my friend Rose grew tired of hearing me whine about being deprived of piano lessons. She announced she would teach me. I was thrilled.

My husband lovingly, although somewhat reluctantly, moved an old upright into our living room. Those things weigh a ton. I could tell by the purple arteries that had inched their way out on his neck.

Not wanting his effort to be in vain, I began my serious study of the piano, certain I would soon be in concert. But I ran into an immediate problem.

It was my teacher. She quite honestly was . . . boring. This surprised me because Rose has a lot of verve. She usually was full of fun but not so as a piano instructor.

She kept insisting I do scale exercises. Either of those words I avoid regularly; combined, they were depressing. Dull, repetitious pinging sounded childish.

I explained to her that this was not what I had in mind, so she agreed to teach me some real songs.

Now, when she said real, I didn't know she was talking about "Old MacDonald Had a Farm."

How do you think it looks and sounds to have a woman in her thirties e-i-e-i-o-ing? After a few weeks of musical farming, I'd had it, and so had my family. I could tell they were stressed when the veins on their temples seemed to pulsate in time to my barnyard plunking.

"I don't want to play 'Old MacDonald.' I want to play 'How Great Thou Art,'" I stated with artistic fervor to Rose.

"You cannot play 'How Great Thou Art' until you first learn to play 'Old MacDonald,'" Rose replied through tight teeth.

"How boring, how unimaginative," I complained.

"Patsy, you don't want to learn how to play the piano. You just want to play the piano," she accused.

Boy, did she hit a chord. No way was I willing to put in the time and effort necessary to become a pianist.

I gave up my musical illusions. Les and the boys joyfully, gratefully and quickly removed the piano. Rose once again became her entertaining self.

What price is your dream?

21

Perks

EVE . . . WHAT A perk-y lady! She definitely had advantages.

Stop and think about it. When she and Adam met, she didn't have to wonder, *Is this the right man for me?* She didn't have any immediate concerns if some sweet young thing was vying for her man's attention.

When they were wed, she didn't have to worry about forgetting someone from the invitation list or deciding who the attendants would be. No decisions were necessary on which photographer, caterer or florist. Talk about simplifying life . . .

Guess what? No mother-in-law or father-in-law conflicts. Never once did she have to hear, "Sure wish you could make applesauce like my mom." They never squabbled over whose family they would spend the holidays with.

She never had to worry about ironing Adam's dress shirts or getting the crease straight in his suit pants. There was no friction about Adam not picking up his dirty clothes, at least not in their garden home. Nor did she have to take any ribbing about where she put Adam's lost snakeskin sandals.

Eve was unique. She's the only gal who didn't have to go through puberty, peer pressure or pimples. She didn't go through the agony of handing her parents a bad report card or the knee-knocking experience of trying to explain why she was late getting home. She never once had to hear her parents say, "Why aren't you more like your sister Ethel?"

When she and Adam talked, it wasn't filled with endless tales of the good ol' days and the good ol' boys. Nor did she have to compete with the World Series or the six o'clock Eden news report.

They had a romance, marriage, honeymoon and home life that was made in paradise.

Eve had it all . . . well, almost all.

Why is it we always seem to want
what we don't have?

22

Quiet Noise

EVEN WHEN I'M still I'm not quiet. My mind is busy embroidering life, one thread at a time, according to the events of a day. Therefore, when I sit down for my quiet time, I have to battle against my mental cross-stitching.

"Sh-h-h," I tell my brain, in an attempt to focus on my prayers. I start to pray for my sons, and my mind somehow switches gears. I'm making a mental grocery list instead.

I've learned to pray with my eyes open and not to get too comfortable. Far more times than I'd like to confess, I've nodded off right in the middle of "and God bless . . ."

Now I pray wide-eyed, sitting in a straight-back chair, which has some drawbacks. I was praying for a family member the other morning when I noticed a build-up of dust under the chair in my living area.

The next thing I knew I had the vacuum out, running it around the room. Then I remembered I was supposed to be praying. I sat back down and resumed talking with the Lord.

Before long I was at the freezer taking meat out for dinner, even though I still hadn't finished my prayer time.

My mind is far too active, and my concentration span is about the length of a commercial.

I tried walking around the house and praying aloud. But then I put things in unusual places, without realizing it, keeping my family confused and frustrated.

One day I found Les looking in the refrigerator for his electric razor. When I raised my eyebrows in surprise, he simply said, "With your filing system, I just had to check."

Kneeling is a proper spiritual position, but for me it is physically defeating. I get leg cramps, go numb and limp pitifully the rest of the day. It seems like poor advertising to tell people I've been debilitated by my prayer time.

What seems to work best is writing my prayers. It helps me focus and finish before I flit off. As I write out my noisy thoughts to free my mind, it untangles the threads of my day for directed prayer. I keep my printed petitions in a notebook. I could add your name if you'd like.

Let's see now . . . where did I put that book?

23

Gotcha

I LOVED THE idea of my two-hundred-pound husband wearing short pants and a whistle. Les had taken a job as Associate Ranger for the Boy Scouts; we would be living on their six-hundred-acre reservation.

Raised as a northern woodsman, Les was more than qualified for his position. Now me, I was a city slicker. But I loved the country atmosphere.

I was determined to adapt to my new life-style. In fact, I began to daydream I would become a world-famous outdoors woman, making valuable contributions to our environment. These were rather high hopes for someone whose past experience included occasional childhood family picnics. Still, I might have fulfilled my dream except . . .

On a beautiful spring day, new life was budding all through our heavily wooded grounds. The birds were singing and so was I, as I strolled around admiring God's handiwork. The daffodils and lilacs were bursting with color and fragrance.

As I approached them, I noticed my nose was running. Within minutes I was having little fits of sneezing. Then I started itching. First my arms, next my face, then my ears. My eyes began to water and feel sandpapery.

Determined not to give in to these unpleasant reactions, I decided to get involved with a project.

I spotted a forsythia bush. Covered in brilliant yellow flowers, it was lovely except for some straggly limbs I thought should be cut off. I didn't realize there is a time to prune and a time to refrain from pruning.

As I looked for a pair of shears, I noticed my head was blocking up, and I seemed to be developing a cough, but I forged on. Finding the tools to my new trade, I began to snip and clip, feeling like quite the botanist.

I leaned down to get an unruly spray, when out of the ground came a stream of yellow jackets. They seemed to be deeply offended that I was pruning out of season and filed their grievance down my scoop-neck top.

I ran through the yard, beating on my shirt like an old Tarzan movie. My sister, who was in the yard a safe distance from me, caught a glimpse of the invasion and began to chase me.

My mom was indoors visiting with her friend Edith when she heard me yelling. She looked out the window as I ran by, quickly followed by my sister, and commented to her friend, "Oh, look, they're playing."

One good thing about living in the country is if you need to disrobe you can. So I did. The remaining attackers had to be plucked from my bod. I then took refuge in my home.

I had spots and dots, was sneezing and wheezing, itching and twitching, and I was riddled with stings. My daydream of becoming Environmentalist Extraordinaire faded with the intrusion of reality.

I had Les screen in our front porch, and that's where I enjoyed the out-of-doors.

Any intruders dive-bomb your dreams lately?

24

Real Estate

MY MOM WAS a mover and a shaker. She loved moving from one home to another, and it would always shake me up! I think moving was a hobby for her. She'd buy a house, fix it up and sell it. Then she would start all over again. It always meant a different school and establishing new friendships. I made friends easily enough, but I hated leaving the old ones.

I decided when I grew up I would live in one house for the rest of my life. Then I married Leslie "The Mover" Clairmont.

Somehow my mom's mobility genes had bypassed me and entered Les. I didn't even realize that was possible.

I had felt safe marrying a man who had only lived in two homes from birth until marriage. But I counted recently, and in twenty-eight years we have moved twenty-three times.

At about house number seventeen, I decided I had moveaphobia, and I wasn't going to pack one more time.

I cried out, "Lord, it isn't fair! You know a woman gets a lot of her security and identity from where she lives."

I tried to validate my opinion with Scripture. If I could do that, I figured the next time Les made me move, I could send him on a guilt trip.

The problem was I couldn't find any Scripture that suggested we should depend on a place, position, possession or even person (other than Jesus) for our security and identity. I had to re-think my house "hold" and learn not to hang on so tightly.

I did feel encouraged when I read, "I go to prepare a place for you."

Notice place is singular. I don't have to take my Samsonite or rent one more U-Haul, y'all. I get to live in one place forever and ever. Amen.

The thought crossed my mind that when the Lord builds my husband's place, He should add on a room for my mom. Then He could put their mansion on rollers, and they could move all through eternity.

When they rolled by, I could lean out of my immovable place and wave. That would be heaven for us all!

Our home here is meant to be a haven . . .
heaven comes later.

25

Atmospheric Pressure

I DON'T FEEL well when I have to say "I'm sorry." I get strong, flu-like symptoms. I become nauseated. My knees get weak, my hands shake, and I get facial ticks.

If I have to say "I'm sorry and I was wrong," it's much worse. Then, along with the jerky behavior, my vision blurs, and my speech patterns slur.

I have noticed, though, that once I've said what needs to be said I make an amazing recovery.

One day Les was feeling frustrated with our eldest son over a work situation and needed to release a flurry of words. He came into my home office and spewed his displeasure about Marty onto me. Once Les said how he felt, he was ready to move past his aggravation.

After he left, I began to process their conflict and decided I could make the whole thing better. I envisioned myself as a Goodwill Angel (not to be confused with the Goodyear Blimp).

I fluttered into Marty's room and announced what he needed to do and when he needed to do it. For some reason Marty was not impressed with this angelic visitation.

In fact, he told me, "If Dad has a problem with me that's job-related, then he can talk to me."

Well, Marty might be twenty-five years old, but how dare he insinuate I was butting in? Setting aside my helping halo, in my loudest mother's voice I trumpeted my heated annoyance. I finally ended my tirade by stomping up the steps. Marty placed his exclamation point on our meeting by slamming out of the house.

I packed away my singed raiment and was still sizzling when I heard Les come in. I went down to make a pronouncement on his son's poor behavior. By the look on Les's face it was obvious he had already encountered Marty.

"If I had wanted you to go to Marty, I would have asked you," he stated through clenched teeth. "Patsy, this was none of your business."

"None of my business!" I bellowed. A cloudburst of tears followed as I ran to my room, tripping several times on my lopsided wings.

"I was only trying to help," I kept consoling myself.

When the tears and excuses stopped, I began to wonder if maybe I could have been wrong. Flu-like symptoms intensified when I realized I needed to apologize to both of them for interfering.

By the time I made my way out to Les and Marty, my vision had blurred. My head was pounding (probably from that heavy halo) as I stammered the dreaded words, "I-I was wr-wrong for interfering, I'm s-sorry, will you f-forgive me?"

Within moments we were all hugging.

As I walked back to the house, I noticed my headache and vexed vision had vanished, and it was almost . . . as if my feet weren't touching the ground.

Hey Angel Face, anyone in your sphere
deserve an apology?

26

Amazing Grace

I WAS SO familiar with our five-mile stretch of country road into town that I developed a rhythm to my driving. Sometimes my rhythm was faster than the posted pace. After following me into town on several occasions, Les mentioned I needed to lighten up on my footwork.

At times when I drove to town, I wouldn't remember the ride in because I was on autopilot. I knew every curve and turn by heart, and my mind tended to wander.

Often I would sing my way to town, and if the song happened to be a bouncy one, without realizing it, I would drive to the beat. This wasn't a problem if I was singing "How Great Thou Art." However, when I got into the rousing chorus of "I'll Fly

Away," my little wagon seemed to be doing that very thing. Les warned me more than once to pay closer attention to my selections.

On one particularly beautiful autumn day, I was on my way to speak for an area women's retreat. My six-year-old, Jason, was in the back seat, looking forward to seeing his friends at the child-care room. I was into the rhythm of the road while I rehearsed my opening thoughts with great enthusiasm.

I glanced in my rearview mirror as something beckoned for my attention. There I spotted someone else who seemed to be quite enthusiastic in his desire to share some thoughts with me. A colorful character. I could tell by the red and blue circular lights on his car.

As he approached my car, I couldn't help chuckling as I pictured Les doing the "I told you so" nod.

Jason questioned, "Mom, why are you laughing?"

"Oh, honey, it's just Daddy told me this would happen one day."

The nice officer was not laughing. He leaned down and boomed with a voice that instantly reduced me to a teeny person, "And where are we going in such a hurry?"

I meekly looked into his convicting face and whispered, "Church."

"You're kidding!" he bellowed.

"I'm the speaker," I confessed. "My topic is 'Renewed Living.' I guess I'm not doing too well . . . with it," I trailed off, wishing I could disappear.

He asked me a series of intelligent questions that I could not answer with any degree of accuracy— things like "Where is your car registration?" and "Where is your title?"

I was totally in the wrong, which was obvious to all of us.

So I was amazed when he announced, "I'm going to let you go without a ticket, but you must slow down and place the proper papers in your car."

That day the officer was like Jesus. He extended mercy when I didn't deserve it.

Need another chance?

27

Bag It

MEN AND WOMEN, generally speaking, approach shopping quite differently. Men see it as a nuisance and yet a necessity. Women, however, see it as a challenge and a calling. Men tend to buy willy-nilly, while a woman investigates, evaluates and meditates her purchases . . . Unless of course it's a once in a lifetime opportunity, and she must buy immediately or lose her chance. It's amazing how many of those "once" chances a woman can find.

It drives my husband wild when I find something I like, but I take several hours looking around at other stores only to circle back and purchase that first item. Recently I resisted this urge and bought the first pair of shoes that appealed to me, only to find out later (after I wore them) that another store in the mall had them for twenty dollars less. To make matters worse, my friend had bought the same shoes—at the sale price.

This would be like a man entering a fishing contest and thinking he had won, only to have his best friend arrive with a catch twice as big and walk off with the trophy.

Sales tags are like trophies for a dedicated shopper. We would have them mounted and displayed if it weren't considered tacky. We've learned to weave our savings in our salutations.

"Nice hat; new?"

"Yes, $15.95 at Kerwin's."

"Really?"

"Yeah. Why?"

"I saw it at Lem's for $9.94."

"No!"

"Yep."

"See you."

"Bye."

You can always spot the devoted ones. They have their own language, called "Shop Talk." Words like "bargain," "grand opening," "clearance," "closeout," "refund," "coupons," "discount" and others decorate their discourse.

For me, shopping can be motivational. At times when I've felt too exhausted to clean up the kitchen, I've been able to make several loops around the two-mile mall to find the right shade of socks to go with my jeans and sweatshirt. To really raise my energy level, announce a five-minute special and watch me become almost aerobic.

Here are a couple of health warnings for shopaholics: If you browse daily, you could get Shopper's Stare from looking at one too many price tags. To prevent this, every couple hundred tags or so, take a brownie break.

Also many avid shoppers are bothered with Blue Light Bursitis from nudging their way to sales tables. They should try taking a friend and sending her through the crowd first, opening up a path.

Worst of all is the dreaded Grip. That's where the buyer and her bags have bonded, and she can't let go of her bargains. If this happens to you, train a loved one to say, "Tomorrow is another day, you can go shopping then," as they gently part you from your parcels.

Oh, yes, one more warning . . . this one from the surgeon general: "It has been proven that shopping is hazardous to your wealth."

Of course, girls, we have to take into consideration the general who said that is a man.

28

Mouth Peace

I RECEIVED A small catalog in the mail from an area home improvement store. I can honestly say I'm not interested in hardware, but the lettering across the front page won my attention.

In bold red print was every shopper's favorite word, "Sale." Above "sale" appeared the word "security." I need security, and I hunt for sales, so I opened their booklet to see what they had to offer.

The first page showed pictures and prices on a line of doors. The one that caught my eye was a steel door. The past week I had released several thoughts to loved ones that I should have kept to myself. If I had a steel door hinged on the side of my mouth, perhaps the next time I felt tempted to say something stinging I could slam that door shut.

The next page offered dead-bolt locks, which seemed like a good investment. Knowing myself as I do, even with the steel door closed I might kick it open to get in the last steamy word. The dead bolt could at least slow down that process.

As I scanned through the pamphlet a second time, I noticed I could purchase a door viewer for a small price. This promised to give me a 160-degree field of vision. I wonder, if I had a clearer view or a different perspective on the individual with whom I was frustrated, would I still want to sound off?

Then I came across coupons for smoke alarms. This could be the ultimate answer. If I had one installed on the roof of my mouth, when my words started heating up, the detector would go off. That would drown out all the sizzling sentences. Then, when my conversation cooled down, the siren would automatically cease and reset.

Steel doors, viewers, dead-bolt locks and smoke alarms, what a security system!

Are you wired for sound?

29

Pollution Solution

I'M TOLD TWO types of people exist—those who proclaim, "Good morning, Lord," when they wake up, and those who exclaim, "Good Lord, it's morning."

Early has never been one of my day's highlights, and the morning mirror has certainly not helped to cheer me on. But I did find Scripture that helped me understand my a.m. reflection: It was "formless and void and darkness was upon the surface of the deep . . ."

I was encouraged to read that things did eventually lighten and brighten up, when God proclaimed: "Let there be light."

For me that's after I apply my blush, mascara and lipstick.

I'm married to the kind of guy who leaps out of bed in the morning, skips down the hall and sings in the shower. For years that got on my nerves.

Plus I didn't think anyone should move that quickly; he could injure something he might need in the future.

Les told people, "Patsy runs around the block every morning and then kicks the block back under the bed."

I limited my exercise to jumping to conclusions, stretching the truth and dodging my reflection.

But slowly I began to realize that Les was a living example, and I would do well to learn from him. I needed a "Good morning, Lord" injection.

If this change was to take place, I'd need a plan. No, make that a miracle!

I began by memorizing, "This is the day which the Lord hath made; we will rejoice and be glad in it" (Ps. 118:24, KJV).

As soon as my brain received the jolt that a new day had begun, I would start to recite my verse—first silently, then in a whisper and finally in a shout.

My recitation started out more like a question, "This is the day . . . ?" As I continued my sunrise salute, it became a proclamation.

Gradually my new routine began to make a difference in my m.o. (morning outlook).

I honestly can't say I leap from the bed now, but I do get up. I don't skip down the hall; it's more like a crawl. I still don't sing in the shower, but I hum, and for me that's progress. No, make that a miracle!

What pollutes your sunrise salute?

30

Good-Bye

WHAT DO YOU mean join the Air Force?" I heard myself trumpeting at my firstborn son, Marty.

"Mom," he calmly responded, "When I graduate, I'm going to sign up. I might even make a career of it."

"Sure, sure, after you finish school and work for a few years then you can join, . . . say when you're forty," I suggested.

If anyone would have told me how difficult it is to release children I would not have believed it. In fact, I had observed families struggling with good-byes and thought they must be overly protective. Now that it was my turn, I was giving the word "possessive" new glue.

I tried reasoning with Marty; when that didn't work I threatened, I pleaded, I cajoled, I bribed, and then I cried. I delayed but did not divert him from finally signing Uncle Sam's dotted line.

I tried to be grown-up in my responses during our remaining weeks, but then I would see Marty, and grief would run down my face and splash off his high tops. Marty did his best to wade through my overwrought behavior. That wasn't easy because when he was home I flooded his every move with my presence, realizing he would soon be gone.

When I would pass him in the hall, I would ask him if I could hug him.

He'd say, "All right, go ahead; hurry up."

I'd quickly squeeze him and then sniff off into another room.

"Patsy, when are you going to grow up?" my husband questioned in disbelief at my Velcro behavior. "Why do you think we had this boy?" Before I could respond, he would answer, "So that one day we could send him out into the grand adventure of life."

He made this announcement dry-eyed and slightly irritated with his weeping woman.

By the time the day came to say good-bye, I had released my emotions and was actually feeling pretty good about Marty's departure. In fact, I marched to the door like a brave soldier, gave him a kiss and even saluted him as he drove off.

I headed back to the house, grinning ear to ear with my new-found freedom. Then I bumped into Les, who was standing in a pool of anguish.

"Don't you have a heart?" he said haltingly. "That's our son leaving. We might . . . never see him again."

Being a woman of deep sensitivity, I realized Les had just gotten in touch with his grief, and so I tried to encourage him.

"When are you going to grow up? Why do you think we had this boy? So that one day we could send him out into the grand adventure of life," I echoed sweetly.

How many of your good-byes have brought you grief . . . how many relief?

31

Hello

OUR SON MARTY was about to return home from the Air Force. He had been stationed in Guam, and we hadn't seen him for eighteen months.

The night before his flight was to arrive, Les and I were at the mall, and I headed for the Party Center Store. I found cone-shaped hats with gala fringe spewing out the top, horns arrayed in sparkling glitter and multi-colored confetti shaped like stars.

This is going to be one fun reunion, I thought, as I headed for the checkout counter.

"What are you doing?" I heard a voice ask behind me. I turned; Les was standing there with his eyebrows bumping together in puzzlement.

It seemed obvious to me what I was doing, but I humored him. "I'm getting supplies for our celebration."

"Just where do you think you're going to use them?" The words sounded more like a threat than a question.

"At the airport tomorrow, of course," I responded uneasily.

"What airport?" he questioned. "Not the same airport I'm going to. If you're taking that stuff, you'll have to go to a different airport by yourself."

I couldn't believe my ears. But I decided at such a happy time we shouldn't be hassling over horns and hats, so I put the party favors back.

When we arrived at Marty's gate, two of his friends were already waiting. We sat chatting excitedly; then I mentioned that ol' Mr. Party Pooper wouldn't let me buy the delightful hats, horns and confetti.

In unison the two young men turned to my husband and said, "Thank you!"

Before I could respond, an airline representative announced the plane had touched down.

I learned that day that mothers don't need party paraphernalia to celebrate. I didn't need hats or horns because I had hands and a mouth. I started leaping in the air, trying to get a glimpse of Marty deplaning. My hands came together like clanging cymbals, over and over sounding out my joy. I began to laugh and whoop out words for the world to hear, "My son is home, my son is home!"

Then I was in his arms baptizing his uniform in a mother's relief.

At this point I'm not sure where Les and Marty's friends were . . . hmmm, now that I think about it, they seemed to have faded back in the crowd.

How about you? Do you welcome loved ones as a loud greeter or a silent meeter?

32

Bird Brain

IT STARTED OFF as a Sunday afternoon stroll in the woods. I had the bright idea that Les and I should go on a bird-watching walk. Because we live on property surrounded by thousands of acres of state land, which has many miles of trails, it's the perfect setting for a leisurely outing.

First the equipment was found and organized: thirty-six ounces of diet pop, two pairs of binoculars, one bird book for ID, a pen to list all sightings and our sanguine Shih Tzu, Pumpkin.

As we headed out the door, Les asked, "Have you ever been on the trails across the road?"

By the look of the trails when we arrived, Crockett was the last one on them. The path didn't seem well defined to me, and I mentioned that to Les. He mumbled something about being a northern woodsman.

As we followed the winding path, it seemed to be closing in on us. In fact, I was thigh-high in weeds. The branches of sinister-shaped bushes and threatening trees began to smack me across the face.

"Les, get me out of here," I whined.

"You're all right. Just keep walking," he instructed, disappearing around a bend.

For a moment I was distracted from my weedy world by the sound of what I thought must be a herd of hummingbirds. It turned out to be militant mosquitoes. They motivated me to move quickly, and soon I caught up with Les. He didn't seem bothered by the mosquitoes. I think it was because of the horse flies that were devouring chunks of his hide.

My resourceful woodsman pulled off two low-hanging branches, and we took turns beating off each others' attackers.

We'd been in the woods forty minutes, and I wanted to leave—now. All I desired was to see some birds. Instead, I was branch-bruised and bug-bitten. This was no fun.

"The closest way out," Les informed me, "is the way we came in."

"No way! I'm not going back there," I stated, forging forward.

Because I had underestimated the heat, the ice cubes in the pop had long since melted. We now had Laodicean lukewarm liquid—not very refreshing but helpful when sloshed through the teeth to loosen the bugs from between our bicuspids. I learned that in certain circumstances it is appropriate for a woman to spit.

I was watching my feet as I moved through the thick undergrowth when something caught my eye. It was the rotting carcass of a mouse being eaten by gigantic black-and-yellow beetles. If I had had any lunch, I'm sure I would have lost it. I increased my pace to something close to a gallop.

We had not seen one bird. Not one!

Sweat began to drip down our branch-whipped faces, when up ahead we spotted sunlight. The woods opened up and deposited us on a dirt road at the bottom of a large hill.

As we stepped from our treacherous trail, three unsuspecting victims passed us to enter the forbidden forest. One of them had her dog on a leash. Our dog took one look at that mutt, turned around and hightailed it right back into the thickets.

Les went running after Pumpkin, making clear reference to her intelligence and her uncertain life expectancy. A short time later he came stumbling out with a repentant pooch.

Now we had to face the hill. To say we limped up it would put us in a better light than we deserve. Les had to carry Pumpkin because she was panting so hard from her run-away escapade that we were concerned she would have cardiac arrest. I was hanging on to Les's elbow for support and motivation.

Halfway up, we sat down on the edge of the road. When we started to discuss our will, I realized this had not been a positive experience for us.

Finally we stumbled into our living room. As I headed for our recliner, something caught my

peripheral attention. I turned and six birds were
. . . in my front yard.

Isn't that funny?
I went looking for something I already had.

33

Color Bind

WHEN LES PICKED me up from the airport, he was dangling the house keys with obvious excitement. He had been out of work following heart surgery, and we felt grateful not only for a job but also that a house was provided for our family. He was to be the director of a Christian conference center, and we would live on the grounds.

But I had not anticipated how quickly my gratitude could seep out.

My first glance of the house left me speechless. Even the cover of night was not enough to disguise the color wheel environment of our "new" dwelling.

My friend Mary Ann summed it up when she stepped in the front door, gasped, screamed and then proclaimed, "This is ghastly!"

Truly it was. Living here would be like trying to live in a kaleidoscope that some child kept twirling. The colors collided so loudly that the place was noisy.

Come take a tour. First, picture the color orange. Got it? Now brighten it. Now intensify that. You now have my kitchen cupboards.

These reflect in interesting patterns off my luscious lime green countertops. The wallpaper in the kitchen is bursting with giant coffee pots in red, rust and orange.

The kitchen is open to the dining area, where the walls are painted powder blue. The carpeting is green and yellow shag, highlighted with oval-shaped animal stains . . . memoirs of Fido and Felix, I presume.

The dining room is also open to the living room. Both the living room and dining area have large plate glass windows with smaller windows above those. The smaller ones are painted deep royal blue with a full moon in the center of each pane (which truly is a pain). Eight full moons gave us a real orbital addition.

Someone must have read that wood adds to the decor. So, that person added a half-wall of gray barn wood, a full wall of red-stained plywood and a high but narrow wall of brown lumber.

Did I mention these walls are all in the same rooms with the moons, stains and colors? Just checking. I didn't want you to miss any of the ambience.

That evening I left there with an attitude. I didn't realize anyone had noticed until just before we moved.

Marty, our eldest, was sitting on the couch when I came downstairs. Like his mother, Marty does not care for early a.m. chatter. We don't usually get into meaningful conversations till noonish. So it was a surprise when I heard words coming from his lips.

"I can't believe it," he stated while staring at the floor.

"What can't you believe?" I inquired, amazed he was talking.

"I just can't believe it!" he repeated with greater conviction, still staring floor-ward.

This short but vague conversation was already getting on my nerves. "Why don't you tell me what you can't believe so I can't believe it with you," I insisted.

Slowly lifting and shaking his head, he gently stated, "I can't believe your attitude."

"My attitude?!" I responded defensively, elevating to my full, intimidating five-foot stature.

"Yes," he went on to clarify, "your attitude about our new home. Here you've been praying for a job for Dad and a home for our family. When it's provided, you allow something as surface as paint to distract you and rob us all of joy."

I turned and headed for the kitchen, feeling unable to defend myself. As I walked away I thought, *Who raised that kid anyway?*

I stood in the kitchen and decided I needed to talk with a woman. I prayed and immediately a name came to my mind.

"No, Lord, that's not it; try again." It didn't seem like the right name. She was a gracious and loving woman but not someone I had ever called for help. Yet the name seemed to stay pressed firmly in the forefront of my mind, so I dialed the phone.

Eleanor was home and took the time to listen to my dilemma. When I got all done with my colorful tale of woe, she simply said, "I have a poem for you."

A poem? I cried inwardly. *See, Lord, I told You she wasn't the one!*

Had she even said, "I have a can of paint for you," at least that would have been practical.

Eleanor began with her compassionate voice to quote a poem that permeated my veneer and exposed the content of my heart.

The woman who can move about a house,
Whether it be a mansion or a camp,
And deftly lay a fire and spread a cloth,
And light a lamp,
And by her loving touch give
The look of home wherever she may be . . .
Such a woman always will seem great,
And beautiful to me.

It was as if the Lord pressed that poem into my heart and did some redecorating. I hung up, knowing I had called the right person.

I pulled a chair to the middle of the room amidst the riotous color and prayed. "Lord, forgive my ungrateful heart, and help me to see what my part is in making this place into a home for my family."

As I scanned my house again, ideas began to flood my mind, and I actually got excited. First, I hired a painter.

I told him, "If you can see it, feel it or touch it, paint it. If it moves, step on it and then paint it."

I had everything painted off-white, even the wood, to give it some continuity. We scraped away our moons. Then we ripped out the stained rug and replaced it with soft gray carpeting.

Now the place looked antiseptic. Adding mauves and blues cured that. Furniture and flowers were our finishing touches.

What started off as a colorful disaster has ended up being a creative delight.

What colors your attitude?

34

Fright Flight

Y OO-HOO, PATSY," I heard someone sing out as I headed for my car in the church parking lot. I turned and saw my friend Claris waving her hand.

"Could you use some sweet corn?" she offered.

"I'd love some," I responded.

"I'll drop off a sack," she assured me as she slid into her pickup and started the engine.

I had a few errands to take care of, but when I arrived home, I was surprised to see Claris had already been there. True to her promise, I saw my bag of corn on the porch propped against the front door.

I repositioned my bag from the drugstore in one arm and embraced the corn sack with the other. I awkwardly unlocked the door and pushed it open with my knee.

Going from the bright sunlight into the dimly lit living room temporarily blinded me. I let the drugstore paraphernalia slide onto the couch, landing gently on the cushion. That freed my hands to open and examine my produce.

I balanced the bag on the back of the couch as I unrolled the top. I was still trying to make my visual adjustment from the outside, so I had to stick my head in the bag to get a corn count.

I'm not sure if my eyes focused first or my nose detected that this was not corn. What I saw were feathers, what I smelled was foul. To be more specific, it was a foul owl.

Reactions can be more rapid than reason. I simultaneously screamed and flung the odoriferous owl ceiling-ward. I went yelling out the door for my husband, who tried to assure me that the worst thing my feathered foe could do at this point was smell—no, make that stink—to high heaven, which was exactly where I had tried to throw that bird.

It turned out that some generous gentleman had found this rotting road-kill on the highway and thought we might like to stuff it for the Boy Scout Museum. At that point, I envisioned mounting the motorist, as a menace to mental health . . . mine!

Caution: Examine carefully before
embracing expectations.

35

Stitches

THE NINE-YEAR age span between our boys didn't keep them from big-time wrestling bouts. I pointed out to eight-year-old Jason that challenging his seventeen-year-old brother was not exactly wise. Jason seemed to have a Hulk Hogan mind-set but the body frame of Pee-wee Herman.

During a body slam attempt, he fell over a footstool and cut his head open on the corner of the wall. Les and I hustled Jason off to the emergency room, because it was obvious he would need more than a Band-Aid.

Jason was shaken and asked, "How bad is it?"

I realized that the location of his injury was to our advantage. He couldn't see it.

"Not real bad," I assured him.

"What are they going to do to me?"

Measuring my words I responded, "Fix it."

"How?"

"They're going to put it back together again," I tried.

"How?" he pushed.

I'd run out of Humpty Dumpty stalls and decided to go for the direct approach.

"They're going to stitch that thing shut, Jason," I declared.

He gasped and then groaned. "Is it going to hurt?"

"Probably," I confessed.

"But what if it hurts more than I'm able to bear?" he pleaded.

"Then you'll reach down inside of you and pull up your courage. Because you accepted Jesus as your Savior, He assures us we can do all things through Christ who strengthens us. So if it hurts more than you can bear, you pray, and He will help you."

Jason became very quiet. We pulled up to the emergency entrance, and I took him in while Les parked the car. The doctor came in, took a look at Jason's injury and began to prepare the wound for sutures. Lest things get active, he had two nurses come in, one to stand on each side of Jason.

Halfway through the process, the doctor realized both nurses were not necessary since Jason offered no resistance. Not once did Jason object to the process or cry or even ask the doctor to stop.

One of the nurses turned to leave when she noticed someone else in the room who was in need of help. I'm not sure if it was my magenta and jade skin tone or my swaying in the breeze that alerted her, but she guided me to a chair and began to fan me. Later the doctor assisted me to the car.

On the way out he said, "I cannot tell you what a privilege it was to work on a boy like that."

My husband shot me a glance as if to say, "Wish I could say the same for his mother!"

As we drove home, I asked Jason, "Did it hurt so bad you had to pray?"

"Oh, Mom, I didn't wait. As soon as you told me, I prayed," he confessed.

"What a good idea. I . . . wish . . . I . . . would . . . have . . . thought of that," I whispered.

Is your life sutured in prayer?

36

Girl Talk

"YOU'RE NOT GETTING older; you're getting better!"

Who said that, and whom were they talking about? I've been looking around, and that's not what I'm seeing.

When I say "around," I mean around me. On my fortyish anatomy are ridges. I thought only potato chips were supposed to have those. These are not even rigid ridges. They're more like Jell-O. They slosh when I walk. They appear to hang in folds round about my waist.

Speaking of waste, I think it's a waste of my energy to carry these waving sacks of cellulite that are drooping off my upper arms.

No wonder women get heavier as they age—everything's turning to liquid. We are like walking washing machines. That's why we are so easily agitated and slosh a lot.

My husband and I were eating dinner the other evening when Les said, "You spilled something on your chin."

I quickly picked up my napkin and dabbed my chin.

He quipped, "No, the other one."

I don't know where those other chins came from. They weren't there when I was thirty.

I've been accused lately of looking snooty in my pictures. Don't they understand I have to hold my first chin that high to smooth out the other three?

Speaking of smooth, what has happened to my thighs? They look permanently puckered, like smocking. I feel speed-impaired at times as one leg of blubber bumps the other. Blubber-bumping can be painful.

Speaking of painful, I now get charley horses. The only place I have muscle left, and just my luck, it knots up!

One thing that has definitely increased as I age is my hair count. I have hair in places I never imagined. Like my neck. I have a three-inch follicle growing from my neck just under my third chin.

I've noticed my mental faculties are slowing down, and now I'm expected to learn a new vocabulary. Words like "menopausal"—sounds like a slow date. "Sputtering ovaries"—sounds like a rare bird or an old car. "Estrogen"— sounds like something you'd drink in outer space.

I don't know. This is all too much for me. I think I'm going to have a case of the vapors.

Gird-le up, gals. There's more to life than meets the eye.

37

Cookie Caper

WHITE CREAMY CLOUDS of marshmallow atop a thin layer of graham cracker, covered and sealed in a smooth two-inch tower of chocolate—the lick-your-fingers-and-catch-the-crumbs kind of cookies.

I have this "thing" for chocolate marshmallow cookies—alias pinwheels. At first I didn't realize I had a thing. I told myself I was only buying them for my family. But when I began to resent sharing those sweet treats with my husband and our boys, I took a closer look at my cookie consumption.

In a let's-get-healthy moment, I decided to give up my prized pinwheels. The problem was, one cookie was left and, well, I sort of thought it would be wasteful to throw it out.

Besides I'm not too good at this denial stuff—at least not cold cookie. But to eat the last cookie right then seemed so . . . so sudden.

Plus, when you know this is your last cookie, you don't want to just devour it. The moment should be more ceremonial. The cookie needs to be savored. It needs to be appreciated. It needs to be mine! And I knew if I did a couple of household tasks, which I should do, I wouldn't feel as bad when I ate the last cookie, which I shouldn't do.

To protect my piggish plan, I went into the kitchen and hid the cookie from my family. I tucked it in the bottom kitchen drawer behind the rolling pin, next to the measuring cups, with two hot pads carefully placed over the top to form a roof for my little sugar shack. Then I quietly slid closed the drawer and headed off to do my chores.

I cleaned my desk, dusted the living room and changed the sheets on the boys' beds. Then I headed for the kitchen, feeling I had earned this moment.

I checked over both shoulders before sliding open the drawer and removing the roof. There was the rolling pin and the measuring cups. And next to them was . . . the spot where the cookie should have been. My cookie was gone!

The next thing I remember I was running through the house, grabbing my purse and keys, and crying out, "But, Lord, I said just one more cookie!"

I sprinted to my car and hightailed it for the grocery store. I heard myself murmuring, "Just one more cookie, just one more cookie."

Finally I was in the store, moving quickly, far too quickly I realize now as I think back on the little children I had to move aside to clear the way to the cookie aisle.

At last! I had arrived and there, where they should be, were the cookies. Only one bag of pin-wheels was left.

As I stood there, faced with my vice, that package packed with chocolate, I reminded myself I was an adult, and I had a choice to make. I could buy them, or I could turn and walk away a wiser woman.

Well, I ate two on the way to the checkout lane and three more on the way home.

By the time I pulled into the driveway I was full, and it wasn't just from the cookies. It was also the guilt. I was mad at myself. To think a grown woman could be controlled by a two-inch glob of chocolate!

I thought I was more mature than that. Funny, the Lord didn't seem surprised at all.

Any sugar-coated secrets in your life?

38

Pulling Strings

I'M MARRIED TO a mellow fellow. It's a good thing, because I don't think our house could take two of me. I'm so tightly strung I need the balance of someone who has his feet on the ground.

I can identify with my friend Cindy, who said her husband, Craig, is like a balloon-man. He has both feet securely planted.

She's like a hot-air balloon, flying off in different directions. Craig watches her until she gets a little too far out, and then he takes hold of the string and pulls Cindy back down to earth.

Even though I'm grateful Les is a mild-mannered man, at times I wish he would show a little more enthusiasm. Recently I purchased a new dress, and I brought it out on a hanger for Les's viewing.

"What do you think?" I prompted.

"That's nice."

"Nice?" I cried.

"Didn't you ask me what I thought of your dress?" he asked, puzzled. "Your dress is nice."

"Les, 'nice' makes me nauseous."

"What do you want from me?"

"I want dramatic; I want dynamic; I want some enthusiasm!" I demanded loudly.

"Patsy, that dress is nice," he said with quiet firmness.

So I took the "nice" dress and stomped back to the closet.

On my way across the room, Les called out, "Patsy, look! Patsy, look!"

I turned and saw my two-hundred-pound husband leaping in the air, arms stretched heavenward, exclaiming, "Wow, what a dress! Wow, what a dress!"

I burst out laughing. My steady, ground-level man was behaving like a helium balloon.

Ever notice when we try to remake a person that we are seldom satisfied with the result?

39

Dynamic Duo

THE FLIGHT WAS full. Every seat was filled with an eager traveler leaving the cold Midwest for a warmer destination.

The flight attendant handed out our lunch trays. My next-seat neighbor and I were trying to figure out our questionable cuisine (by its freeze-dried taste), when someone screamed in the back of the plane.

Ever notice when someone screams the quiet that follows seems so loud?

People react differently to a nervous moment. My seatmate began to eat faster and faster. My fork stopped in midair, and I'm sure I appeared frozen in time.

Actually, I was making some fast decisions. My first decision, because I am a great woman of faith, was "I am not going to look."

I knew if I looked I would see that the plane's back section had fallen off, and I would be sucked out. But, if I didn't look, we might land safely before I found out.

That might have worked, except the next time the girl screamed she was standing beside me. Do you know how hard it is to ignore a fellow traveler who's screaming inches from your frozen fork?

By now my seatmate had managed to place all of the food from her tray in her mouth. She had not chewed or swallowed. She looked like she had stored up enough in her cheeks for the winter.

As you might guess, the attendants busily tried to take care of the emergency. It turned out the girl was traveling with her grandmother, who had become ill, and it had frightened the young woman.

As a precaution and to make them more comfortable, they were moved to first class. Soon we noticed grandma and granddaughter were in comfortable conversation with the flight attendant. All was well.

Well, almost all. I had lost my appetite, and my seatmate was looking mumpy.

In an emergency, do you freeze, feed or
face it with faith?

40

Weighty Matters

SCALES THAT ANNOUNCE your weight? You've got to be kidding! How humiliating. I bet some ninety-pound, undernourished model came up with that winner.

The only thing worse than a robot voice announcing my tonnage is a robot with recall.

I was staying with my friends, the Hootens in El Paso, when Joyce announced, "Patsy, we have a new scale you must try."

"Oh, really," I replied with skepticism. "Why is that?"

"It's just wonderful. It talks," she joyfully reported. "It will not only tell you your weight, but it also has a memory and will tell you tomorrow if you have lost or gained."

She was thrilled. I was appalled.

I find it depressing to think that, as Righteous Robot trumpets my weight, everyone in the home hears the results. This isn't the final score for the World Series, for goodness' sakes.

"Patsy has gained five and a half pounds!" I imagined it broadcasting.

Yes, it even calls you by name.

I believe in being friendly, but calling me by my first name in the same breath as my weight is a little too intimate for me.

Next they'll put a microchip in our driver's license that heralds our age every time we pull it out of our wallets.

After a number of creative stalls, I finally responded, "No, Joyce, I'm only here for a few days. I don't think it would be productive."

Translated that means, "Ain't no way I'm leaving Texas with that information left behind."

What weighty issue tips your scale?

41

Buggy

I CRAWLED INTO bed after midnight. Clicking off the light, I dropped my head onto the pillow. As my ears adjusted to the quietness, I began to drift off.

Then it happened. A small but definite noise. The kind of noise that causes me to become irrational and unreasonable.

I sat up in bed and shook Les.

"What's wrong?" he questioned.

"I hear a mouse."

"I don't hear anything," he stated before he even listened. He knew from experience he would get no rest if we had a mouse.

I slipped out of bed and began to move across the creaking wood floor. I stopped several times and tried to detect from which direction the chomping was coming.

This was behavior befitting a Purple Heart. In the past I would have not only insisted Les get up but also that he immediately list the house with realtors.

As I stood statue-like, I glanced down and saw something moving. No, I saw many somethings moving.

"Les, quick," I summoned.

Les jumped to his feet, motivated by the urgency in my voice. Much to our surprise, a long procession of large carpenter ants was pouring out of our heat register, doing double time across the wood floor and under the bedroom door.

We each grabbed a shoe and began to decrease their population. One of them must have yelled "run," because they scattered in all directions.

After a few moments, we stopped to listen. Once again I could hear chomping. This time the noise was very close. The sound seemed to come out of the door.

I placed my ear against the wood, and the mouse-sound magnified. Then I realized the ants weren't going under the door but inside it. The chomping wasn't a mouse, but a colony of carpenters eating their way through the door's inner layers.

Now I wanted to move!

Les, being far more reasonable, did some carpentry work himself. He retrieved some tools, took the door off the hinges and dragged it out into the night. (I was lucky he didn't drag me out.)

We were now door-less and hopefully ant-less. That night I dreamed that Les borrowed a gun and was trying to shoot the invaders out of the door.

The next morning I got up and went to my desk to work. After only a few minutes I heard a familiar sound—like chomping. I walked to my office door and realized it, too, was harboring a colony. Les then unhinged and removed that door.

Now I was coming unhinged! I was feeling antsie. I began to listen at every door, drawer and floor for the pitter-patter of little feet. I couldn't believe we could have that many unwanted guests and not know it.

Our creeping invaders were using the heat ducts as freeways. The ducts gave the critters, who traveled "antnonymously," access to every room. Since we had only seen a few here and there, we didn't realize that they had moved in their relatives. While we were sleeping, they were devouring . . . our house.

Beware of creeping little things
that splinter your house.

42

Airborne

EDITH'S COMBINATION OF qualities drew me to her—her courage, creativity and confidence in God. Besides, she was fun. When I had the opportunity to be her roommate at a women's retreat, I leaped at the chance.

But when I saw the skyscraper we would be calling home, I felt "building dread." I get dizzy when I stand up straight and certainly had not planned on a high-rise experience.

Edith was delighted. For her, everything in life was a grand adventure.

As the clerk mentioned we would be on the twenty-fourth floor, I felt nauseated. Edith was elated. I hate elevators. I tried to figure out how I was going to backpack my luggage up twenty-four flights of steps.

Edith had no idea what I was going through as she headed confidently for the elevators. I had never mentioned to her that I avoided anything that elevates, levitates or regurgitates.

When the elevator arrived, a woman stepped out and proclaimed to me, "That's the fastest elevator I've ever been on!"

I immediately did not care for this woman. She obviously had not been raised properly or had chosen to ignore the commandment "Thou shalt not talk to strangers."

Edith bounded into the elevator and held the door for me. I suggested by my behavior that my suitcase had become so heavy I was unable to get to her. She stared with obvious doubt and confusion. Other people boarded the elevator and glared in my direction with growing agitation.

I knew I would have to get on or be humiliated. I sent emergency prayers heavenward, which by this time I believed to be the twenty-fifth floor.

I tugged at my luggage as I swallowed hard and reluctantly stepped on, closing my eyes so I wouldn't have to see the door seal me in.

Before I could work up a good fear, we had arrived.

Edith opened the door to our room and exclaimed with delight on finding a wall-to-wall, floor-to-ceiling window. I clung to the doorframe to keep our room from sliding off its platform.

She galloped toward the window, thrilled with the view. I began to wonder what I thought was so fun about this woman. She pressed her nose against the glass and beckoned me to join her. Then she turned, surveyed the room and suggested with enthusiasm that we take the bed closest to the window before our other roomies arrived.

"Won't that be fun," I lied.

That night I dreamed I fell off the bed and rolled out the window.

By the time the weekend was over, however, I was grateful I hadn't bolted and run but had stayed and won. I even gradually made my way to the small table next to the window and ate lunch with Edith. This was a mountaintop experience for a former agoraphobic, who couldn't wear high heels without needing oxygen.

Given a choice, I still prefer the first floor; but I've since learned being up doesn't have to be a down experience.

What has you up in the air?

43

Revenge

I'VE ALWAYS BEEN a talker, so it was natural for me, as a teenager, to take a job in telephone sales work. The goal of my position was to interest home-owners in a salesman coming by to explain our service.

Each phone girl had a script to simplify the job, to increase confidence and to keep on target. We sat in a line in front of one long desk that had partitions so we could lean forward and have some privacy when phoning. At the end of the room was a master phone where our boss could listen in on our calls.

The first week of work the boss, without warning, listened in on one of my pitiful attempts. When I hung up, he announced in front of the entire office,

"Patsy, that was the worst sales presentation I have ever heard."

I was humiliated. I was infuriated. I was motivated. I attacked that phoning with fervor and determination.

At the end of the week I had more sales than anyone in the office. By the end of the month I was the top sales girl.

And then in childish revenge . . . I quit!

How do you handle criticism?

44

Birthday Baby

WHEN MY NUTRITIONIST said, "No more sugar," I didn't have a sweet response. I did notice I was feeling better, though, when I followed her advice. But there were times. . . .

We had been invited to Mary Ann and George's for a couples' Bible study. After the study we surprised our mutual friend Burt with a birthday salute. We gave him cards and sang and . . . then it happened. Mary Ann had baked a huge chocolate supreme pudding cake.

George was helping to serve, not only because he's a good host but also because Mary Ann was on crutches, recovering from an injury. Every time George entered the room with generous mounds of cake, applause and groans of gratitude filled the air.

Something began to happen inside of me as I observed this dessert distribution. It annoyed me that everyone was making such a big fuss over a sugar-infested gooey-gob of chocolate.

And why Mary Ann felt led to add super-sized scoops of vanilla ice cream was beyond me. Excessive, that's what it was.

Just look how silly they were behaving, oohing and ahing like children. It seemed to me that it wouldn't hurt a few of them to skip dessert for a while.

It was at this point that my husband was handed his mountainous masterpiece. His eyes were the size of dessert plates. He lit up with glee. Then he leaned over to me and said, "Would you mind getting me some coffee?"

"Get it yourself!" I shot back so quickly and abruptly that it surprised even me.

Les looked at me with the eyes of a rejected puppy. I felt embarrassed and ticked. I grabbed the cup and headed for the kitchen.

When I returned, Les was face first in his dish, having a lip-licking time.

I thought, *How sad that adults behave out of their addictions.*

Mary Ann called from the other room, "Patsy, could you help me?"

I walked into the kitchen, where she pointed to her dessert and sweetly asked, "Would you carry that to the living room for me?"

The injustice of it all! If you can't carry your own cake, then you shouldn't have any, is my theory.

Now, I know one should not think about tripping a person on crutches, but for one moment that thought scampered through my mind.

Grudgingly, I raced back to the main room, got rid of the calorie-crammed cake and took my seat next to Les, who now reeked of chocolate.

Then George decided to close our loving time of fellowship in prayer.

The little child inside of me throwing the temper tantrum stopped long enough to listen. As I walked out the door, I realized I was the only one with cake on my face.

Better check a mirror. I hear it's contagious!

45

Sandal Scandal

JONAH MAKES ME giggle.

Here was a prophet waiting for orders from head-quarters.

When they came, he strapped on his Reebok san-dals and hightailed it out of town—in the wrong direction.

Jonah was a man who decided to live below "see" level, as he boarded the boat and went down into the hold.

I felt a little down myself when my husband came in recently from the mailbox waving a letter. I rec-ognized the telephone company's insignia on the envelope.

"No thanks," I called sweetly. "You can take care of that."

"No," he replied, "I think you need to see this."

"It's really old news when you stop to think about it," I suggested.

"History is valuable; we can learn from it," he insisted.

I tried a spiritual approach. "Forgetting that which is behind, I press on."

By now he was dangling the expansive sheet of long-distance calls in front of my face. I felt "see" sick.

Have you ever noticed when you don't do what you know you should, you lose your vitality? Look at Jonah. After running away and going below see level, he was plum worn out. He was so tired he snored through a life-threatening storm.

My doctor used to tell me, "Patsy, you're like an ostrich. Every time life gets hard, you want to jump in bed and cover up your head."

I would think, *I must be anemic, I must be hypoglycemic, I must have PMS or TMJ or IRS or FBI.*

All I knew was I was one tired woman. Denial and disobedience are draining.

When Jonah climbed onto his ship of self-pity, he had no idea how low he could go.

I wonder if the Lord said, "Jonah needs some time by himself. Gabriel, reserve him a suite at that new Sea Sub Inn. I understand it has a lot of atmosphere."

Jonah didn't seem thrilled with his accommodations. His room didn't have much of a view, but he had plenty of running water and free transportation. The experience must have been inspiring, because he became a motivated prophet and seemed in a hurry to Reebok down to Nineveh.

All ashore that's going ashore.
Or you can stay below see level.

46

Color-Coded

DOES TURNING FORTY bother you?" Les asked on my birthday.

"You've got to be kidding. Everyone has thought I was so much older for so long, it's a relief. It makes me feel legitimate," I insisted.

"You know what I hope never happens to you?" he added wistfully.

"What?"

"I hope you never get to the point, when you wave your hand to say good-bye, your underarm waves in the opposite direction."

"That quite honestly has never entered my mind," I assured him.

My husband may be prophetic, because about two weeks later, during my morning shower, every bit of tone rinsed out of my body and down the drain.

It's truly an aggravating attribute to be moving in one direction and feel your body waving in response. Stopping is the challenge, because it takes several seconds for the fleshy momentum to slow to a jiggle and finally stop. One could suffer from "whip flab" if one were not careful or stopped too quickly.

I realized Les noticed his fear had come true when Mother's Day came that year. He bought me a set of dumbbells. Actually, mine were called "smart bells." I didn't think it was a smart move on his part. I was insulted. No, make that ticked!

Finally I decided to do the scriptural thing with my heavy gift and take the writer of Hebrews' advice, "Let us lay aside every weight . . . which doth so easily beset us . . ." I put them in storage in my bedroom closet.

I had put other things in there never to find them again. I was hoping for that kind of fate for my "bells."

Les never mentioned that I wasn't using them. I think he knew better.

Christmas came, and the memory of my Mom's Day gift had almost faded. For a moment, though, I felt some initial apprehension when he handed me a beautiful package, lest I find a tummy tuck coupon book or a fanny fixer or some other anatomy adjuster.

To my delight, however, I found a multi-colored dress with a shimmering fabric that was feminine and lovely. I was impressed. I was speaking for a luncheon in the area for a holiday celebration, and this would be perfect.

I still remember standing on a small platform speaking on "Jesus Is the Reason for the Season." To add emphasis to one of my points, I made a sweeping gesture only to notice, for the first time, the full draping sleeve.

That's when it hit me; Les had given me colorful camouflage. He had taken a more subtle approach to fleecing my flab. I laughed to myself and thought, *I'll get him later!*

What colorful cover-ups are you using?

47

Alert

BREAKFAST CAN BE dangerous to your health. It can look innocent enough, flakes and raisins floating in milk, like the breakfast I had one morning. If I had left those raisins floating, all might have been well.

I'm not sure now if I coughed or just took a breath, but one of those rebellious raisins ran down my airpipe and wouldn't move. I hacked and coughed. I jumped up and down. Then I realized if I got real still I could breathe. My heart, which had been pounding madly, began to find its rhythm again.

I remembered a doctor was staying on the grounds (we were living at a Youth for Christ camp). If I could get to him, he would help me.

I made it to the dining hall without another fruit fit, and gratefully the doctor had just sat down to eat.

"Doctor," I whispered, "I have a raisin stuck in my windpipe. What should I do?"

He looked at me thoughtfully. After a moment of sizing up the situation, he gave his professional evaluation. "We can do a tracheotomy," he offered calmly, as he reached for his juice glass.

My heart began to palpitate wildly.

"Any other options?" I stammered.

"I could try forceps, but there's a chance the raisin would go into your lung, causing it to collapse," he concluded, as he buttered his toast.

Sweat began to appear on my deeply furrowed brow.

"Doctor, is there anything else I might do?" I whimpered weakly.

"Well," he said, hesitating while he salted his eggs, "you could try relaxing and see if it comes up on its own."

Out of all his medical insights, this one was the most appealing to me. I headed back to my apartment, wondering how that doctor could eat his breakfast while I was obviously terminating on mine.

When I got home, I positioned myself in my rocker to contemplate my fruitful dilemma. My mind began to wander to the future. . . .

I was looking into a cemetery where two women were talking.

The one said, "What's that?" pointing to a large tombstone.

"Oh, the one shaped like a raisin?" the other responded. "I can't remember her name, but she was bumped off by her breakfast."

My heart started to jump again, and I realized I was not helping my situation with my daydreaming. I wandered into the bedroom and cautiously lowered myself onto the bed. It felt like I had a baseball in my throat. I decided to go to sleep so if it didn't work out in my favor I'd never know it.

To my amazement, I fell sound asleep. I woke up a couple of hours later—absolutely fine. I could breathe, the baseball feeling was gone, my lung had not collapsed, and I didn't need a tracheotomy. I checked all around me in bed but found no raisin. I don't know where it went; maybe it was resurrected.

All I know is I learned a good lesson—eat oatmeal.

What's difficult for you to swallow?

48

Scared Silly

WHEN CAROL'S MOM invited me to go on vacation with their family, I was thrilled. Carol was one of my best friends, and I thought a week with her would be an adventure. Carol and I were fifteen. We considered ourselves quite grown up; others seemed to find that debatable.

More than once her mom warned us that we would be staying in a ghost town. There wouldn't be much to do, and there would be no boys. We didn't care, because we enjoyed each other's company, and besides her mother could be wrong about the boys.

We arrived at the little deserted town after dark. Street lights were few and far between. Carol and I took one look at the silhouette of the tall, narrow, rickety house we were to call home that week and announced we weren't going in. It looked spooky to us, and we were scared.

The only thing more intimidating than this haunted-looking house was Carol's mom when she got angry. We had just completed a ten-hour drive, and she didn't want to argue with two sniveling teenagers regarding their accommodations.

Hanging on to each other's shirttails, we inched our way up the rotting steps into . . . a fairly pleasant home. We began to breathe easier until someone mentioned that the bathroom was in the basement.

This was not good news. Carol and I don't do basements. Who in her right mind is going to use a basement rest room in a declining house in a ghost town, especially at night? We decided then and there to exercise great restraint for the next week.

Eventually we realized the futility of that thought and had to make the downward trek. We always entered the cement and stone basement together; and while one went into the water closet, the other sat on the steps nearby.

We talked nonstop and loudly until we came back up, feeling our noise level kept us safe from the basement boogies.

One day Carol and I took a walk through the woods to Lake Superior. On such a beautiful summer day we figured we had no reason to be afraid until . . . we heard noises.

Crackling noises. Crunching sounds. Brush movement.

We glanced at each other as we remembered the stories about area bears. We turned around and began to head back to town with a quickened pace.

The suspicious sounds seemed to quicken, too.

We grabbed hands and began to run and sing loudly. Somehow we both believed that volume was a deterrent to danger. Besides, it had worked so far on the basement boogies, so may be it would work on the backwoods bears.

We thought a popular song about Yogi Bear was appropriate for the occasion. "I'm a Yogi, I'm a Yogi Bear. Hey Boo-Boo," we sang again and again, hoping to distract and deter our assailants.

By the time we reached town, we could hardly catch our breath, our hearts were pounding wildly, and we were laughing and crying with relief.

We never did see anything . . . well, not with our eyes. But in our minds, every bush had become a bear.

What a week we had! One we would never forget. We created much of our own fun . . . and fear.

Any boogies in your basement?

P.S. She was wrong about "no boys." I'm married to him!

49

Misdirected

I HAD JUST disembarked from a rather bumpy flight. Les was waiting to pick me up, and I shared with him about the growing storm clouds around Chicago. He looked at me puzzled and inquired, "How would you know about the weather patterns in Chicago?"

I responded with sarcasm, "Well, isn't that where I've just been?"

"No," he stated with authority, "you've been in New York."

"I was? I thought I was in Chicago," I confessed in a somewhat lower voice.

Shaking his head in disbelief, he walked ahead of me mumbling something about not knowing how I got from one place to another without him.

Well, come on now. They are on the same side of the country. It's not like I mixed up Pittsburgh and Pasadena.

Besides, I can't help it if I came packaged with directional deficiencies. More than once Les has thought he would have to file a missing-person report on me when we have gone browsing.

The new one-stop shopping system offers, under a single roof, everything a couple could want as long as they both shall live, if they don't get hopelessly lost in the aisles in the process. With the size of today's stores, they should offer us maps, guides and skateboards as we enter.

I can't tell you how embarrassing it is to hear your name announced over the intercom. "If Mrs. Clairmont is in the store, Mr. Clairmont would like her to find her way to the front door, and he will lead her to the car."

The one-stop shop in our area is like an enclosed wilderness. I find myself wandering the aisles wondering, *What am I looking for? Why am I here? Where is my husband? How do I get out of this maze?*

Getting out of the store is just the first phase of testing your survival skills. Next is the biggie—finding your car in the parking lot. I have learned to play Car Bingo.

It works like this: Line up your vehicle with a letter on the building or an object. For instance, you might see a trash can at the end of your lane. You then count how many parking spaces between your car and the receptacle.

Let's say there are fourteen. When you come out of the store, you stand in front of the trash can. Then walk fourteen spaces . . . bingo, your car.

This is not exactly foolproof, though, because I notice that malls have a sensitivity to litter. Our mall has sixteen identical garbage bins, which if you have your calculator handy, means I could (did) look in 256 parking slots before I could shout, "Bingo!"

It's taken years, but I can sort of read a map now. If I get to you, however, don't ask me to get back to where I came from. I don't know why, but I can't reverse directions. I'm a one-way lady.

My husband believes that when I was being "knit together," somebody dropped my directional stitches.

Would you mind if I followed you . . .
that is, uh, if you know where you're going?

50

Sew Simple

A STITCH IN time saves nine, unless they're mine!" This quote was said by me, about me, and seconded by my high school home economics teacher.

Our class project was to make a simple straight skirt. Six weeks later, when everyone else was wearing her designer original, I was still trying to sew the darts.

My teacher was not happy. In fact, at times she didn't even look human. Her eyes seemed to glaze over and dilate when she checked my seams.

She made me tear them out so many times it was difficult to find enough solid material on which to try my next stitches.

Finally, a neighbor woman took pity on me and finished my skirt. My teacher knew an adult had sewn it, but she didn't seem to mind. In fact, she looked relieved—until she found out I had enrolled in sewing for another semester.

After announcing to the new class its sewing project, she took me aside and told me I would be doing something different. She decided I should knit a little pair of slippers. The problem was I didn't know how to knit. She assured me it would be simple.

Six weeks later I had a healthy square of knit—— too large for a slipper, too small for a rug. I never did figure out how to fit it around my foot.

But my teacher didn't want it on my foot any- more. She mumbled something about putting it in a time capsule, because future generations wouldn't believe anyone could get that many stitches per square inch. I guess I held my needles a little too tight.

When I married Les, I didn't mention my home ec experiences. It didn't seem relevant——until he asked me in our first week of marriage to sew a tear in his pants' seam. I obliged, because I didn't want him to think I couldn't handle my wifely duties.

Several times he came in to see if his pants were ready. I took my time to make sure the stitches were secure.

A little while later Les came hopping out of the bathroom, unable to get his foot through the leg. It seems I stitched through one too many layers. Sometimes it's the thought that counts.

After years of Les doing our mending, the Zander family came into our lives. Margret is a seamstress, and George is a tailor.

Margret assured me that my schoolteacher was wrong, and Margret had never met anyone she couldn't teach to sew. It would be simple.

Margret began to work with me. She was patient. She was kind. She was thorough.

Then one day she looked at me and said, "Patsy, there are exceptions to every rule. From now on you bring your sewing to me."

Feeling unraveled?
There are those He sends to sew and mend.

51

Subpoena

ORDER! ORDER! ORDER in the house!

Those words echoed in my head every time I opened a drawer, closet or cupboard. The gavel of conviction was pounding out my disorderly conduct.

I confess my house got away from me. It happened a little at a time, like mold slithering over some elderly eggplant in the back of my refrigerator. Because a person could do dust etchings on my bookshelves and grease engravings on my range, it was clear evidence was piling up against me.

I don't think all of the household disarray was my fault, though. For instance, take the socks . . . actually, you don't have to. Someone already did.

Every third pair of socks, correction, that's "sock," in our home lives a solitary life.

If professionals were brought in on this case, they'd discover my dryer has a latent aggression problem. When it surfaces, the heating element disintegrates individual stockings, leaving me holding the spouseless sock. My dryer is selective and careful never to destroy two of the same kind——a true sign of a criminal mind.

I plead guilty to the webbing on my wall hangings, but I had an accomplice. My friend Norm Crane told me, "Never kill a spider. They are wonderful house guests because they are like having your own built-in silent exterminator."

Norm obviously doesn't suffer from arachnophobia.

My husband and two sons struggle with basketphobia. They can't get close enough to my strategically placed baskets to toss in their dirty clothes. They prefer corners, chairs and doorknobs.

It does give a certain lived-in look (the kind you might find in a high school locker room after a losing game). They drape their used sweat suits and socks so that any movement of air might permeate our home with their own personal fragrance.

My junk drawer in the kitchen has overflowed, spilling shoe horns, screwdrivers, safety glasses, soda straws and squirt guns onto the countertops. This gives the room an antiquated ambience.

I'm drowning in our clutter. I think someone should provide a household suction service in which workmen could pull up in their garbage truck-type vehicle, attach a giant suction tube over the opening of the front door and then throw the switch.

The machine would create a vacuum, sucking up everything that wasn't put away. A second switch would then be activated, and the disorganized debris would be compacted into filler for highway potholes.

We would improve our environment, recycling our clutter while providing a service. Then, instead of tripping over our junk, we could drive on it.

Perhaps I could get probation if I volunteered to work on the Household Suction Service crew. We could start on my house.

Need any debris suctioned from your life?

52

Culprit

I HAD NEVER kidnapped anyone before, and I was quite excited at the prospect. All the details had to be set in motion if I was to pull it off. This would require accomplices.

I called my victim's workplace, and the secretary (alias, the boss's wife) agreed to schedule a bogus meeting for the employees on Friday at noon.

Next, I lined up my mom to stay at the house with Jason while I was on the lam. I then packed a suitcase, smuggled it to the car and stashed it in the trunk.

I included only a few conspirators to help prevent a leak that would blow this whole operation. I didn't need a traitor; I had too much riding on this to let someone squeal and mess up my action.

A couple of hours away from the scene of the crime was a hotel. I called the innkeeper and told him to get things ready and to make sure I wasn't disturbed after I arrived. I promised him if he followed instructions I'd make it worth his while.

Finally the day arrived. My heart was racing with anticipation. Everything was going as planned.

I arrived at the victim's work at 12:01. Entering the front door, I asked him if I could speak to him for a moment in my car.

I had left the engine running, and when he got in and closed the door, I sped off.

At first there were verbal objections. "You can't do this! You can't do this!"

I handed him a hand-scrawled statement:

Dear Husband,
You have just been officially kidnapped. All necessary people have been notified. All business matters have been covered. Your clothes are in the trunk. Take a deep breath. Relax. I'm in charge now, and you must do as I say.
Love,
Patsy

We arrived at the Victorian bed-and-breakfast, which was decorated for the holidays. We had our picture taken in old-fashioned garb to commemorate my crime. I showered him with gifts—a shirt, pants, robe and slippers. I purchased a tape of old funny radio broadcasts. We reminisced and giggled and had a wonderful time.

I wonder if this would be considered a crime of passion? If so, I plead guilty.

Sometimes crime does pay.

53

SWAT Team

Z-Z-Z-Z-Z-ZZZZ

I had just slipped into bed when I heard the dreaded hum of a mosquito.

Z-Z-Z-Z-ZZZ

I knew it was no use trying to go to sleep until the enemy had been eliminated. I flicked on the light, which woke Les with a start.

"Whas-amatter?" he slurred.

"There's a mosquito in here . . . listen," I whispered.

Z-Z-Z-ZZZ ZZZ-Z ZZ-ZZZ

"Les, either this is the biggest mosquito God ever created, or he has friends," I speculated.

Les grabbed his discarded T-shirt to snap at the little varmints.

I spotted one and alerted Les, "There it is on the ceiling over the washstand."

At the same time, he was zeroing in on two more by the dresser. A few spectacular leaps and swats took care of our troublesome trio.

Since it was already after midnight, we were glad to turn off the light and go to sleep.

z-z-z-zzzz

"You're kidding," Les growled.

I reached over to my nightstand, running my hand down the cord to the switch and once again illuminated the battlefield.

It was us against them, and they had come armed for battle. Their entire platoon had been called in. They attempted several strategies—the old dive-bomb-the-head maneuver and the tricky blend-in-with-the-wood-and-wallpaper routine.

Les outdid himself with breathtaking counter-attacks. I think the most impressive ones were as he bounced up and down off our mattress and in one swipe wiped out two of those little scoundrels. Of course, his shocking-pink, striped boxer shorts definitely added flashes of color as he leaped back and forth about our boudoir.

I acted strictly as a spotter, carefully camouflaged under the sheet, lest I become their next juicy victim. Some of their kamikaze pilots had come in and were doing suicidal spirals at our anatomies.

But no fear . . . Les was here! My husband was taking his call to active duty like a real soldier, with true dedication. He was now a two-fisted fighter, T-shirt in one hand, fly swatter in the other.

I became a little nervous, though, when he leapt over me in attempts to get escaping prisoners.

About 2:00 A.M. my dedication faded, and I fell sound asleep. I woke at 8:00 A.M. to find my husband standing over his trophies.

He had killed more than forty mosquitoes before he discovered and closed off their access point. He had twenty-three bodies lined up for all to see. The rest were splattered in various spots in our bedroom. Unlike me, who had gone AWOL, he had stayed faithful until the war was won.

Are you steadfast in life's battles?

54

Sow's Ear

THE FLIGHT ATTENDANT struggled to position my purse under the seat, insisting it must be stored before takeoff lest it "get loose" and endanger fellow passengers. I noticed a smirk at the corners of her mouth as she said, "I bet you can hold a lot in there."

I'm sure it must look comical to see a five-foot lady carrying a six-foot purse, but I find it a necessity. I remember a fellow passenger once commenting as I struggled to the ticket counter, "Lady, it's hard to tell if you're carrying that purse or it's walking you."

Men don't understand; women have stuff. Important stuff. One never knows what one may need when one leaves home.

In my purse I carry practical provisions, like a pencil sharpener, nail polish remover, vitamins, flashlight, collapsible scissors and drinking cup, five tubes of lipstick, tweezers, floss and other stuff too numerous to mention and too valuable to leave at home.

My purse is an extension of my home. I have every room represented in the folds of my hand-bag.

I tried a few smaller purses, but I had to carry two, and even then the tops wouldn't close.

My friend Emilie recommends you carry little purses inside your bigger purse to keep the contents organized. I tried that, but I needed so many little ones, it made my paunchy purse look like it had a fertility problem.

Some purses are designed with compartments. I owned one with so many built-in pouches and pockets that I needed a directory to remember where I had stored my stuff.

Today's fad is belly bags that tie around your waist, leaving your hands free. Great concept . . . for those who have a waist. There's no way I'm going to add inches to the bag already permanently affixed to my bod.

Businessmen understand purses better than they let on. Take note of their briefpurses—excuse me, briefcases. That's where they carry their stuff. Pens, paper, passport, paper clips and paraphernalia.

I was almost cured of my handbag hang-up when I was diagnosed with purse-itus. That's when your purse straps embed themselves in your shoulder, leaving you bound to your belongings.

After a temporary separation, my bag and I have

been reunited and are working out a contents settlement. I've agreed to lighten its load; and in return, my purse has promised not to be such a weight around my neck.

What kind of "stuff" are you carrying?

55

Vantage Point

Winter . . . BRRRR . . . I never liked the cold.

For years I whined my way through winter, feeling justified as I listened to many others complain about the cold. Then we moved to a Boy Scout reservation on six hundred twenty-five acres, and I realized it could be a long, lonely winter if I didn't find some way to use my time. I decided to take up cross-country skiing.

First, I had to purchase my equipment. That was fun. I chose adorable powder blue ski pants, matching jacket, a sweet little knit hat, fluffy mittens, groovy goggles, floral long johns, cute color-coordinated shoes, darling little poles and oh, yes, some skis.

Les did not think it was wise for a non-athletic novice to go sliding off by herself into half a mile of heavily wooded acreage. I kept assuring him I could handle this.

I can still hear him calling to me as I glided out of sight, "If you get lost out there, I'm not looking for you till spring."

There's something about having the right equipment that can give one unrealistic confidence. I felt as though I looked professional—besides, how hard could it be to walk in the snow?

I was amazed how quickly I picked up a rhythm. The snow must have been just right for gliding, because I was moving well, and my overrated view of my ability was growing with every stride.

At this point I passed the hill . . . a sizable hill . . . a steep hill. It seemed to be beckoning me, tempting me, daring me. What could there be to tucking my poles and bending my knees? Life was meant to be lived. I decided to go for it.

I positioned myself confidently and then learned forward. Who would think one little lean could start one in such a downward direction? The wind blowing briskly about my face reminded me of the exhilarating challenge of life. I believe it was at this moment that I spotted the lake, which reminded me of the excruciating pain of death.

I seemed to be headed for the thinly ice-covered water at an increased rate of speed. I meant to learn how to swim, I really did. (This though seemed a little hindsight-y.)

Being perceptive, it didn't take me long to tune into one fact—whoever designed these skis forgot an important feature: the brakes. You would think that a backup parachute would be required at the time of purchase. Where's Ralph Nader when you need him?

No fear though, for there, before my eyes, was an escape route—a grove of fir trees. Actually, I could see now that I couldn't miss those babies if I wanted to.

Leaping sideways to try to slow my momentum, I bounced off almost every tree trunk in the woods. Limbs met my face and body with a whipping force.

Finally I came to a stop. Wrapped securely in bark at the base of a tree, I lay very still. Snow is not as soft as it looks.

Slowly I tried moving body parts that just minutes before were gliding merrily along with little effort. Now some parts had no feeling while others had a great rush of pain.

Les's face flashed through my mind. I could almost see that "I warned you" look, followed by a smirky smile. I determined then to keep this story under my skis.

Discomfort began to attack all parts of my body. Nothing seemed to be broken, just painfully rearranged.

The hill had acquired mountain proportions. I was scaling it on my knees while dragging my slightly abused ski equipment behind me. I had the suspicion that someone was videotaping this escapade, and the next time Les was watching sports, I would be featured in the "thrill of victory and the agony of defeat" segment.

I buried the bent equipment in the snow beside the house and slipped onto the porch. Swallowing my groans, I made my way through the house to my room, sat down on the bed and started the uncomfortable task of disrobing.

Just then Les walked in.

I'm not sure if it was my lopsided groovy goggles, the pine cones hanging off my sweet little hat, or the evergreen needles protruding from my front teeth, but he sensed things had not gone well.

He was actually quite merciful. He only sang thirty-two rounds of "The Old Gray Mare."

When he left the room I looked down and saw the packaging my goggles had come in. It read, "High-altitude glasses." I thought, *That's what I need.* Not ski equipment but the advantage of a Higher perspective. Perhaps then I would have chosen tatting for my winter sport.

What was that again, the thing that
goes before a fall?

56

Weather Watch

MY FRIEND DON Garrett tells me I talk twenty-five miles per hour with gusts up to fifty. My husband says that is ridiculous—my gusts are at least a hundred.

Gusty people are easy to identify. We are the ones broadcasting our biographies to the world. Our friends run from us in the grocery store. We are part of the reason Reeboks are so popular. People spot us by the cereal and quickly jog three aisles over to the dog food just to avoid us. They give up their Wheaties for WoofWoofs and figure it's a small price to pay.

Usually friends feel guilty playing dodge-'em cart, but they know if they ask how we are, we'll start at birth. Most people don't have that kind of time, interest or attention span.

When two Gusties meet up, sprint for cover. Even a windbreaker won't protect you from their gale-force exchange.

They start talking before the grocery baskets stop rolling as each attempts to get his or her news out first. This is an important part of the strategy, so that at the end of the first speaker's whirlwind of words, that person can announce, "Have to run!" The plan is to escape the blast of babble from the opponent.

Gusties have incredible lung capacities. They know if they take a breath, someone else might get control of the conversation. They speed-speak, which requires them to mentally remove all punctuation, enunciation and hesitation.

When two prolific Gusties visit, they often speak in overlap. That's where before one can finish a thought, the other speaks over the top of the victim's words and runs away with the spotlight. The main objective is not what is being said but who gets to say it.

Receiving a telephone call from a Gusty can leave you feeling blown away by the velocity of verbosity. It's amazing that a person can utter so many words and actually say so little.

The good news about Gusty callers is that you can lay down the receiver, complete several tasks and pick up the phone without having them miss you. They are what you might call self-contained conversationalists.

If you meet a Gusty with PMS or one in mid-life, watch out! It adds a whole new meaning to "the winds of adversity." Meeting one is like trying to hug a hurricane. Storm warnings should be posted during these seasons for the safety of the public.

Do you leave people with a wind-blown look?

57

Visitors

L ES AND I have been married . . . forever. Our
marriage didn't start in paradise but in a basement. It didn't start out like Eden but more like
eek.

Our first apartment was in a monstrous, ancient,
decrepit, mansion-type house. Ours were the only
basement quarters. That should have made us cautious, but we were young, inexperienced and poor.
We had to live in the inner city to be close to the
bus station so Les could get back and forth to the
military base.

After we paid the rent, we had five dollars for groceries and bus fare. We bought milk, bread and
bologna. That simplified meal planning.

Les spent every other night at the barracks,

which meant I was alone. This was a new experience for me.

Our apartment was furnished in early ark artifacts. We had three rooms and a bath. Because the rooms were lined up on one wall of the basement, the floor plan was like a conveyor belt. We had to go through the living room to get to the bedroom, and through the bedroom to get to the kitchen, and through the kitchen to enter the bathroom.

Our bathroom was unique in that you had to stand in the doorway to take your shower. It seemed the shower head was permanently jammed in a northeast direction.

One night when I was alone and bored, I decided to eat something. I thought my big menu decision was whether to have my bologna sandwich with or without a glass of milk. I was wrong.

When I opened the cabinet that housed my bread, I found other tenants. Roaches. Hundreds of roaches. The bread bag hadn't been retied securely, and it was alive with these pilfering pests. They were feasting on my valuable staple.

I was repulsed and angry. Slamming the cupboard shut, I flicked off the light and fumed back to the living room.

As my hunger increased, I reasoned that those nasty varmints couldn't get into the refrigerator where the milk and meat were safely stored. So I went back to the kitchen.

As I turned toward the refrigerator, I saw something move. I froze in my tracks and so did it. I was about three feet from the biggest rat I had ever seen. Well, actually it was the only rat I had ever seen.

In slow motion I climbed onto the tabletop as a scream moved through my body and out my lips.

My new roommate decided to vacate by scrunching under the kitchen door. This door led to the rest of the basement, which was a dark maze filled with furnaces for the upstairs apartments.

While perched on my platform I cried . . . profusely! I didn't know anyone, we had no phone and no money, it was late, and Les wouldn't be home until the following day. We didn't even have a TV or radio that I could turn on to scare the rat and give me a diversion.

When I ran out of alternatives, I remembered the Lord. It had been a while since I had talked with Him, but I wanted to now.

After an emergency prayer time, I cautiously made my way off the table. Then I quickly turned on every light in the apartment. I stuffed towels in the scrunch space under the door. Then I sat in the living room and plea-bargained with the Lord.

Eventually, I braved my way to bed, praying all the way. As I lay back against my pillow, an incredible peace came over me. I felt so safe and cared for. I could feel the stress of my trauma ease out, and I felt myself falling asleep.

Have you noticed when you run out of places
to turn, He's always there?

58

What a Pain

BEFORE I EVEN opened my eyes, I knew I was in trouble. My stomach felt as though it was an automatic butter churn. The paddles were doing double time, and everything in there was clabbered. My head felt light, and when I opened my eyes, my body seemed to jounce.

I sat up abruptly, hoping to recall my head from the ceiling. It didn't work.

I carefully inched my way to the edge of the bed and tried to figure out what was going on. My twirling head made it difficult to reason.

I thought may be I'd feel better if I got up and moved around. I slid off the side of the bed onto legs like Jell-O and hugged the wall. I decided I was dying.

"Les, Les," I groaned pitifully down the stairs.

"What?" he called back cheerfully from his office.

"I'm sick. I think I'm dying," I whimpered, resenting his good mood.

I'm into group suffering. If I'm not doing well, it's not that I want you to be sick exactly . . . miserable will do.

Les bounded up the steps and then walked too heavily down the hall, hurting my now throbbing head. He took one look at me embracing the wallboard and announced, "You look like you're dying."

I didn't have time to thank him for his words of encouragement, because I had a physically compelling desire to visit, if not move into, our bathroom.

I have always found kneeling in front of a ceramic centerpiece humbling.

Finally I moaned my way back to my bed where I found Les trying to stifle a case of the giggles under his pillow.

"I'm sorry," he confessed, "but if you could only hear yourself."

I personally find it helpful to moan if I am in pain. The more pain, the louder I moan. Besides helping me deal with my discomfort, it alerts everyone within a one-mile vicinity that I am not doing well. I am certainly not opposed to get-well gifts.

I reminded Les of that and told him he had better hurry because I wasn't sure how long I could hang on.

Turns out that my terminal illness was a short-term flu. Just about the time I thought I was taking my last breath . . . I was well.

Can you handle pain, or . . . are . . . you one?

59

Wild Bunch

I'M STAYING ON beautiful grounds that belong to my friend Verna. While I'm resting and writing, I'm in a home tucked in the woods. God's fingerprints are all around . . . as well as His sense of humor.

I was reading one morning when I heard what at first sounded like a squeaky wheel. As the sound moved closer, I went to the window.

Much to my surprise and delight I saw a flock of wild turkeys. Counting heads was hard because they were moving so quickly, but I figured there were at least forty of them.

They appeared to be having an intense meeting. Having divided into opposing sides, they were in a heated debate. One group would aggressively storm their opponents, gobbling forcefully. The others

would then respond confrontationally, their gob-
bles sounding at times more like screeching. It
seemed as though those yelling loudest were the
most intimidating.

One small group separated from the others in
pursuit of a lone turkey, apparently trying to whip
him into shape or get him to submit. They surrounded him, backed him into several trees and
didn't let up until he hightailed it to the back of the
pack.

Then one of them spread his masterful tail
feathers and began to strut. Immediately the flock
settled down and followed the flamboyant one single file into the woods.

As I observed these turkeys, I couldn't decide if I
had just witnessed a political rally or a church
board meeting.

Gobble Gobble

60

Bus Stop

JASON, OUR YOUNGEST, has two goals in life. One is to have fun, and the other is to rest. He does both quite well. So I shouldn't have been surprised by what happened when I sent him to school one fall day.

As Jason headed off for the bus, I immediately busied myself, preparing for a full day. The knock on the door was a surprise and disruptive to my morning rhythm, which is not something I have a lot of. I flew to the door, jerked it open, only to find myself looking at Jason.

"What are you doing here?" I demanded.

"I've quit school," he boldly announced.

"Quit school?" I repeated in disbelief and at a decibel too high for human ears.

Swallowing once, I tried to remember some motherly psychology. But all that came to my mind was "A stitch in time saves nine" and "Starve a fever, feed a cold," or something like that. Somehow they didn't seem to apply to a six-year-old drop-out dilemma.

So I questioned, "Why have you quit school?"

Without hesitation he proclaimed, "It's too long, it's too hard, and it's too boring!"

"Jason," I instantly retorted, "you have just described life. Get on the bus!"

Well, I cannot tell you how many times the Lord has had to echo that counsel back to me—times when I've questioned, "Lord, You say You'll never give us more than we can bear. You must not be looking. This is hard, very hard!

"By the way, Lord, it's been lasting a l-o-n-g time. And truthfully, it's getting bo-ring!"

About that time, in the recesses of my mind, I hear the refrain, "It's life; get on the bus!"

Bus token, anyone?

61

Prophet Profile

God purchased His people to plant them in the place of His prosperity. Let's peer into the power-packed pages of our Protector's priceless promises to see this very thing.

In His publication, on the first page of Exodus, we see God's people pleading in prayer, as prisoners of pharaoh because of population problems. When God's people pray, He delights in providing.

But point two becomes perplexing when the provision for His people is put in a pond, pulled from the basket and placed in pharaoh's daughter's arms. She beats a pathway back to the palace to prepare him to become a prince.

Problems arise for Moses when he becomes a perpetrator. The palace becomes a perilous place, so he heads for the pasture.

Now how could pasturing stupid sheep ever prepare you to lead God's people? Perfectly!

We begin to see the process to become one of God's VIP's . . . plagues, Passover, pillars and piled-up water that became a pathway for some and a precarious place for others.

Perhaps you've been pondering your future plans and feel perplexed. Well p'shaw y'all! Just remember Moses, who went from the pond, to the palace, to the pasture, to the pinnacle, to view the promised land before entering paradise. Praise the Lord.

Normal
Is Just a Setting
on Your
Dryer

To my mom
Rebecca McEuen,

housekeeper, homemaker,
& humorist
extraordinaire

Contents

Acknowledgments

Writing a book is never a normal experience, nor does its completion express the efforts of just one person. It took a lot of above-normal people for this project to become reality.

My husband, Les: thank you for your love and all the creative ways you find to express it.

My firstborn son, Marty: thanks for all the hugs when I felt discouraged.

My younger son, Jason: thanks for believing the best in me and for me.

My sister, Elizabeth Vegh: thanks for laughing at my stories.

My editor, Janet Kobobel: thanks for your above-and-beyond-the-call-of-duty involvement. You are not normal; you're exceptional.

My computer specialist, Mary Low Schneemann: thanks for responding to a last-minute, frantic call with sacrificial generosity.

My adviser, Ruth Ann Davis: thanks for your insights that you wrap in life-giving humor. You have been a healing gift to me.

Thanks also to friends who nudged, nurtured, and prayed:

Carol Porter	Nancy Berrens
David Berrens	Ginny Lukei
Jan Frank	Lauren Hess
Danya Voigt	Joanie Karpanty
Lana Bateman	Debbie Wirwille

Thank you also to Verna Paul for giving me an anything-but-normal hideaway. It was truly a little bit of heaven.

Finally, a big thank-you to Focus for including me in the family. A special thanks to Al Janssen, Gwen Weising, and Larry Weeden.

1

Normal Nonsense

LORD, IF ONLY I could be normal like other people!" That was my constant prayer during the years I hid away in my home with agoraphobia (a constricting circle of fears that leaves one housebound). Then I got out of my home, into the flow of people, and found out "ain't nobody normal." Unique, yes. Special, definitely. Normal, no way!

Normal is just a setting on your clothes dryer and has nothing to do with people. Try as we might, we remain peculiar people with distinct differences.

I was peeling tomatoes in my kitchen one day when a friend began to laugh. Surprised, I asked what was so funny.

"I've never seen anyone take the skin off tomatoes before adding them to the salad," she said. She thought that was abnormal.

But when I was growing up, my mom always removed the peel for our guests. She considered it good manners to make things special and convenient for our company. Peeling tomatoes was the norm for us.

I had a neighbor we nicknamed Mrs. Ickity-Pickity because of her seemingly abnormal need to have things clean. We used to laugh because she even washed the soap in her soap dish.

Today I don't think that's strange at all. I find it unappealing to spot a grimy gob of gooey soap stuck in the sink. It is now my normal procedure to follow Mrs. Ickity-Pickity's example and douse my Dial.

My husband, Les, not only felt it was normal to rise up early, but he also was certain other people's character was flawed if they didn't leap out of bed at the first glimmer of light. Normal for my family, on the other hand, mean that on days when schedules permitted, a late morning snooze was a treat to be enjoyed. You can imagine the conflict these two "normals" caused as they—and we—collided.

As an agoraphobic, I felt anything but normal. I didn't know of anyone else who was afraid to go to the grocery store because the aisles seemed to swallow them up. I didn't know of anyone who listened to 30 weather reports every day and then hid under the table from approaching storms. Nor had I talked with anyone who couldn't ride elevators or stay alone at night. Then when I had to give up driving because of panic attacks, I knew I was hopelessly abnormal.

Yet if you could coax agoraphobics into a room together, there would be a "normalcy" among us in that our behavior would match in many ways. Just goes to show—normal is only a setting on a dryer.

I believe abnormal is normal. Think about it. Consider your friends—great people, but don't they have some pretty curious ways? Abnormal is not an isolated occurrence but a constant reoccurrence. It's something we share in common . . . our differences.

I kept trying to attain normalcy by being what I thought others thought I should be. How exhausting! Everyone seemed to have his or her own definition of my normal, leaving me feeling like an isolated emotional abnormality.

That's what this book is about—emotions and how they affect and infect our lives and our need for a healthy balance. We'll look at a variety of emotions and how, if we deny them, we end up out of balance, and yet if we indulge them, our pendulum swings too far the other way.

This *isn't* a book on how to be normal. (I haven't figured that out yet.) Rather, it's an encouragement to be the best "us" we can. We think we know ourselves so well, yet we find our emotions often mysterious. And sometimes our emotions surprise and overwhelm us.

You may experience different feelings in response to these stories of others who struggle, fail, start over, and celebrate. You'll see that life is seldom as simple as setting your dryer to normal. And my prayer is that you might laugh, cry, think, remember, and come to understand yourself better as you move through the pages of this book.

2

Sure I Can!

MOST OF US over 40 find it difficult to believe we're losing our youth. Our minds are still spunky, at least in a sputtering kind of way, and tend to send inaccurate information to our bodies like "You can still leap buildings in a single bound." Right. I can hardly step into an elevator without having my arches fall.

At 47 (at the time of this writing), my mind is marching to "The Battle Hymn of the Republic," while my body is humming in the background, "That'll Be the Day." Even with my increasing physical disruptions, I keep holding my thumb over the birth date on my driver's license when I'm cashing a check.

My friend Claris, a heroic woman who drove school buses for 19 years and has lived to tell of it, forgot her age. It had to be amnesia that caused her to be coaxed into going roller-skating in her forties. An hour later she was in an ambulance, and she wasn't driving. A cast, crutches, and several months later, Claris was back wheeling around in her bus, which has the only size wheels she now trusts to hold her up. Speaking of holding up, . . .

Jim was certain he could reach a little higher than his arm span while tottering on the top rung of the ladder. Need I tell you any more? Our fiftyish friend came down like the Jericho walls, but instead of broken pitchers, he had broken ribs. After being taped back together, he felt every breath he took. Speaking of breathtaking, . . .

Meagan decided to take up downhill skiing . . . at 40. Her first time out she fell backward on her skis, but they didn't release. That was not good. Meagan had to be removed from the slopes on a stretcher by the ski patrol. She wore a mega foam collar for months.

You would think we would learn from our friends' examples. Well, actually I did. I don't roller-skate, climb ladders, or ski downhill. No, not me: I'm too smart to try those tricky feats. Instead, I decided to ride a five-speed bicycle. My infamous ride would have been a cinch had I ever before ridden a bike with the brakes on the handlebars, which I had not. That became quite clear to who knows how many.

My son Jason and I rode our bikes to a nearby store, where, instead of braking when the bike slowed down, I side-saddled it and jumped off like

Annie Oakley. I ran into the store and bought a couple of small items. We didn't have a basket, but I was confident I could manage the bike and the bag. It had been many years since I had ridden a bicycle. (Actually, I was eight when I got my last bike.) But you know what they say: "Once you learn, you never forget."

We were almost home when my bike began to pick up speed. Evidently there was more of an incline on our street than I had realized. For a moment I felt like a kid again, with the wind whipping through my tresses and the houses passing by in a whirl of colors. Suddenly I recognized the whirling greens as my house. I instinctively pedaled backward to brake. Nothing happened. I mean, nothing happened! My acceleration was such that I could see I was headed rapidly for the side street. If my calculations were correct, I would cross it at the speed of light.

Feeling I was losing control of this ride, I kind of panicked. Then I recalled Les's reminding me, as I rode away, that the brakes were located on my handlebars, and that I should squeeze them to stop. I could only grip on one side because of the bag, and when I squeezed, nothing happened. Seeing my life skate-board past me, I grabbed for the other grip, bag and all, and pulled as hard as I could. Sure enough, something happened!

I became airborne. Over the handlebars and into the wild, blue yonder. I'm sure I looked like a 747 wide-body. That is, until my landing. I did a belly-flop glide down my sidewalk/run-way, stopping just before I became a permanent design on our front steps.

Jason looked down at me in utter amazement. I'm not sure if he couldn't believe I could ride a bicycle that fast or fly that high.

If this had happened to you or you had observed it happening to someone else, what would you expect the first words out of the person's mouth to be? Perhaps "Call 911!" or "Get your dad!"

Well, that's what a normal person might say. But not me. The first words out of my swelling lips, while my face was still ingrained in the cement, were, "Is anyone looking?"

Is anyone looking! Give me a break! The sidewalk/slide had torn my pant leg off, my knee was ripped and gushing, I had skid marks on my stomach, my elbow felt like Rice Krispies, my ribs had a Vise-Grip on my lungs, and I wanted to know, "Is anyone looking?"

With Jason's help, I limped into the house, carefully lowered myself into a chair, and cried. My tears were as much out of embarrassment as from pain.

From my emotional response, I had obviously damaged something more than my body. Mine was a giveaway statement of someone suffering from fractured pride.

But then I wondered: Isn't that true for any of us who can't accept our limitations?

3

Ouch!

"PAIN IS GOD'S megaphone," C.S. Lewis said.

If that's true, then, folks, I've heard from heaven!

Last year I went through months that were a literal pain in the neck. I've been accused of being one, and now I know what it feels like to have one.

I hauled too many suitcases, briefcases, purses, word processors, and carryon's through too many airports and hotel lobbies. I exceeded my recommended load limit, and in doing so, I stretched my back and tendons. I then spent painful months learning the importance of listening to my body.

My physical therapist asked why it took me so long to seek medical help. To tell you the truth, I thought I was just being wimpy, and that if I kept bench pressing my luggage, eventually I would look as fit and fabulous as Stormie Omartian. Instead I complicated my recovery, as the tendon damage spread from my shoulder to my elbow, and then to my wrist.

Our bodies protest when we do things that are beyond their ability to perform. Body signals alert us in many ways. Our muscles, tendons, ligaments, and back scream when we try to lift or carry things that are too heavy.

Les is a strapping fellow who, during his younger years, was so strong (how strong was he?) he could lift buffalo. What he shouldn't have tried to carry was the two bundles of shingles for our roof. Actually, he might have achieved that hefty task if, after he slung both bags of shingles over his shoulder, he hadn't had to climb up two stories on a ladder. Even then he might have made it if, when he put his foot on the roof, the ladder had stayed still. Which it didn't. And neither did he.

The first part of Les's fall was broken by a porch landing. He then proceeded to tumble down a flight of steps and collide with the less-than-cushy earth.

Stunned, Les lay very still to assess the damage. After a few breathless moments, he rose slowly, slung the bags over his shoulder again, and climbed back up on the roof.

Les's friend Tom Wirsing had witnessed this acrobatic feat. But because Tom was on the roof when it happened, and Les took the ladder with him when he fell, Tom couldn't come to Les's aid. He spent several harrowing moments as a helpless bystander. When Les stepped back on the roof, Tom had just two words for him: "Go home!"

The next morning, Les's body was buzzing with messages. Les needed a headset to keep up with all the incoming data. His back went on strike, and his legs, sympathetic to the back's protest, filed their own grievance. Muscles he didn't know were a part of the human structure reported their existence. Bruises the size of roof tiles added color to his battered frame. The bruises served for quite a while, like Post-It notes, as a reminder never to do that again.

Along with Post-It notes, our bodies have built-in alarm clocks. Instead of waking us up, they're designed to insist on rest. These alarms go off every time our heads nod dangerously behind a steering wheel, we fall asleep in class, or we drag through a day with the enthusiasm of a yawn.

When Les and I were a young married couple (versus the relics we are today), Les worked a long way from home. One morning, as he neared work, he began to nod. We had stayed up late that week, and his need to sleep sat on his eyes like sandbags. The sound of the early-morning traffic became a lullaby, and Les took a nap. It didn't last long. He woke abruptly when he hit a parked car, which hit a parked car, which hit another parked car.

Les called me on a pay phone from the scene of the crash. "Patsy, I've been in an accident."

"Are you okay?"

"I'm not sure. My head is bleeding. Here come the police. I have to go." And he hung up.

I was seven months pregnant and beside myself with concern. I had no idea where the accident happened or if he truly was all right. My body soon announced that if I didn't settle down, our family would be having more than an accident.

Five hours later, my smiling husband walked in the door. I hugged him and cried with relief. Then I wanted to lambast him for not calling me back. It all worked out well. Les decided it was easier to hit the hay than a lineup of cars.

Mood swings can be the body's beeper, reporting possible hormonal havoc. I remember three sisters I met at a retreat who were concerned their fourth sister was in spiritual trouble because she wasn't her usual bouncy self. They kept her up late at night and prayed with her over every possible hidden sin in her life. Later they found out she was just pregnant. After a couple of months and some uninterrupted sleep, her hormones settled down, and she was back to her perky self.

I'm not saying the all-night vigil was a bad idea, but there are times when mood swings beep attention to a legitimate health issue.

There's no doubt we are fearfully and wonderfully made. All we have to do is listen to our bodies and respond with good choices. Some of you already are disciplined and wise in caring for yourselves. But, like me, many of you don't listen until you're in trouble. We could all benefit by answering the following:

How much water do you drink in a day? (No fair counting the water in coffee or cola.)

How many hours of sleep do you require a night to feel "normal"? (Les requires seven hours but prefers six. I need eight hours but enjoy nine. Les catapults from the bed each morning, while I have to be jump started just to ignite a pulse. Remember, normal is just . . .)

Do you have an exercise regimen? (Getting out of bed each morning does not qualify as weight lifting.)

When was your last eye exam? (I took my mangled glasses in last week for repair. I had sat on them . . . for the third time. The woman looked at them and said, "Lady, do you know which end these were made for?"

"Evidently not," I replied sweetly, "or I wouldn't be here again.")

Write down the date of your last dental appointment. (If B.C. follows the date, it has been too long.)

Are you listening to your body when it says, "Enough is enough" (food, work, rest)?

When was your last physical? (Talking to a friend who once took a first-aid course does not count.)

Did it include a pap smear? (This is an uplifting experience.)

Have you had a mammogram? (That's where the technician thinks she's a magician and tries to turn a cup into a saucer.)

Have you ever had a change in your weight without a change in your eating? (My mother-in-law thought she was fat. Her "fat" turned out to be a tumor the size of a watermelon. My husband was losing weight while eating like a buffalo. [Maybe that's why he could lift them.] It turned out he was diabetic.)

Are you having frequent headaches, stomachaches, backaches, rashes, sleeplessness, spotting, mood swings, urination, unquenchable thirst, and so on? It's time to find out why.

How many pills do you take in a week? in a month? Are you masking a growing health issue? (Our plop-plop, fizz-fizz mentality covers our pain but doesn't resolve it.)

Trust the way God has designed your body to let you know when you need to make a life adjustment or a visit to your family doctor. This body is just a temporary time suit. (Can't you hear it ticking?) It's the only one we get before heaven's new, improved version, which will be complete with eternal vision.

Speaking of vision, remember that in this life, your glasses belong on your nose. Take it from someone who knows.

4

Jumpin' Jehosaphat

SOME FRIENDS WERE getting ready to move and needed a home for their dog, Fredda. We already had a dog (Fredda's mama) but felt obligated to take Fredda back since we had given her to them fraudulently. See, I thought she was a he when I gave Fredda to them, and they therefore named her Fred. After arriving home with their little guy, they noticed Fred had problems that would require surgery or a change of names. They kindly opted for a name change.

Fredda was a kind-of-cockapoo. Actually, she thought she was a kangaroo (no doubt the result of her early identity crisis) and developed a unique straight-up-and-down leap. She was a very sanguine dog and hated to be left outside. So she used her incredibly high leap to peek in our windows at what was going on. It wasn't unusual to be sitting at the table eating and, out of my peripheral view, glimpse a set of eager eyes and fluffy, flying ears. By the time I could turn to look, Fredda would have dropped out of sight. She repeated this Olympic feat frequently.

This caused many visitors concern about their sanity. We tended not to mention our "kangaroo" to guests until their eyes looked dazed. You could see them trying to process whether their minds were leaving them or we had been invaded by seeing-eye fur balls. With quick jerks, our friends would whip their heads to the side in an attempt to catch our mystifying mutt. Eventually we would confirm their UFO sightings to ease their troubled minds.

Fredda became our son Jason's dog (he was eight at the time) and would escort him to the bus stop. Jason would have to leave early because it takes longer when you're with an animal that insists on leaping up instead of forward. One morning, Jason came bursting back into the house crying, "Mom, Mom, come quick! Fredda's been hit by a car!"

I grabbed my housecoat, and as I secured it, Jason added, "I think she's going to be all right, because I saw her tail wag!"

Halfway up our driveway, a lady I had never met came running toward me and right into my arms. She was crying, "I hit your dog! I'm sorry, I'm sorry." I held her for a moment and assured her we knew it was an accident.

She sobbed, "Yesterday my cat died, and today I've hit your dog!"

"I'm sorry this has been such a painful week for you, and I know you didn't mean to hit her," I responded. I hugged her one last time and encouraged her to go on to work.

I thought how disconcerting as well as disastrous it must have been for that lady to have a flying dog, all eyes and ears, leap out of nowhere.

By the time I reached the road, Les had arrived and was gently placing Fredda in his pickup. He looked at me and shook his head to let me know she was dead. I turned to look for Jason and saw that he was back in line for his school bus. He had his eyes squished tightly shut, and his little arms were pressed firmly against his body in his attempt to not see or know the fate of his beloved, bouncing buddy.

"Jason," I said softly.

He didn't move.

"Jason, honey, your doggie is dead."

He fell into my arms, allowing the swell of tears out of his flooded eyes. Then his tense little body let down and began to shake. I took him by the hand, and we walked down the hill to our house to grieve.

Many times I, like Jason, have wanted to just close my eyes and not look at reality. Reality is often harsh, filled with unfairness, pain, and loss. But when I refuse to face truth, I find myself rigid with anxiety and unable to deal with life. Acknowledging and letting go of what I can't change is the beginning of the grieving process.

5

Crafty

I DO CRAFTS. No, wait, that's not quite right. I own crafts. Yes, that helps to bring into focus the blur of materials stuffed into assorted baskets, drawers, and boxes in my attic and basement.

My craft addiction has left partially done projects pleading for completion. I have snarls of thread once meant to be used in needlepoint and gnarly-looking yarn intended for an afghan. I have how-to books worn from my reading and rereading of the instructions. (I love reading; it's the doing that bogs me down.) Swatches of material, florist wire, paint brushes, grapevines, and (every crafter's best friend) a glue gun—along with a myriad of additional stuff—greet me whenever I open my closet.

Every time I'm enticed into purchasing a new project, I think, *This one I'll do for sure.* I've attempted everything from oil painting, floral arranging, quilting, and scherenschnitte (the German art of paper cutting) to quilling.

"Quilling?" you ask. For those of you unfamiliar with it, this craft requires you to wind itsy-bitsy, teeny-weeny strips of paper around the tip of a needle. Once they're wound, you glue the end, using a toothpick as an applicator so your paper coil doesn't spring loose. Then, with a pair of tweezers, you set your coil onto a pattern attached to a foam board, securing it with a straight pin. You are then ready to start the paper-twirling process over again. To be a good quiller, it helps if you, the crafter, are wound loosely. I believe quillers (at least this one) have to be a few twirls short of a full coil to attempt this tedious art.

You may be wondering how many of those paper tidbits one needs to finish a piece. That depends on the size of your pattern. I chose a delicate, little snowflake. Taking into consideration that I'm a beginner (which is still true of every craft I've ever tried), I decided to select a small pattern and not overwhelm myself. (This would be like saying, "I think I'll go over Niagara in a barrel rather than a tub in hopes I won't get so wet.")

When I started my snowflake, I thought, *I'm going to make one of these for each of my friends and put them on the outside of their Christmas packages.* After five hours and a minuscule amount of noticeable progress, I reconsidered. *I will give these only to my best friends and include them in their gift boxes.*

A week later, I realized I didn't have a friend worth this kind of effort; only select family members would get these gems. And they would be all they'd get. I thought I would also include a contract for them to sign, agreeing to display their snowflakes well lit, under glass, in a heavy traffic area of their homes, all year.

Fifteen hours into my little winter-wonder project, I decided this would be the first and last paper wad I'd ever make . . . and I'd keep it for myself. It could be handed down in my family, generation after generation, in a time capsule, after my passing. I often wondered who the flake really was in this venture.

I suppose you're asking yourself, *Did she finish it?* Not yet, but I plan to (great inscription for tombstones).

I once attended a retreat where I was persuaded to join a wooden angel craft class. The angel done by the instructor (art major) as an example was adorable. Mine (craft minor) looked like an angel that might join a motorcycle gang.

Even that angel didn't get completed, because they ran out of heavenly parts. She had only one wing and was minus her halo. Actually, it was kind of sad. Today my fallen angel lies at the bottom of a box in my basement, covered with rotting quilt pieces and plastic ivy, still waiting for her ordination. May she rest in peace.

I took a painting class for credit and received an A. Finally, something I could succeed in! Of course, if that was true, why didn't I have a picture to hang?

It hit me that I didn't have a painting anyone could identify, much less display. For one of our projects, we painted apples in a bowl. When I took it home, my friend thought it was a peacock.

I approached the instructor and asked how I had earned an A in her class. "For showing up every week," she responded. She must have the gift of mercy.

Les and I started hooking a two-foot-by-three-foot rug 25 years ago. We're almost to the halfway point. We figure, in a joint effort, that we have hooked less than an inch a year and should complete it in the year 2012. You may want to get on our gift list.

I seem to be more into ownership than completion . . . and then I feel guilty. I've noticed I'm not alone in that. Some kindred spirits could stuff a landfill with their forsaken artistry. I wonder if that's why we have so many garage sales and so much garbage in this country. We sell off and throw away our unfinished business, and then we go buy more.

Words like *responsibility, follow through,* and *moderation* get lost in the shuffle as I push back one box of crafts to move in my newest project. Every time I haul out or hide away another abandoned endeavor, it reinforces a negative quality within me.

Besides, what happened to the notion "Waste not, want not"?

That's a great line. I wonder how it would look in cross-stitch? Oops, there I go again.

6

Snappy Answers

SOMETIMES I FEEL as though my emotions are a tangled wad. I guess that's why one night, while I was in bed praying for a creative way to visualize emotions, I thought of knotting rubber bands together. I jumped up and found a bag of 100 red, blue, green, and yellow rubber bands. Then I climbed back in bed and began to tie them in a long, snarled chain (probably the closest I've ever come to knitting or crocheting).

My husband came into the room and saw me busy at my stretchy task. He shook his head and muttered, "I knew one day it would come to this."

I often ask my audiences if they brought their emotions with them to the retreat. Usually they giggle, and a number of women raise their hands, signifying they did. Then I ask how many of the gals brought their hormones, and the rest of the hands go up.

When I next pull my emotions out of a bag in the form of my rubber chain, the women titter and nod their recognition. I demonstrate, by tugging at the bands until they appear they will snap, how people sometimes get on my nerves. As I pile the long, variegated snarl into a five-inch-tall heap on my hand, I show them what happens when I don't stay current with my emotions—they become so entangled that I can't tell what I'm feeling. And when I can't identify what I'm feeling, I can't resolve it, which means the knotted mess is growing inside me.

I remember coming home one evening after being with a group of friends and telling Les how angry I was with one of them.

"Really, what did she do?" he inquired.

Well, I told him in no uncertain terms what she did.

When I finished, he said, "I don't think you're angry."

"You don't?" I asked.

"No," he reinforced.

"I feel angry," I assured him.

"I think you're jealous," he stated boldly.

"Jealous?" I screeched.

"Jealous?" I hissed.

Then I slunk into another room to file my nails in private. Alone, I finally asked the Lord if what Les suggested could possibly be true. Immediately I realized he had caught the cat by her claws.

I've been able to work through my jealous feelings in regard to this friend thanks to Les's confrontation. Otherwise, I'd still be rationalizing my anger and not facing the real issue.

When issues aren't faced, they build inside us, which means somebody's going to experience emotional whiplash when we get crossed. The way buildups become blowups is that one day a family member, co-worker, friend, or total stranger makes one teeny-tiny comment, and we let that person have it with our entire rubber-band arsenal. He or she doesn't know what happened.

When the person asks, "What's wrong with you?" we shout, "Everything!" shaking all our tangled emotions in his or her face.

Have you ever noticed how quiet a room gets when you overreact? All eyes are on you. Even though no one says it, you know they're wondering what your problem is. But then, so are you, because more often than not, the time and place where you explode are side issues.

I once had a disagreement with a co-worker, and when I came home, I started nit-picking on my teenager Jason. I hit him with a lengthy list of criticisms. Baffled, he asked, "What's wrong with you?"

Those words caught my attention, and I realized I was the one with a problem. Jason was the victim of my misdirected frustration.

Sound familiar? Does to me.

I find that when I have a gob of feelings overlapping, I begin to highlight one or two emotions. I then work those feelings overtime and ignore the rest. That's why I thought I was angry with my friend instead of jealous. Besides, jealousy is so—so—well, petty, whereas anger is more respectable (righteous indignation) and gives me a feeling of being in control.

I find it fairly easy to say to someone, "My friend Jane makes me angry." (I'm in control.) But it's hard to confess, "I am jealous of Jane." (Now I feel vulnerable, and that's scary.)

For years, I majored in fear. I seldom felt another emotion during my agoraphobic days. I was afraid of everything, or so it seemed. Later, I began to get in touch with anger, joy, sadness, and other equally important feelings. As I identified them, my wad of rubber bands became smaller. That gave me more inner space for the things of God.

What is your most-frequently-expressed emotion? Do you find yourself erupting in anger? enveloped in fear? engulfed in guilt?

If we don't deal with our raggedy strands, we react like turtles—our answers have a bite to them, and then we pull our heads back into hard shells of denial until our next snappy performances.

7

Step Right Up

I CAN IDENTIFY with Zacchaeus in that I have a difficult time finding a place high enough to let me see a parade. Visibility is limited when you're five feet tall. I've spent a lifetime on my tiptoes, calling up to others, "What's going on?"

I know I'm supposed to take comfort in the saying "Dynamite comes in small packages." But I don't want to blow up; I want to grow up.

Sitting tall is also a challenge because invariably, a seven-foot-two fellow will plant himself in front of me at church. I then have the joy of staring for the next hour at the seams in his shirt and his nappy neck. It's like trying to watch a ball game through a billboard.

Hugging is often a strain as we shorties have to reach past our stretching points to squeeze a neck. It's such a rumpling experience and requires read-justing everything from hat to hose.

As a speaker, I frequently find myself peeking over lecterns in my attempts to spot the audience. It's difficult to retain the interest of people when their view consists of your forehead and eyebrows. I have stood on many creative booster stools so I could see and be seen.

At one retreat, the kitchen workers brought me a box of canned juice to stand on. It worked fine until my high heel poked between two cans and I jerked sharply backward. I grabbed the lectern, catching myself just before doing a topsy-turvy somersault. My disheveled appearance from my stage aerobics made me look juiced.

I have perched on many piano benches to speak. Because they're pieces of furniture, I always remove my shoes before stepping up. Smooth nylons on shiny-finished wood equal slick chick in action. It's like trying to speak on ice skates—pos-sible but risky.

To elevate me enough to be seen at one church meeting, the staff quickly piled up two stacks of hymnals, five deep. As I turned to look at my audi-ence from one side of the auditorium to the other, the books would swivel. At one point, the right-foot stack headed east while the left-foot stack headed west. Those shifting stilts kept me divided in my concentration, as I was concerned I would leave with a split personality.

I've stood on milk crates, suitcases, tables, and kiddie stools. Once I was precariously placed on a wooden box whose weight limit I obviously exceeded. It creaked threateningly throughout my presentation. As I closed in prayer, a soloist began to sing, and I cautiously stepped down. Relieved that I hadn't burst the boards, I walked down the platform steps to take a seat. At the last step, my heel caught in the microphone cords, and I crash-landed in the front row as the singer was belting out "Amazing Grace." I obviously was not Grace, although in a discussion later, we thought it was amazing I could survive my teeter-totter platform and then splat when I arrived on solid ground.

It's difficult to be taken seriously when you're 60 inches short. People have a habit of referring to shorties as "cute." "Cute" is what you call a toddler, a house without a future, or the runt of a litter.

I tried to increase the presentation of my stature by wearing tall clothes. But more than once while walking up the front steps in sanctuaries, my heel slid into the hem of my long skirt, toppling me across the altar, where I looked like some sort of short sacrifice.

I shortened my skirts and added shoulder pads to my jackets in an effort to give an illusion of tallness without tripping myself.

Then one time I was in Washington, and when I was introduced, I grabbed my suit jacket and slid into it as I headed for the stage. I had been speaking for about 15 minutes when I turned my head to one side and noticed that my left shoulder was four inches higher than my right. Evidently the pad, rather than conforming to the shape of my shoulder, perched on it. Up to that point, I was the only one in the auditorium who hadn't noticed. I was speaking on being dysfunctional and suggested this perched pad was proof of my expertise in the subject.

When I finished speaking, the mistress of ceremonies approached the steps with the back of her dress tucked into her pantyhose. That took a lot of pressure off me.

Another time, I was sharing the stage with a statuesque and elegant friend who, as I was speaking, noticed my mega shoulder pad had slid off my shoulder and into my blouse. She reached in through my neckline and fished down my back in her attempt to retrieve it. I was stunned but continued to speak as if I didn't notice she was shoulder deep into my clothing. Well, I lost the audience as everyone became hysterical watching her catch my illusive inches and pat them securely back into place.

I wish my height were my only struggle with smallness. Unfortunately, I'm also shortsighted in my faith. I'm one of those "If I can see it, then I can believe it" people.

Zacchaeus was a small man who shimmied up a sycamore tree to give himself a boost. To that extent, I can identify. But his next move made the difference for him in a way lengthened robes or mountainous shoulder pads under his togas never could. He inched out on a limb to glimpse the Savior. He risked the shaky-limb experience of faith and responded to the Lord's invitation not only to come down, but also to grow up.

That day he stepped down from his own efforts to see and be seen and stepped up to the call of the

Lord. Zacchaeus still lacked inches, but he gained insight and walked away a giant of a man.

Faith is a believe-it-first proposition, with no promise I'll get to "see it" regardless of how many boxes I climb. That's scary . . . like going out on a limb, huh, Zac?

8

Short(s) Circuited

KNOWING MY FRIEND Nancy is like embracing a waterfall.

She splashes over with energy, excitement, and enthusiasm for life and people. She's filled with joy, and also mischievousness. Her mind and wit are quick and memorable. David, her husband, is a courageous man who has survived and been blessed by Nancy's outrageous humor. We all remember when. . . .

David is mellow and usually cooperates and enjoys his wife's wishes and whims. But one day the two of them had a tiff, and neither Nancy nor David would budge from the feeling of being in the right. Several days had passed since the difference between them arose, and static hung in the air, droning out communication.

David would normally give in under such circumstances, but not this time. Nancy was amazed he wasn't talking, but she was equally determined not to speak first.

Then it happened. David came home and started to pack his suitcase. Nancy was confident he wasn't leaving her; he was often sent on business trips. But she couldn't believe he would go without resolving their conflict first. David, however, jaw set, silently prepared to leave. Nancy fumed.

Most of us, when we fume, have to verbally spew so we don't become combustible and explode. Not Nancy. She uses her hostility to create . . . well, let's just say *memories.*

That night, they went to bed without a word. David was feeling a slight advantage in their "cold war," because he knew what his travel plan was, and she didn't. He also knew this would bug her, because she's a detail person and likes to be fully informed. David fell asleep that night with a smirk on his face. I don't think he would have rested as well as he did, however, had he seen the grin spreading across his stalemate's lips.

David rose the next morning and went in to take his shower. While he was washing up, Nancy was quietly yukking it up. First she counted his undershorts in the suitcase to see how many days he would be gone. Finding that out, she then could determine where he was going. He always went to one of two places, each requiring him to stay a different length of time.

Once she figured out his destination, she quickly lifted the neatly folded underwear out of his luggage and replaced it with a note. Stifling giggles, she stashed his confiscated shorts in a drawer, zipped his case closed, dashed back between the bedsheets, and used a pillow to muffle her pleasure.

David emerged showered and shaved, picked up his suitcase, and left for his trip. This was the first time they had parted company without hugs, kisses, and promises to call. They were both finding a bit of comfort, though, in thinking they had a secret the other didn't know.

The outbound flight put David in a confined place with time to think. He began to feel bad about their stormy week and his stony departure. He dearly loved Nancy and promised himself and the Lord that he would call and apologize as soon as he arrived at his hotel.

Nancy meantime busied herself around the house, stopping occasionally to imagine David's reaction when he unpacked. Chuckling, she waited for the phone to ring, both dreading and delighting in the prospect.

She didn't have long to wait. "Mom, it's Dad; he wants to talk to you," her son yelled.

Nancy wasn't sure if she should run to the phone or run for cover. But she made her way to the table and picked up the receiver. What she heard was not what she had anticipated. On the other end, David confessed his regrets at their spat and expressed even greater sorrow at leaving without making things right.

Nancy's heart sank as she was warmed by his tenderness and sincerity. She decided she had better 'fess up, too.

"David, have you unpacked yet?" she inquired.

"No, not yet."

"Maybe you should," she suggested.

"Why, what did you do?"

"Just go open your suitcase; I'll wait on the line."

David came back chuckling. "Very funny, Nancy. Where did you put my shorts?"

"Oh, they're here in the drawer," she admitted.

"No, really, are they in a side pocket?"

"Honest, I took them out before you left. Isn't that funny, David?" she said with failing confidence.

The line was silent, and then, much to her delight, David broke into gales of healing laughter.

The note? Oh, yeah, it read:

"David, your attitude stinks, and now so does your only pair of underwear!"

9

Middle Man

BECAUSE OF A delay in taking off, my home-bound flight was late, leaving me at risk of missing my second plane. When we landed at the connecting airport, I did an O. J. Simpson through the terminal, arriving at my gate just as they were closing the doors. Relieved I'd made it, I headed down the aisle in search of my seat. I stopped at my assigned row and, to my dismay, found I had the middle seat.

There are some things I don't do. Middle seats head my "no way, I ain't gonna!" list. Middle seats make me feel like an Oscar Mayer wiener advertisement. My mood swing went from "I'm so grateful I caught my plane" to "I don't care what this ticket says, I'm not sitting in that center seat!"

I glanced around and realized, however, that this was the last available seat on the flight, and I would sit there or on the wing. Previously I always had an aisle seat; this just wasn't normal. All things considered, though, I prayed for an attitude adjustment. I remembered that God will operate on our attitudes but that He requires us to cooperate.

To do my part, I tried to think of a way to make this irritating situation fun. I took a quick survey of my seating again and thought, *What could I do with a person on each side of me?*

Then it came to me that I could pretend I was Oprah Winfrey and my seat partners were my guests. I would interview them. Now, this had possibilities!

Right off, there was a problem. Evidently the lady by the window didn't recognize my Oprah impersonation, because she wasn't a very cooperative interviewee. She was reading a book, and she let me know with sighs and downcast eyes that she didn't want to be disturbed. I thought Oprah wouldn't allow that to stop her, so I continued.

"Are you married?" I inquired.

"Yes," she mumbled.

"Do you have children?" I persisted.

"Yes," she grumbled.

"How many?" I pushed.

She stared at me with a strange look on her face, and I thought maybe she didn't know. Then she leaned in to me, lowered her voice, and said, "Nine."

"*Nine!*" I bellowed, surprising even myself. "Nine," I repeated, this time to myself. I don't think I had ever met anyone with nine children before . . . and she was pregnant. I was impressed!

Now, I also have this problem in that whenever I'm given noteworthy news, I feel led to pass it on. As I sat there trying to mentally contain those nine children, it seemed as if a balloon was being blown up inside me. I would explode soon if I didn't tell someone about these kids.

I leaned back toward the woman and said, "Would you mind if I tell this man on my left that you have nine children?"

Startled, somewhat confused, and slightly irritated, she whispered, "If you feel you need to tell that man!"

"Trust me," I responded, "I need to do this."

I then leaned to my left and said, "Excuse me, I thought you might like to know that this woman has nine kids."

"*Nine!*" he exclaimed, leaning forward to view this productive female, much to her consternation.

That was the kind of enthusiastic response I was looking for. I decided right then that he was a kindred spirit, and I turned my interview efforts toward him. Besides, I now realized that Multiple Mom was too pooped to participate in my game show (she had nine good reasons to be).

I had already observed something about this young man when I was being seated. He called me "Ma'am." At the time I thought, *Either he thinks I'm ancient, he's from the South, where they still teach manners, or he's in the service.* I decided the latter was the most likely, so I asked, "You in the service?"

"Yes, Ma'am, I am."

"What branch?"

"Marines."

"Hey, Marine, where are you coming from?"

"The Desert Storm, Ma'am."

"No kidding? The Desert Storm!" Then I thought, *This interview stuff is great!*

"How long were you there?" I continued.

"A year and a half. I'm on my way home. My family will be at the airport. I'm so scared." As he said this last, he took in a short, nervous breath.

"Scared? Of what?" I asked.

"Oh, all this hero stuff. I'm not a hero, I'm just me, and I don't want my family to be disappointed."

"Take it from me, Marine, your parents just want you to come home safe."

Nodding his head in hopes I was right, he looked at me and asked, "What do you do?"

I had been waiting for someone to ask this very question. I had just completed my first book, and I wanted to announce that I was an author. Here was my big chance. Sitting as tall as a five-foot person can, I said clearly and possibly a little too loudly, "I'm an author."

"An author! An author!" the Marine proclaimed. "An author," he repeated, obviously impressed.

I loved this kid!

Changing the topic back to him (as Oprah would do), I commented that he must have thought about returning to his family and home many times while he was in the Middle East.

"Oh, no, Ma'am," he replied. "We were taught never to think of what might never be, but to be fully available right where we were."

What great instruction, I thought, *whether you're in the armed forces or the army of the Lord.*

Then Michael (that was his name) told me that when he lived at home, he and his mother were friends. When he joined the service and was stationed in Hawaii, they had written to each other and had become good friends. But when he went to Desert Storm, they became best friends.

"She will never know how she affected my life while I was away," he continued. "I've never thought of myself as a religious person, but while I was in the Storm, I learned to pray. The example I followed was the one my mom set for me when I was growing up."

"What was the most difficult time for you?" I inquired in Oprah fashion.

"There was a four-month space when we had not seen a woman or a child. The day we drove into Kuwait was very emotional for us. The women stood in the doorways, waving, but even more moving was when the children ran to greet us," he said, his voice still filled with the feeling.

I wondered if the children affected the soldiers so deeply because children give us such a sense of a hope and a future.

"Since I've been stateside waiting to go home," he continued, "I've been thinking about my nephews, and I can hardly wait to hear them call me Uncle Michael. The title *uncle* means even more to me than being called *sergeant*."

About that time, the flight attendant was passing by, and I tugged at her skirt. She looked down, and I said, "Know what? He"—I pointed toward Michael—"is returning from Desert Storm, and she has nine kids." I gestured in the direction of Super Mom.

The attendant evidently knew people with nine children, because that didn't hold her attention.

But Michael sure did. She asked him several questions and then requested that he write his name on a piece of paper. Taking his signature, she headed toward the front of the plane. She reminded me of a woman with a balloon inside her that was ready to pop.

Moments later, the pilot came on the intercom and, with enthusiasm and sincerity, said, "It has been brought to my attention that we have a VIP aboard. He is a returning GI from Desert Storm."

Michael groaned and began to inch down in his seat.

I sat up taller.

"Sergeant Michael is in seat 12F," the pilot continued.

All heads swung in our direction. Michael had slunk so deeply into the upholstery that he was about two inches tall. In contrast, I was six-foot-two. (Visibility is always good for ratings.)

Then the pilot said, "As a representative of this airline and a citizen of the United States of America, I salute you, Michael, and thank you for a job well done."

At that point, the entire plane burst into applause.

Wow! I love this Oprah stuff.

The pilot came back on and said, "We are making our final approach into the Detroit Metro Airport."

Michael's breath caught.

I looked up and saw his eyes had filled with tears. He peeked through a tear to see if I had noticed, and of course there I was, goggling at him.

He said softly, "I just don't want to cry."

"It's okay," I told him. "I checked a Marine manual on this one, and it's all right to cry. Some of the most admirable men I've ever known have shed tears at appropriate times, and Michael, this is a right time."

"Then you don't think I need to blame this on my contacts?" he responded, grinning.

"I don't think so," I said with a giggle.

As our plane taxied in, I told him the best gift my son brought me when he returned from 18 months in Guam was that after he made his way through the waiting crowd, he scooped me up in his arms and held me for a very long time.

It was time to deplane, and when Michael stood, men all around us slapped him on the back and pumped his arm, thanking him for his contribution.

We made our way to the front, where the pilots came out to meet the sergeant and shake his hand. The flight attendants encircled him and told him he was great. I noticed that he didn't seem to mind this last gesture. In fact, he seemed to be getting taller.

Because of security precautions, no one was allowed to meet us at the gate, which meant we had to walk down a long corridor before we reached Michael's family and my husband.

Michael's homecoming included a lineup of relatives armed with video equipment, flags, cameras, and banners. When we were close enough for eyes to focus in and distinguish which one was Michael, his family began to chant, "Michael, Michael, Michael."

Michael stopped dead in his tracks. I got behind him and pushed. "C'mon, soldier," I said, "this isn't the enemy. This is your family."

He started walking again, but his shoes seemed to be full of cement, and he was moaning quietly with every step.

Even from a distance, I could identify his mom. She was the one leaping the highest in the air. A guard leaned against the wall, watching to make sure no one stepped over the security line. But every time Michael's mom jumped into the air, she came down with her toe just over the line to let that guard know who was really in charge.

As we got closer, she stopped jumping, and her hands went over her mouth to muffle the building sobs. Tears poured down her arms and dropped off her elbows . . . just over the line.

I realized that this was not my party (or Oprah's) and I needed to step back. When I did, in his nervousness, so did Michael.

I gave him a final nudge toward his family, and they engulfed him, everyone in tears.

I made my way through the other waiting people, wiping my eyes. When I saw my husband, he spotted me dripping emotions. "I'm part of this," I sniffed, nodding toward the reunion.

"You think you're a part of everything," he proclaimed.

That was true, but this time I really was . . . sort of. I wanted to stand and watch as I saw Michael find his mom in the crowd and pull her into his arms and hold her.

"That's tacky, Patsy," Les reminded me. "It's rude to stare."

Mr. Manners guided me over to the escalator and prompted me on. I turned backward so I could watch for as long as possible. As the moving steps drew me away from the celebration, I saw Michael still holding his mother, and he had held her for a very long time.

When we got to the baggage claim area, I prayed for the first time ever that my luggage would be delayed. Before long, the whole Desert Storm entourage came down to claim Michael's duffle bags.

Yes! I thought. *My big chance to be part of the finale.*

Michael was still surrounded by family when I saw a youngster toddle over and pull on his pant leg. I realized this must be one of the nephews he was so eager to see again. When I noticed how young the boy was and remembered that Michael had been gone for a year and a half, I held my breath to watch how the boy would react to his uncle. (I thought about my sons when they were that young and how, if I left them with a sitter for more than an hour, they acted as though they didn't know me when I returned.)

Michael's face lit up as he reached down and picked up the young boy. His nephew wrapped his chubby legs around the sergeant's waist, and his arms encircled Michael's neck. Then the boy's mom came over, and I heard her ask, "Honey, who's got you?"

He looked up, his young eyes reflecting his hero, and said, "Uncle Michael."

I could breathe again.

A few minutes later, as Les escorted me to the car, the thought hit me that I almost missed being a part of this tender event because I hadn't wanted to sit in the middle.

I wonder how many divine appointments I've missed because I found my circumstances not to be what I expected (just not normal), and my defiance robbed me of His greater plan?

10

Yuk It Up!

WE ALL HAVE moments we'd rather not remember—the kind that when we do recall them, we get embarrassed all over again. Like finding you're dragging a long sweep of toilet tissue. Spike heels are great for that. You shish kebab the tissue on your way out of the restroom, and you can literally parade it for miles before anyone will tell you.

Having dragged my pantyhose behind me through my hometown has left me with empathy for other dragees. I remember a gentleman and his wife who approached me at a convention and related their adventure.

The man said, "If you think it's embarrassing for a woman to drag her pantyhose, how do you think a man feels when it happens to him? I went to work and walked through the office when one of the women sang out, 'What's that, Bill?' I turned to look, and dangling out of my suit-pants leg were my wife's pantyhose. I casually ambled over to a wall, shook them out, and walked away. I left the hose huddled in the corner to figure out their own transportation home."

Evidently his wife didn't pick up her pantyhose, but the static in his slacks did. Half the hose clung to his pant leg, while the remaining leg danced behind him. The man, his wife, and I laughed long and loud as he relived his tail.

There's something so healing about laughter. When I can laugh at an event that has the potential to turn my pale face flashing red, somehow the situation doesn't record itself in my memory with as much pain.

My friend Ann is a good example. She flipped her melon and lived to laugh about it. While she was shopping for groceries one time, she spotted a large, elongated watermelon. She wanted the melon, but it looked heavy, and she wasn't sure she could lift it. No stock boys were around, so she decided to give it the old heave-ho. Either the melon didn't weigh as much as she had thought, or she was stronger than she realized. Anyway, she grabbed hold of the watermelon and slung it up and toward herself. With torpedo speed, the slippery melon slid out of her hands and up her shoulder to become airborne.

Once again, Sir Newton's theory of gravitation proved true. The melon headed for earth with great rapidity. When a melon is dropped from more than five feet onto a tile floor, "splat" doesn't begin to describe what occurs. Not only did it explode, but everything in a 15-foot radius was affected as well.

As Ann turned to look at her Herculean effort gone awry, she spotted . . . a victim. Or should I say the victim was "spotted"? A nicely dressed businesswoman looked stunned as ragged chunks of watermelon dripped down her pantyhose.

Ann didn't mean to laugh, but the whole scene struck her as so absurd that she couldn't help herself. The lady was not laughing, which seemed to tickle Ann all the more. The woman marched off in a huff, leaving a trial of seeds behind her.

Ann was now leaning against the rutabagas, trying to catch her breath, when the manager walked up and said, "This is not funny."

Well, that was the wrong thing to say. Poor Ann howled. Her sides were splitting, her face was red, and she was hysterical. She said she was trying to gain her composure so she could find the lady and apologize to her. But finally she had to just leave the store.

Laughter can make moments more memorable. Whether laughing alone or with others, it helps us feel good about our memories.

I remember walking through the mall once when I noticed a quarter on the floor. Had it been a penny, I might have passed it by. But a quarter? No way. I stooped down and swooped my hand across the floor to scoop up the coin, but it didn't budge. I tried again. I could hear laughter coming from a nearby ice cream shop, but I didn't look because I was focused on the shiny coin. I tried to pick it up again, but it held fast. I tried prying it with my nails. I even took out my emery board and used it like a crowbar, trying to dislodge this gleaming coin.

As I stared at George Washington's immobile silhouette, I thought I saw him smirk. Then I realized George was not alone. The laughter nearby had grown to unbridled guffawing. I looked up and realized five teenagers were watching me and laughing at my financial struggle. It was the kind of laugh that told me they knew something I didn't.

I could have flown off in a fury or resented their intrusion. Then again, I could find out what was so hilarious and join the fun.

I asked, "Okay, what's the deal?"

One girl confessed they had glued the quarter to the floor and had been watching people try to pick it up. The kids dubbed me the "most dedicated to the task." I giggled with them as I thought about my 25-cent antics.

Laughter is an incredible gift. It helps us to not take ourselves too seriously and makes it possible for us to survive life's awkward moments.

11

There's a Reason

WHEN MY HIGH school teacher's eyes suddenly met mine, my heart began to palpitate. I slowly slid down in my seat, trying to disappear inside my open textbook.

"Patsy," she sang out, "let's hear your report."

This was not music to my ears. During my school years, I had developed creative avoidance skills in an ongoing endeavor to escape up-front presentations. Not making eye contact was a crucial part of my strategy. In a careless moment, however, I had glanced toward the chalkboard, only to find myself in eye-lock with this dear but determined teacher.

Realizing I would have to respond, I slowly rose and, on knees of silicone, made my way to the front of the room. My topic was "Quinine."

Fear had collected in my throat, which I forgot to clear before announcing the title of my speech. The "Qui" came out like the deep rumblings of Mount Saint Helens, and the "nine" screeched at a pitch that attracted dogs from three counties.

The class howled. My face flashed lipstick-red. I speed-sputtered through the report, never looking up.

By the time I finished, the jelly in my knees had congealed into blocks of cement. With 50-pound knees, I stiffly hobbled back to my desk. I plopped into my seat, dropping my eyes in humiliation. For the remainder of the semester, I studied the designs in the tile floor, not daring to glance up lest I be called on again.

When people don't make eye contact, there's a reason.

I had been cleaning my bedroom and headed for the kitchen to find the glass cleaner. As I passed through the living room, I glanced in the direction of my two-and-a-half-year-old (at the time), Marty. He had been watching cartoons and playing with his cars. Something about his looks made me stop in my tracks. I realized it wasn't what I saw but what I didn't see—his eyes. Marty stared down at his toys. I called out, "Marty."

He lifted his head but avoided my eyes. I walked toward him, and he sheepishly peeked up at me. Then I saw it. Lying on the floor behind Marty was an open bottle of baby aspirin. Little, pink pills were strewn among his play-things. I pulled Marty to me and looked into his mouth. Crushed aspirin particles were stuck in his tiny, white teeth. My heart began to pound wildly.

This was a new bottle of medicine, and only a few tablets had been used before now. I scooped up the remaining pills and quickly counted them. It appeared Marty had ingested 69 aspirins.

I drew him into my arms and ran to my neighbor's apartment. We didn't have a telephone, and Les had taken the car to work. I ran into Sharon's home and frantically called my physician. The woman who answered the phone instructed me not to bring Marty in but instead to induce vomiting by running my finger down his throat. She informed me that the doctors were too busy to talk to me. I thought, since she worked for the doctors, that she must know what was best, and I followed her directions.

I hung up feeling sick to my stomach but with a sense of urgency rushing through my mind. I dialed my mom's number and yelled, "Marty has an overdose of aspirin in him! Help me!" I slung the phone down without waiting for an answer and ran with Marty in my arms the two doors back to our apartment.

When my mom arrived, I was in the bathroom working with my little guy. It was necessary to do what I was doing to him, but very unpleasant for both of us. Mom and I took turns helping him bring up the potential poison until, in one effort, Mom's fingernail jabbed his tonsil, and Marty started to spit up blood.

Mom and I were unsure if we should continue, so we picked him up and ran back to the phone. This time I was able to speak directly with the doctor. He was appalled to hear we had been told not to come in. Now too much time had passed, and the aspirin remaining in Marty had gone into his bloodstream.

The doctor said to let him play but to watch his eyes and not let him go to sleep. He said that if Marty's breathing became difficult, we should rush him to the hospital's emergency room.

I hung up the phone, and as I was telling Mom what the doctor had said, Marty's eyes closed and his breathing became erratic. I firmly shook him awake, and we headed for the emergency room.

That had to be one of the longest nights of my life. The hospital wouldn't allow me to be with Marty, so I camped out all night in the waiting room. By daybreak he was out of danger. Mom and I had been able to get enough of the medicine from his system that he had no long-term damage. But it would take him a while (us, too) to recover from the trauma of this event.

When we returned home, I investigated how Marty had managed to get to the aspirin. We didn't have childproof bottle caps at that time, so as a precaution, I had placed the bottle in the highest cupboard of our home. Marty, however, had ingeniously pulled a high stool over to the cupboards and climbed up on it, taking along his play golf club. From what we could determine, he had then stepped up on a shelf and, while holding on with one hand, swung his club, knocking the bottle off the upper shelf. The drop must have loosened the top, and the rest, as they say, is history.

What alerted me to our emergency was not the stool or golf club but Marty's eyes—especially when he wouldn't look at me.

When people won't look at you, there's a reason.

I can tell when my friend is angry at her husband, because she won't look at him. She avoids visual acknowledgment of his existence until he somehow works his way back into her favor.

Others aren't sure of what to do with how they feel, and they find themselves dodging eye contact to avoid giving away their hidden emotions or getting into conflict. Lack of visual involvement is a screeching smoke detector, alerting us to smoldering relational issues. How many times have you heard or said, "If you're not upset, why won't you look at me?"

Some folks are so full of shame that they don't feel worthy of personal eye contact. Then there are those who have been traumatized and feel frightened and abnormal. They only allow themselves quick peeks at those around them.

Guilt can be another visual barrier that keeps people from our view. Whether false or genuine, guilt affects our connection with others.

The way I see it, when people won't look at us or we won't look at them, there's a reason!

12

Heigh-ho Silver

I LOVE PLAYING word games, though Les would rather go to the dentist and have all his teeth extracted than join me. So once a year, whether he feels like it or not, we play a game of Scrabble. That is, until. . . .

It was twilight, and we had been playing a short time (hours if you asked Les) when our eight-year-old, Jason, questioned, "What's that noise?"

I was in eye-lock with my letter tiles and didn't even look up. Les, who had been staring at the ceiling counting cobwebs to entertain himself, took an immediate interest in Jason's noise just in case it offered him a way out. Sure enough, it did.

Jason went to the window, and then, with eyes the size of saddles, he hollered, "The horses are out! The horses are out!"

That broke any concentration I had, as we all rushed to the window to see for ourselves. Our hearts began to pound, and we stood frozen for a moment. We watched as a dozen horses stampeded across our yard and toward the road.

The potential for disaster sent everyone scrambling. Les yelled for our oldest son, Marty, and his friend Steve to try to head them off. The boys hightailed it out the back door, and Les sped out the front.

I, being of great value during a crisis, ran back and forth in the house, shouting, "Oh, my! Oh, my!"

Then I went out on the porch to peek, but I couldn't see what had happened because the horses had galloped out of our treelined yard and onto the well-traveled road. But I could hear. Screeching tires first, and then a sickening thud, followed by breaking glass. A shudder went through my body, and my mind kicked into high gear.

I flew back into the house and phoned our friend Tom across the lake. "Come quick! The horses, ran, road, thud, glass . . . ambulance, vet, tow truck . . . Come quick!" I sputtered like a stenographer.

Panting, I made my way out to the line of trees, but I was too scared to look. Jason leaned out to see what had happened, and I snatched him back. "No, Jason, this is too gruesome for a child. Go back to the house," I instructed firmly. Then, considering the wisdom of those words, I went with him.

By the time I reached the front door, Marty and Steve were coming up the hill after corralling the remaining herd. Then Les walked in, shaking his head and mopping his brow. He proceeded to explain the runaway results.

It seems a neighbor was on his way home from work when he came over the top of the hill by our house. As he crested the hill in his Volkswagen, all of a sudden he was part of a stampede. He hit his brakes, and as he skidded, his little car scooped up one horse, slung it over the roof, and gently deposited it back on the road, heading in the opposite direction. As the horse skimmed the top of the rounded vehicle, it tapped its hoof through the passenger's window, leaving splintered glass piled neatly in the empty seat.

The car came to a stop long enough for the uninjured but dazed driver to regroup and then drive home (with quite a "guess what happened to me on the way" tale to tell). The rattled runaway, wide-eyed and wiser, was ushered back to the barnyard to rejoin the rest of the herd.

Les and the boys had just caught their breath when up drove Tom and his troops. His wife, Joyce, their kids, and some friends had all piled in the car to see the horse-rendous accident and do what they could to help.

But now the car, driver, horses, and even the glass were all gone. The road was humming with traffic, the horses were grazing innocently in the pasture, and Les was lounging next to the Scrabble board . . . grinning. It appeared to be a normal evening at the Clairmonts'.

Our friends looked at me as if I had imagined the whole thing. I began to wonder myself. Les finally confessed, but only after I released him from any future spelling games.

When emotions stampede like wild horses in the night, one may end up with hoof prints in one's mouth.

I had made assumptions based on what I had heard but hadn't actually seen, and then I had passed on that information. I had the sinking feeling this wasn't the first time I had done that.

13

Clean Sweep

FEELING ZONKED, I decided to zone out when I boarded the plane bound for home. I found my row and secretly checked out my seat companion. She was a normal, fiftyish-looking woman. (I immediately liked her for being older than me.) I peeked at her so I wouldn't be obligated conversationally. I didn't want anything to disrupt my siesta in the sky.

Doesn't it just drive you bonkers when you have a hidden agenda and someone toddles into your space and trips up your plan?

This time my "toddler" was a flight attendant who came scooting down the aisle offering treats. My stomach won out over sleep, and I ended up chatting with my neighbor, Susan. Am I glad I did! This was no normal woman.

Susan told me an incredibly sad story with a surprise ending. She said her beloved husband of 30 years decided he loved someone else and wanted a divorce. The feelings of crushing betrayal deepened when Susan found out his affair had been going on for years. He was also a clever businessman and had prepared himself for this decision so that he would come out the financial winner.

Susan was first numb and then paralyzed by her grief. Her husband used her shock to his advantage, swooping down fast and furious to get all he could. Much to Susan's dismay, she was notified by the court that she would have to turn over to her husband and his girlfriend her cherished home of 23 years, where they had raised their five children.

Reeling from grief upon grief, Susan moved into a tiny, furnished apartment. There she tried to figure out what had gone wrong. In the divorce settlement, she was awarded a small, failing business, and that was to be her source of income. To add not only to her dilemma but also to her pain, her ex-husband and his female friend opened a new, competing business just down the street.

Now, folks, I don't know about you, but that's where I would throw up my hands and spit.

Not Susan. She reached inside and pulled up her faith. She decided she couldn't allow others' choices to extinguish her joy or decree her future. She was determined not to be a victim but to be victorious and begin with a grateful heart. No, she wasn't grateful for her tremendous loss, but that God is a healer of fractured hearts.

One day while doing dishes, Susan turned on the small TV near her sink. As she changed channels, she came to a musical presentation and was caught up in the contagious melody. But now she had no dance partner.

Then she spotted her companion leaning against the cupboard. He was the tall, silent type. She waltzed over and embraced the kitchen broom, then twirled about the room, laughing and singing. Around and around she spun, dizzy with delight. Suddenly she realized she was not alone.

Susan saw she had been joined by three of her married daughters, who were standing in the doorway, giggling at their mother's antics. (They checked on her regularly those days for fear her losses would be more than she could bear, driving her to an act of despair.)

As she stood holding her silent partner, Susan looked at her girls and said, "In the years to come, may this be the way you remember me . . . dancing."

Susan didn't want to leave a legacy of brokenness or despair. Instead, she chose to give a living heritage of courage, conviction, and, yes, celebration. Her circumstances were anything but normal, but then, so was her response.

By the way, she was able to turn the little business around, buy a lovely home, and enjoy a full and active life. She chose not to stay in her sorrow or linger in her loss, but in the midst of devastation, to dance.

14

You-Turn

I AM ALWAYS going. Going places, going to town, going up, going down, and even going bonkers. But one going I don't do well is going back. I'm a forward person, and I'm married to a fast-forward kind of guy. If Les and I are pulling out of our driveway and realize we've forgotten something after we've passed our mailbox (affixed to our front porch), we don't go back; we go without.

Since I'm an "Onward Christian Soldier," you can imagine how difficult it is for me when I have no choice but to go back.

Janet, a friend, and I had just completed four glorious days of study and fun. We stayed in a beautiful, wooded setting that we thought was paradise.

The grounds were complete with English gardens, wild turkeys, deer, and swans.

The most attentive creatures were the swans—especially the male fowl, who truly was foul. He changed our thoughts forever about swans' being gentle beauties. Good-looking he was; good-natured, guess again.

We nicknamed him "Dick the Bruiser." Dick's walk was an overstated strut. He would flex his chest feathers and then swagger. To further intimidate us, this bully would stretch out his S-shaped neck until it became an exclamation point. The feat made you wonder if there were a giraffe in his family closet. He seemed to be of the mind that the grounds were his and we were intruders. After he backed us into the kitchen and didn't allow us to leave until he finally became bored with us, we decided it *was* his place. We did our best to stay out of his way the rest of the time we were there.

When it came time for Janet and me to leave, we were reluctant because it had been a perfect writing place for us. With the Bruiser's permission, however, we eventually packed the van and said our good-byes. We hugged Zona (the best cook in Michigan), waved to Dick and his willowy wife from the safety of the van, and hit the dusty trail.

We had a three-hour ride in front of us, and we decided to use the time brainstorming. Janet and I had been chatting for an hour when I noticed my gas gauge was registering a little skimpy. I chose to fill up then to prevent any delays later.

I swung into a country service station and ordered ten dollars worth of gas. Then I reached for my purse. It wasn't there. I panicked. Janet prayed. Then Janet paid. No purse, no moolah.

I pulled away from the pumps, parked the van on the side of the road, and began a frantic search. I rummaged through the boxes, bags, and baggage in an attempt to force my purse into existence. While I ripped apart the van, Janet was nervously tossing animal cookies into her mouth.

I finally had to admit I had forgotten my handbag back with the Bruiser. Ol' Beak Face was probably picking through it while I was ransacking my vehicle. (I wonder how swan feathers would work for pillows?) To make matters more frustrating, buckets of bone-chilling rain were coming down.

Looking for an easier answer than going back, I decided to call Les. The only available phone was an unprotected one that I couldn't reach from the van. So I jumped out into the downpour and grabbed the receiver, only to realize I had forgotten my home number. I jerked open the van door, my hair hanging down my face like wet feathers, and asked my California guest if she knew my number.

Janet was still munching morsels. (I don't think she was hungry but thought it best to chew on the cookies rather than chew me out.) She dipped into her purse and pulled out my number. She tried reading it but instead showered me in hippo crumbs. I took the sticky scrap with the scrawled numbers and hurried back to the phone. I reached Les as the rain washed away the writing, leaving the paper as blank as I was feeling.

After a quick but soggy talk, Les and I agreed I would have to return to claim my belongings. I sloshed my way back to Janet, who appeared to have stored the cookies much like a chipmunk storing acorns in his chubby cheeks. I announced my backtracking plan to her. She swallowed hard and smiled weakly.

Once I made the U-turn and aimed the vehicle in the "wrong" direction, we tried to cheer up. We remembered we had passed a bakery advertising homemade pies. We had valiantly declined the chance to have a piece on our first drive by. Now we agreed we should not only stop, but we should also each have our own pie as a source of comfort. In preparation for this highlight, we talked about what kinds we hoped they had, and we tried to imagine the light, flaky crust.

Our mouths were watering when we spotted the bakery ahead. I sped up and turned into the driveway, only to spot something else. The bakery had closed. I began to wonder how swan pie might taste.

I know an hour's distance is not that far, but when I have my mind set on forward, I find it exasperating to switch directions. My mistake added two unnecessary hours to our travel. With each mile back, we felt the emotional impact of going the "wrong way."

Janet was kind and didn't say I was a nitwit. But I found it difficult to forgive myself for this stupid stunt.

"If only I hadn't left my belongings," I whined repeatedly. Yet my purse was too valuable not to retrieve. It was full of my identification, as well as my finances. I had to drive the long road back before we could continue our journey.

I find this is also true when we're working on issues from the past. We have to be willing, at times, to look back so we can go forward. If we don't, we leave valuable pieces of our identification behind.

It's not unusual to feel angry about going back to retrieve our emotional "bags," because most of us have our indicators set on forward. Returning seems like such a waste of effort. But it's the same as when I recovered my purse; once I had what was mine in hand, my anger began to subside, and I was more fully equipped to move ahead.

The temporary inconvenience of returning put me in a much better place than if I had gone home and arrived there both angry and without my personal belongings.

Unresolved childhood conflicts can leave us in cycles of anger, guilt, shame, or fear. Those feelings use up more of our time than if we made the ride back and took care of our personal stuff. They also add stress to our relationships, leaving us stuck in negative emotional cycles without an exit.

Angie felt like a mouse in a maze. She was caught in her unmanageable emotions, and she couldn't find a way out. Her husband, Rich, was exhausted from trying to understand her and was threatening to leave.

When Angie first called me and confessed her bizarre behavior, I suggested she talk to a counselor about some childhood pain. She instantly became irate, declaring, "My childhood was like being brought up in Ozzie and Harriet Nelson's home. It was perfect."

Angie's strong response indicated that the past was a painful and scary place for her. Her proclamation showed an extreme need to avoid not only going back, but also checking her rearview mirror.

Her reluctance to consider yesterday as an answer for today was as normal as my hesitancy to back-track for my bag.

Later, out of desperation for her own emotional well-being and for the sake of her marriage, Angie made the journey "home." She claimed "her belong-ings," which turned out to be far more valuable than she had imagined. She also felt a sense of inner relief, making it possible for her to move ahead.

The strange thought patterns and behavior that had plagued her lessened and then stopped. When Angie was able to change channels (from "The Nel-sons"), life came into clearer focus for her. She began to tune in to reality and see how her life actually had been. Living in truth, although ini-tially painful, helped her emotions to heal. Today Angie enjoys healthier thoughts and improved rela-tionships.

Back is, at times, the most forward step we can take.

15

Accidental Perspective

I BOUNDED OUT the door, energized because I had completed a writing project and motivated by a purchase I was going to make. I had been working on a story for two days, and it had finally come together. While I was writing, in the back of my mind, I kept thinking about a used piece of furniture I had been in town that would be just right for my office. I needed a book and display case, and this piece offered both, plus more. The price was right, too.

I was excited as I headed into our little town full of delightful shops offering wonderful "deals." I was almost to my destination when, in my rearview mirror, I noticed a car come up behind me at a fast clip. I remember thinking, *That guy is going to hit me if I don't scoot out of his way.* I added a little pressure to the gas pedal and turned my wheel to hurry into a parking space. That's when it happened. A loud thud was followed by crunching, scrunching, grinding sounds as my minivan rearranged the front fender of a parked car.

I am of the belief that if you're going to hit a vehicle, you should select one with someone inside. When you smack an empty, parked car, you pretty much rule out the chance the other person may have been at fault. All eyes are focused on you. Also, if you must have an obvious accident, it's better not to do it on Main Street in your hometown.

I jumped out of the van and ran over to look at the smooshed car. The victim's vehicle had two silver beauty marks streaking down the side, and the chrome fender curled out instead of in, giving it a flared appearance.

Then I ran inside an office and asked if the car belonged to anyone there. It didn't, so I headed for the next building, when I heard someone call my name.

A lady I had just met at Bible study two weeks prior waved and ran across the road in my direction. She gave me a hug and told me everyone in the ladies' dress shop heard me hit the car and came to the window to see what had happened and who had done it. When I had stepped out of my van, she had squealed and announced, "I know that woman!" In a small town, anonymity is difficult.

Then she added as she checked out the crumpled car, "You could tell this story at conferences."

Trust me—at this point, I was not eager to tell my husband, much less the world, what I had done.

I dashed into the shop where the bookcase was and called to the clerk, "I have to go turn myself in at the police station, but would you please measure the bookcase for me? I'll be right back to purchase it."

As I headed for the front door, I heard a sweet voice say, "I just sold it."

"No!" I exclaimed. "You don't understand! I hit a car in my attempt to get here and buy this piece" (as if that would make a difference). Then I whined, "The buyer wasn't driving a dark blue Buick, was she?"

The saleswoman assured me she wasn't. I could tell she felt bad about my situation, but I felt worse. On the way to the police station, I thought, *Maybe I'll have them throw me in the slammer and sleep off this trip to town.*

When I arrived, I confessed to a woman behind a barred glass window that I had committed a crime. She called for an officer to come and write a report. While I was waiting, I noticed the zipper on my pants was down and my red shirttail was sticking out like a road flag. I quickly turned away from the men sitting in the waiting area to "fix" myself and tried not to think about how long my red tail had been waving. A fleeting recollection of me looking like Wee Willie Winkie as I ran from one store to the next, trying to find the car's owner, darted through my head.

The officer appeared and began to ask questions. Near the end of the inquest, he asked, "How much damage did you do to your vehicle?"

"I don't know," I answered.

"You don't know?" he echoed.

"I don't know," I validated.

"Why don't you know?" he pushed.

"Because I didn't look."

"Why didn't you look?" he asked in disbelief.

"I'm in denial," I confessed.

"You have to look," he told me. Then he sent me out to get my registration.

I returned, paper in hand.

"Well," he said, "how much damage?"

"Sir, I didn't look," I said with polite resignation.

He shook his head and gave me back my registration. As I was leaving, I heard him say, "You'll have to look."

When I got home, I asked Les to go out and look.

It turned out I had swiped her car with my running board. The board wasn't off, yet it wasn't on. It was neither here nor there but suspended in air. Threads at each end dangled the board precariously.

Afterward, I realized that when we spend too much time looking in our rearview mirrors, we may hit something right in front of us. Looking back is an important part of conscientious driving, but it's not the only safety precaution.

Likewise, it's important for us to benefit from our past, but we don't want to get so stuck staring at yesterday that we collide with today in a destructive way.

Unlike the situation with my van, I can't send Les to check my past and assess how much damage was done. That's my responsibility. As the officer said, "You'll have to look." But once I take care of what I can do to repair the past, I then need to drive on, benefiting from occasional rearview references and perspective.

16

High Flyer

WHEN MY BROTHER-in-law, Bryan, was sent to Saudi Arabia during Desert Storm, my sister, Elizabeth, and their three children came for a visit. Elizabeth and the youngsters—Steven, eight; Nicholas, two; and Lindsey, four months—stayed for five weeks.

It didn't take me long to decide that combat gear would be helpful not only in Saudi, but also at our place. It had been a long time since Les and I had experienced young ones for days on end, and we had forgotten how much energy they're capable of expending. The visit also highlighted Les's and my need to consider a retirement village . . . soon!

Elizabeth, being a conscientious mom, strapped on her Reeboks every morning in her attempt to keep up with the fast-paced, creative escapades of her little munchkins.

In my effort to be supportive of this never-ending challenge, I invested in some baby furniture. First, I bought a small crib, then a highchair, and lastly a walker.

I had noticed Nicholas, the two-year-old, thought his four-month-old sister, Lindsey, made a cushy trampoline. So I thought I would spare her little body squash marks by tucking her in the walker.

When I arrived with the walker, I was eager to try it out. Fortunately it didn't require assembly, and all I had to do was open it up and slide her in. Seemed simple enough. Little did I realize I was under surveillance for the purpose of sabotage.

I innocently turned my back on the open walker while I stooped down to pick up Lindsey. In that unguarded moment, the saboteur, Nicholas, catapulted his two-year-old frame into the walker. He then pulled it up like a pair of pants and tore off running at a high speed that set the walker legs flapping in the breeze.

Much to my amazement and horror, Nicholas headed for the stairway. He evidently thought the word *landing* meant "runway" and the term *walker* was a code name for Lear Jet, because he ran right off the landing into midair.

At that point, Nicholas learned a scientific concept . . . gravity. Nick and his floppy-fitting flying machine dropped into the stair-well, crashing on the cement floor below.

My heart stopped for the split second of silence that followed. Then my feet began to gallop as screams came trumpeting up the steps. As I neared the landing, I envisioned Nicholas in a pile of little

broken bones. But what I met was an enraged con-
sumer stomping up the stairs, registering the loudest complaint I had ever heard. Evidently Nicholas
wanted money back on this faulty piece of equipment.

Nicholas didn't have a mark on him and didn't
even seem to be in pain . . . but he was livid this
contraption didn't fly. I tried to console him, but he
was intent on revenge. He kicked the plastic tires a
couple of times and called it names in toddler jar-
gon. I believe he referred to it as a "swachendinger."
Finally, we were able to divert his attention while
Les stowed the abused apparatus.

I find it interesting how young we learn to blame
something or someone else for our behavior, and
then how long we hold onto the habit. The other
day I saw a grown man behaving much like my little nephew. The man's car had a flat tire, and when
he stepped out of the vehicle, he proceeded to kick
the tire and bang the hood with his fist. I'm glad my
windows were up and I couldn't hear the names he
was calling his car from his adult arsenal.

That scene was both funny and sad. Here was a
grown-up conversing with an inanimate object as
he tried to beat it senseless. Smart, huh? And yet
he's certainly not alone. . . .

A friend came over one day, steaming because
the bank had dared to bounce her check. "Did you
have money in the account?" I asked.

"That's not the point," she insisted. "I've done
business there a long time, and they should have
overlooked it."

Instead of seeing her poor bookkeeping and
spontaneous shopping sprees as the problem, she

pointed an accusing finger at the bank's "un-friendly tactics."

My check-bouncing friend, the flat-tire man, and my flying nephew found it easier to shift blame than to see how their actions played a part in the outcome. Blame is a common defense. I know, I've used it. In fact. . . .

Recently I was running a little late for an appointment. Just before I ran out the door, I stopped to put away my mail. I noticed an unopened letter and took additional moments to open, read, and write a quick response to it.

On the way to the meeting place, I ran into heavy traffic and then had to wait at a train crossing for 100 cars to chug by. When I arrived at my destination, I was stressed out and frustrated. I heard myself accusing the stand-still traffic and the stretched-out train for my delay.

As I thought about it later, however, I realized that if I had left when I should have, I would have missed the train and had enough leeway to inch through the traffic and still arrive on time . . . minus my jangled nerves. I find that I'm often guilty of creating the chaotic atmosphere that sets me up for emotional frenzy.

In the blame game, everybody loses, and nobody changes.

17

My Way

JOANIE HAD A magnetic beauty. People often stared at her out of admiration. She also had a spunky personality and was known for being a little headstrong. Her dynamic beauty and bouncy determination made her quite popular.

Jeff was a successful businessman and real-estate investor. He was brought up in a dysfunctional home, but he had chosen a different life-style from his family's. He was well respected and loved by his friends and co-workers. When Joanie and Jeff married, everyone felt they were a perfect pair.

Joanie and Jeff had it all, with one exception. They were unable to have children. This grieved them both, but especially Joanie, who felt she had let Jeff down. Jeff remained devoted to her, but she became preoccupied with her infertility. She wept often. Her housekeeper, Karen, would hear her cry and try to console her. Karen's gentle care touched Joanie's heart, and they became friends. Joanie found herself confiding in the other woman.

Joanie and Karen's lives were very different. Karen was much younger, she lived a meager lifestyle, and she had only been in the U.S. a short time when she began to work for her wealthy employer.

As the months passed, Joanie's desire for a child only increased. One day, as she watched Karen arrange flowers in a vase, an idea swept through her mind. At first she was startled at her own thought, but as she entertained the idea, it began to comfort her.

Joanie wanted Karen to have Jeff's baby. That way Jeff would have a child, and Joanie would not have to live with the nagging feeling of failure.

Artificial insemination had not yet been perfected, and Joanie felt she had waited long enough. Besides, she knew Karen and Jeff loved her, not each other. So how could it hurt?

Both Karen and Jeff agreed to Joanie's plan. In fact, neither seemed to hesitate or object. And so it was that Karen became pregnant with Jeff's first-born.

Joanie initially was pleased with her decision. But then she noticed a change in Karen's attitude toward her. At first Joanie thought she was imagining the change. Or maybe it was just the mood swings of a pregnant woman.

But time told a different tale. Not only did Karen's tummy puff, but so also did her pride. Karen felt superior to her childless friend.

Joanie was first crushed and then livid. In a fit of fury, she fired Karen.

Jeff, Joanie, and Karen's lives had turned into a tragedy. What started out as the perfect pair seemed to end as brokenness and despair.

Actually, there's more to this story, much more. If you'd like to see the end of the saga, look in an age-old book, the Bible (Genesis). Joanie (a.k.a. Sarah), Jeff (a.k.a. Abraham), and Karen (a.k.a. Hagar) are presented in all their sadness and eventual celebration.

It's a story that tinges the reader's heart with sorrow over their choices but gladdens the heart over God's grace.

When you think about it, this trio doesn't sound old. In fact, Sarah, Hagar, and Abe's choices remind us of the tabloid headlines we see as we move through the grocery store checkout. This proves once again that Scripture offers counsel generation after generation.

"There's no new thing under the sun."

18

Flight 326

I HAD JUST finished a demanding three days of teaching in Indiana and was headed for my home in Michigan. As I stood in the airport looking out at the runway, I became aware of how exhausted I was. But I comforted myself with the thought that I would soon be home.

While standing at the window, watching for my plane, I noticed a tiny Tinker Toy-type plane putt up and park at a gate. I told myself, *See, Patsy, things could be worse. Instead of being just tired, you could be booked on that pretend airplane.*

As that thought crossed my mind, I heard an airline hostess announce my plane's arrival. I picked up my belongings and headed for my gate. Even my purse seemed heavy as I dragged along. When I arrived where I thought I belonged, I noticed I was all alone. I backtracked to the check-in desk to ask about my gate. The lady behind the desk told me that someone would be escorting me and some others outside.

Confused, I asked, "Why would I need to go outside?"

"To board your flight," she said dryly.

"I don't understand," I replied, feeling mentally deficient. I thought, *Surely I can't be so wiped out that I'm unable to process what this gal is saying to me.*

She spoke slowly, hoping, I'm sure, that a light might go on signifying someone possibly was home. "Your plane has arrived," she reannounced, directing my attention to the window. "We'll have someone take you out to board."

My eyes followed her outstretched arm, but I couldn't see my plane. I thought my mind had left me, and now my sight was impaired. I decided to be blunt. "I don't see my plane," I said, bewildered.

"Aren't you on flight 326?" she inquired.

I looked at my ticket and verified by bobbing my weary head up and down. Evidently she felt sorry for me, because she took me by the arm, walked me to the window, and pointed to the plane.

Suddenly I came to life. It was as if someone had stuck my finger in an outlet. She was aiming her sinister finger at the play plane I had seen earlier.

"No, I don't fly in anything but a jet," I shot at her.

"You are today," she smilingly bubbled back.

"No, no, there's been a mistake. I only fly in normal airplanes." I stammered the words, starting to panic.

She seemed to take my "normal" statement personally. She told me I could call my travel agent on the pay phone, and then she turned and walked back to her desk and the waiting line.

I was nauseated. How could this have happened? Then I heard the announcement that the guide was ready to take us outside to board.

Not knowing what else to do, I followed several businessmen out to the waiting plane. The Bible verse "All we like sheep have gone astray" came to my trembling mind as I followed on the gentlemen's heels. When we arrived at the portable steps, I knew by seeing it up close that this was what is referred to as an "aircraft." That means, "something a couple of space cadets glued together in their garage while watching Big Time Wrestling."

I had to bend down to enter the aircraft. (Excuse me, but I'm only five feet tall.) Then I made my way (a distance of 12 inches) to my seat. Because of restricted space, I had to embrace my purse and briefcase in my lap. I could feel the vibration of the engine shaking my armload of belongings. Then I realized the engine wasn't running yet, and what I felt was my own pounding heart ricocheting off my clutched parcels.

I peeked around and noticed the men aboard didn't seem comfortable, either. They looked like sumo wrestlers bent forward and stuffed into seats not designed to hold them. Their knees seemed to be growing out of their chins.

The cockpit was open to us, and it appeared that if the pilot got into any problems, we, the flyees, could lean forward and take over.

I peeked out my lens-sized window as an airline employee approached the propeller and gave it a mighty whirl. I was not encouraged to know this apparatus had to be hand wound. The engine kicked into an ear-deafening rhythm.

Instead of just vibrating, I now felt as though I were being shook silly on one of those weight-reduction belts. The plane wobbled out to the runway and began to taxi. (I wished at that point that I was *in* a taxi.) I had the distinct feeling, as we sputtered ahead, that the businessmen and I would each have to sling out a leg and paddle to get this baby airborne.

That wasn't necessary. Suddenly a hose broke loose outside the plane and spewed liquid across our windows. The tiny craft reduced speed and hightailed it back to the terminal.

The next thing we knew, the pilot and copilot had evacuated the plane. Their desertion removed any question about whether they planned on going down with the ship.

Somehow, when the pilots left us, we passengers were in no mood to stay. One of the pilots ran around to the side of the plane, wiped his finger through the liquid, and smelled it. Then he disappeared.

A businessman looked at me and said, "It's a good thing none of us is smoking."

That pretty much did it for me. I was getting off if I had to stuff myself through the porthole window next to me. That wasn't necessary, though, because an airline worker opened the door at that moment and asked us to quickly evacuate the plane. I gave new meaning to the word *quickly.*

As we gathered inside the terminal, we were told there would be a short delay while they fixed the plane. I could just picture them pushing this craft back into the garage so the space cadets could safety pin the hose back in place.

In about 15 minutes, they lined us up and marched us back to the Tinker Terminator. Only now there were fewer of us, because several men refused to get back on.

That was the most purging ride of my life, as I asked the Lord to forgive me for every offensive thing I had said or done. All this confession was in preparation for meeting Him, which I knew I was going to do at any moment. The flight felt as if we were sky surfing. And then we made a roller-coaster drop from the sky, thumping onto the runway.

Les told me he was looking out the window, watching for my plane, when Tinker bounced in. He said that out of boredom, he was watching the handful of people squeeze out of the hatch when I emerged. "Boy," he said, "was I surprised to see you in a plane like that!"

"You!" I squealed with weak knees. As we walked to the baggage area, I Velcroed myself to Les's arm. I was grateful to be back on earth with my husband and my squeaky-clean heart.

Interesting how disruptive events can give us a more grateful perspective and a renewed commitment to our families and faith. Could that be what they were designed for?

19

Hold Your Tongue

WHEN JANET AND I arrived at the house in the woods to work on a manuscript, the bear rug in the living room caught our immediate attention. It was large, furry, and cuddly looking. But when we viewed our new friend from the front, our assessment changed. The black bear didn't look so friendly with its huge head and ferocious, open, growling mouth. We dropped "cuddly" from our list of descriptives.

Janet and I tried to guess what might have caused this bear to look so testy. Maybe someone had swiped its Smoky the Bear poster, or perhaps it had sat on a hive and the bees had made their point. Finally we decided this was a she-bear, and someone had criticized her cubs and ticked her off.

Her gleaming teeth were bared as though she were seething with anger and eager to rip off someone's limbs. But we both agreed the most despicable feature of this animal was her long, glistening tongue. Yuck!

After hours of concentration on our project, my head felt clogged with words, and my mind was skipping beats. Janet and I were losing our enthusiasm and focus. That wasn't good, because we had a lot of writing to accomplish before proclaiming our work complete.

As the gaps in my thinking process widened, I began to hit wrong keys and misspell simple words. It was obvious I needed a break.

I pulled away from my computer and walked across the room, being careful to inch around the intimidating animal skin sprawled on the floor. I shuddered as I passed. Pulling a couple of tissues from the Kleenex box, I turned to say something to Janet while walking back to the table. My eyes were on her, and for a split second I forgot our fiendish floor friend. In that unguarded moment, my foot slipped into the bear's open jaws, sending me catapulting over its head. The tongue flew out of its fierce mouth and slurped down my leg as I screamed in disgust. Trying to catch my balance, I staggered against the fireplace and cringed as the tongue slid to my feet.

Janet howled!

I broke my grisly gaze to look in Janet's direction, and we both came unglued. We laughed and laughed, the kind of laughter in which it's hard to catch your breath, and your insides jostle around like an unbalanced washing machine on spin cycle. Tears cascaded down our now-blotchy faces. Gasping, I jumped around in an attempt to jump-start my breathing. As we both caught our breath, we noticed the bear staring at its own taunting tongue lying three feet from its head, and we burst into laughter again.

After our 15-minute seizure of guffawing had passed, we felt great! The laughter had amazingly flushed our heads, refreshed our attitudes, and relieved our emotional humdrums. Janet and I went back to work with renewed interest and creative results.

Laughter lightens the load.

20

???'s

GOD ASKED A lot of questions in Scripture. That
intrigues me. He who has all the answers, asked.
Did you ever wonder why?

For instance, the Lord called out to Adam and
Eve after they had sinned and hidden from His
presence, "Where are you?"

Whenever I've read that portion of Scripture, I've
wanted to tattle and call out, "They're hiding
behind the blaming bush!"

The bush must really have been a dandy hiding
place if our all-knowing, all-seeing God didn't have
a clue to their whereabouts. I'm sure it was a big
garden, but c'mon, we know God knew. So why did
He ask?

The Lord questioned Eve in regard to her disobedience, "What is this you have done?"

Do you actually think God was stumped? I wonder why He didn't just dangle in front of her guilt-ridden face a Polaroid snapshot of her and the enemy dining on fruit flambé. Or run an instant replay of Adam's eating out of his wife's hand.

I notice God didn't stop asking questions in the garden but continued throughout Scripture. Curious response from a sovereign God who can not only tell us what we've done, but also expose the content of our thoughts and hearts. Consider Hagar. . . .

Hagar was in trouble. Death was knocking at her door, as well as at her young son's, when the angel of God called to her, "What is the matter with you, Hagar?"

Isn't it rather obvious, especially for an overseer like an angel? Hagar and Ishmael were a couple of crispy critters after crawling in the scorching sun. The only moisture was the boy's tears, and they evaporated before they could drip off his face.

Maybe the angel was wearing shades or was momentarily blinded by the sizzling sun. But wait, something even stranger happened next. Before Hagar could give the angel an update on her ordeal, the angel mapped out her future, answering his own question.

I'm getting more confused. If the inquiring angel knew the answer, why did he ask?

Let's see, we have Eve in arrears while the enemy leers, and Ishmael in tears while Hagar sears. Boy, do I have questions.

The story of Elijah doesn't help. Elijah had a fiery faith until Jezebel doused his flames. Jez Fed-Exed

Elijah her plan to snuff him out. Elijah's faith flickered, allowing fear to flame up, and he fled.

We find Elijah headed for high ground in an attempt to control his own destiny. He was pursued not by the enemy but by the questions of God.

"What are you doing here, Elijah?" the Lord probed. Not once but twice, He asked Elijah what He already knew.

Even in the midst of death, God asked questions. We find Ezekiel in a valley of death, meandering among the corpses. The voice of the Lord solicited what sounds like advice from Ezekiel when He asked, "Can these bones live?"

Excuse me, but He who formed our skeletons from the dust of the earth and breathed into mankind the breath of life wasn't sure if the bones could live? Perhaps He misplaced His recipe. Can you hear Him pondering, *Was it one part dust to every three breaths, or three parts dust to every one breath?*

I think not. I'm the one left pondering.

God sent us His Son, Jesus. The family connection is obvious, because Jesus, our Answer, came asking questions. Like Father, like Son.

The Lord asked impetuous Peter, "Who do you say that I am?"

Still later He penetrated Peter's heart with the words, "Do you love Me?" Evidently the Lord thought Peter was hard of hearing, because He repeated Himself, "Do you love Me?" Twice I can see, but the Lord pushed Peter a third time. "Do you love Me?"

This loving interrogation left Peter stumped. He responded as we might have, "Lord, You know all things; You know that I love You."

What I hear Peter saying is, "Why are You asking when You know me better than I do?"

If we truly believe the Lord knows us, we must realize these questions have a purpose. And it certainly isn't that the Lord is forgetful and needs us to remind Him. Nor is He stuck and in need of our feeble insight. I think He questions us so we might think—think through our choices, our responsibilities, and our beliefs.

Maybe, if we try to answer some of these questions in regard to our own lives, we will better understand their wisdom:

"Where are you?"

"What is the matter with you?"

"What are you doing here?"

"Who do you say that I am?"

"Do you love Me?"

"Do you love Me?"

"Do you love Me?"

Well, what do you think?

21

Risky Business

MY HUSBAND IS a risk taker. Usually that has enhanced his life. Occasionally, though, his on-the-edge attitude gets him into a jam. And I'm not talking strawberry preserves.

One day Les was working on a project that required him to do some welding. In his desire to expedite things, he took a risk and didn't wear his safety glasses. He thought it might not matter since it wasn't an involved welding job. *Nyet.* It mattered.

The tingling in Les's eyes began about ten o'clock that evening, but he decided to brave it out. The sandpaper feeling began about eleven. He thought he could endure it. The feeling of hot coals sizzling his eyeballs hit about midnight. He finally requested to be taken to the hospital or shot, whichever was fastest. I debated and then settled on the hospital.

We lived at a Boy Scout reservation in the country at the time. Our two young sons were asleep, and they both had school the following day. I decided to call in a friend to take Les to the clinic. I chose our dear friend and pastor, Marv. (Don't you know how thrilled he was to receive this honor.)

Les and Marv had been friends for years. They share a common interest in getting the other's goat. They are both playful, fun-loving fellows who genuinely care for each other, although the casual observer might think there are moments when their jokes outweigh their caring.

Marv came immediately, extending concern and support. After arriving at the hospital and going through an eye check, Les learned there was no permanent damage. The doctor filled his eyes with cooling salve that immediately eliminated the pain. Then he taped Les's eyes closed, covering them in bandages that wound around his head. Les looked like an escapee from King Tut's tomb. The doctor instructed him to leave the dressings on for eight hours.

Picture the opportunity this gave Marv—Les blindfolded and needing Marv to lead him around. Marv guided Les to the parking lot and then let him go, suggesting Les find the car. It was now 1 A.M. There were only three cars in the lot. Les couldn't find any of them. (Remember Pin the Tail on the Donkey? Les's childhood training in this important game must have been inadequate. Car trunks and donkey rumps alike eluded him.) Marv finally ushered Les to the vehicle and brought him home.

At 2 A.M., I heard laughter rolling in through my bedroom window. I was dozing, waiting to hear the outcome. I had expected the best, but I was not prepared for laughter.

I pulled back the shade and saw Marv holding onto Les's arm. Marv was telling Les how to avoid obstacles in his path.

I head Marv say, "There's a step, Les; lift your foot."

Les lifted his foot in blind obedience. But there really wasn't a step, which left Les high-stepping it around the yard like a drum major.

Marv and Les were both guffawing, although Marv seemed to be laughing harder.

After I received the good news on Les's eyes, Marv headed home. We listened as he chuckled his way out to his car. Les and I laughed our way to bed.

The memory of that night could have been an eyesore for us all. But thanks to Marv, as we think back on it, we smile rather than wince. A little levity applied at the right moment can be a balm that lasts longer than the hurt, soothing a heavy heart. And yes, Les found a way to pay Marv back.

22

Blue Light Special

MOVING? NOT AGAIN!" That was my first reaction when Les suggested we go house hunting. After 23 moves in 30 years, I could hardly grasp the thought that it was time to pack another U-Haul. For years we had worked in camps where we lived on the grounds in camp housing. But Les felt we should buy our own home.

Purchasing a place sounded exciting, exhausting, and scary. This was to be our "grow old together" home. That meant I had better be sure I loved it, because I probably would spend a good long spell there.

I decided to make a list of everything I'd like in a home. I started my lineup with a maid, a cook, and a masseuse, but then the words "Get real" came to mind, so I chucked that list and began again.

Location was important to both of us. We had been living in the country the past five years, which was glorious in many ways but had a few disadvantages. For instance, like the pioneers, going to town was a big deal for us. That may have been due to the wagon-train-sized ruts in our road. The ride jostled you so hard, your cheeks bounced up and down and hung like jowls by the time you disembarked.

Also, we had a large hill just before our home. During the winter it could be treacherous, often causing guests to leave before they ever arrived, as their vehicles glided backward down the icy incline. During the summer, the hill made us a target for every storm that blew through our country. The winds rattled windows and snapped power lines, plunging us into darkness in the middle of the woods. Dark darkens in the woods—trust me.

I decided to wait till glory for my next mansion on a hilltop. For now, I wanted to stand by my man on level ground.

I knew I wanted a first-floor master bedroom and bath, as well as a first-floor laundry room. (I wanted Les to have easy access to the laundry in case he ever felt led to clean up his act or mine.)

Next, I thought a pantry and a dishwasher (which I had never owned before) would be great. I knew a fireplace would be fun. We'd had them before, but it had been eight years since the last one. I missed all the ashes, soot, log chips, scorching sparks, and the smoke when the flue wouldn't stay open. There's something romantic about a fireplace.

I also wanted a shower separate from the tub. Don't ask me why; I just did. A yard with trees seemed important, and I love porches. We hadn't had a garage in years, so I added that to my wish list as well. Then I jotted down a basement, because they're valuable for storage and shelter from storms. I wanted all this with a blue-light-special price tag.

As I clutched my "all I want in a house" paper, we began our search. We looked at all kinds of homes, always feeling hesitant for one reason or another.

Then, as we were driving down a street in town weeks later, I noticed a vacant home. Les took down a phone number off a building permit and called. We found out the house was for sale and had not been listed. The builder offered to show us the place in an hour. The home was not new but one a tree had squashed, and the builder had made it like new.

When we stepped into the home, my husband's face lit up. For him, it was love at first sight. I was "in like" with the house but certainly hadn't decided I wanted to live there. After the tour, Les was ready to sign on the dotted line, while I was still trying to remember what color the carpeting was. In the evening, we placed a deposit on the home, and I felt numb.

The next day, we took another walk through Les's house to see where we would be spending the next century of our lives. As Les paced off the property line, I sat on the floor of the living room, staring. Then I remembered my list, which had been buried in my purse when this whirlwind house purchase occurred. I shook out the wrinkled and crummy paper and started to check my requirements.

First-floor bedroom, check. Well, at least I did have that. In fact, it was the largest bedroom we had ever had. It had a door that opened into the first-floor bath, which isn't exactly what I had in mind, but it worked, so I checked that one also. The separate shower was incorporated into the home . . . on the second floor.

Pantry. Hmmm, I was thinking walk-in. This one had a bifold door with a single line of shelves. It was a pantry. Check.

Hurray, a dishwasher! It pleased me to check it off.

First-floor laundry, check. Of course, it was only large enough for the washer and dryer. I was thinking it would be nice to have space for things like the dirty clothes and a basket. I couldn't deny, though, that there was a laundry area.

The home had a basement, check . . . a Michigan basement. That means that once your furnace and water heater are in, it's full.

The garage sits in the backyard and will hold Les's tools and our boxes of storage. No room for a vehicle, but still a garage. Check.

Porch, check. Seats two people.

Trees, double-check. Yard is three inches deep in fallen leaves.

Fireplace, check. It's modern; I'm country. Sigh and check.

As I gazed at all the marks on the page, I realized the Lord had given me everything I had asked for. It was just packaged differently from what I had expected. Rather than seeing this house as a problem, I began to see it as a provision. And do you know what happened? I fell in love with this darling home.

I wonder how many times I've received from the Lord what I had asked for but just didn't recognize it?

P.S. Our home is on low ground, in town, and was a blue light opportunity!

23

Bucket Brigade

WHEN I WAS growing up, my big brother Don had a favorite record he would play repeatedly. It was sung by Johnnie Ray and was entitled "The Little White Cloud That Cried." Over and over, that poor cloud would weep its little heart out. Just about the time you thought you couldn't bear to hear the cloud squeeze out one more teardrop, Don would turn the record over, and Johnnie would sing his hit song "Cry." We needed a bucket brigade just to handle the tears of this one crooner.

Some of you reading this will remember Johnnie Ray performing "Cry" on television. He would truly get into his song. Dramatically he would pull at his tie, open his shirt collar, drop to his knees, and finally fall to his face while pounding the floor with his fists. Don't you just love a man who can show emotion!

Okay, okay, maybe that's a little more emotion than I'd be comfortable with, but I wonder how many of us wouldn't benefit from a good gully wash.

While some of us have cried a river already, others of us have lost touch with this vital resource. I remember doing a retreat in central Georgia during which a number of tender and endearing things transpired that moved almost all of us gals to tears. But I spotted one young, attractive woman whose posture was like a robot's. She appeared to resist emotions positive or negative. I chatted with her and mentioned her "composure." She announced stoically, "I don't ever cry."

It was obvious she needed to, however, although I'm sure it would have been like releasing Niagara Falls. The torrent of tears would have eventually subsided, emptying out space for her to feel again.

I realize this crying thing can also be taken too far the other way. There's nothing sadder than a sniffing saint who's stuck inside herself and sees her sniveling as spiritual. Some soggy saints could be rented out as professional mourners. Grief was not meant to be an address but a process.

I used to think that because I cried so easily, I was deeply sensitive. Instead, I've learned that when someone told me a sad story, I was so full of my own unshed tears that the first tear I shed was for them, but the rest were for myself. Other people's pain kept tapping into my own unresolved issues.

I remember one night watching a movie on TV. Toward the end, the star was treated terribly by someone she loved. I felt her pain, and I began to cry. The story continued, and so did my tears. Building sobs were difficult to hold in. The movie ended, but I kept crying. My husband came into the room, and I blubbered, "I just feel so bad about that girl."

Tenderly Les said, "Honey, I don't think this is about that girl."

That did it. My dam burst! Les's words seemed to make it safe for me to feel my own pain. I began to realize that my first response was more than "sad movies make me cry." This girl's injury triggered my own buried memories. I wept and wailed for almost an hour. It was great! It wasn't great while I was crying—in fact, that was kind of scary. But the release I felt afterward was liberating.

Of course, most painful issues can't be resolved in an hour of crying, but many times it can be a good place to start.

Try this: List the last three times you cried. What did you cry about? Whom were you crying for?

Maybe you're a soggy saint. If so, it's time to call in a bucket brigade and get on with life.

Or maybe it's time for your tears, and you need someone to give you permission to let loose. Well, here it is. Go ahead . . . have a good, soul-washing cry!

24

Soup's On!

I HATE FEELING rejected. I'm so overwired in this area that when I approach a traffic signal and it turns red, I take it personally. Okay, I'm not quite that sensitive, but I do like to be liked. I'm always grateful for the cheerleaders in my life—the people who root for me and believe the best about me. But into each person's life must come a few pom-pom pilferers.

I love speaking and have had the privilege of sharing the stage with many outstanding people. Usually we speakers are so busy that we don't have time to get to know each other. We fly into a city for an engagement, eat, speak, eat, talk with some of the audience personally, eat, and then go. (We leave with more "tonnage" than we came with!) I'm always overjoyed when I have a chance to "talk shop" with someone who shares the same type of ministry. So when a platform personality came to me after I spoke at a large event and wanted to chat, I was pleased.

She was warm and affirming and asked if she could recommend me to groups as she traveled. I was complimented and grateful. We chatted non-stop, then hugged and agreed to meet the following day for another visit before our departure.

When I met with her the next day, there seemed to be a problem. By her actions, I could tell I was it.

She went from cool to cold to curt. I went from confused to hurt to ticked. The ticked part came afterward, as I tried to figure out how I had fallen from favor. Later, I learned an acquaintance had spent some time with this speaker discussing me. I guess "Poached Patsy" didn't taste too good, because she certainly seemed to have indigestion.

The more I thought about the injustice of this encounter, the angrier I became. The incident stirred up memories of every unfair situation I'd ever experienced. I brooded, I boiled, and occasionally I blew up as I retold the story to Les. He got tired of receiving the residue of my rejection. So I set the incident on the back burner of my emotions and let it simmer. Once in a while, I'd lift the lid and stir the soup.

One day, while having lunch with cheerleading friends, the topic of unfair situations came up. I ran for the stove to check my pot, and sure enough, it was still hot. As I spewed my injustice all over them, they were taken aback by my intensity.

Finally one friend asked, "When did this happen?"

I had to stop and think for a moment, and then I realized it had been three years! My friends were surprised I still carried such animosity, because I had not seen this woman since that encounter.

After lunch, I thought through what my friends had said. I began to see that keeping this issue hot within me had left me with a pressure-cooker personality (minus the gauge). Instead of letting my rage diminish, I seemed to have used time to refine and define it.

Something about injustice convinces us of our right to hold onto our anger and even embrace it. I'm learning anger is not necessarily a wrong response . . . until I choose to harbor and nurture it. When I enfold anger, it drains my energy and takes up valuable inner space. Brewing anger taxes my physical, mental, and emotional well-being. It also hampers my close relationships with others and God.

Some of us don't have a handle on living skills that equips us to deal with our emotions appropriately. We tend to deny we're angry or defend our right to be so, leaving us frustrated, misunderstood, and stuck in the muck of our own emotions.

I understand now that the woman's momentary rejection of me was not as damaging as my long-term choice to raise rage. When I think of the people I have formed opinions of or changed my opinions about because of what someone else has said, I'm aware of what a human response it is—often not fair or loving, but human.

When Les and I were first married, we lived in a mobile home park. Just after we moved in, I was warned about the unfriendly neighbor next door. I was told she kept to herself and was snobbish.

Remembering what I had been told, it took me a while before I tried to establish communication with her. It turned out she was shy and very dear. She and I enjoyed a warm friendship that I almost missed out on because someone had told me her stunted understanding of my neighbor.

When the platform speaker and I had our puzzling encounter that second day years ago, I felt hurt by her change of heart, which is an appropriate feeling when you're rejected. But I quickly put the lid over my hurt and turned up the burner of my anger. Rejection felt too cold; at least anger had some self-generating warmth. But I must have stood too close to my own heat, because my emotions felt scorched. I'm slowly learning to take my hurts to the Healer before I hide them under my unrighteous rightness.

Relationships, like alphabet soup, spell out "opportunities." It's just that some are easier to swallow than others.

25

Fired Up!

PLUCKY: "HAVING OR showing courage or spirited resourcefulness in trying circumstances" (*American Heritage Dictionary*).

Elijah was plucky. After all, he's the guy who challenged Ahab and Jezebel's wise guys to show up or shut up. Elijah laid out a game plan with the end result of winner takes all.

Allow me to set a little of the scene. (For inerrant accuracy, read 1 Kings 18 and 19.) Wicked Ahab, king of Israel, was miffed at Elijah for declaring a drought on the land and then disappearing. Ahab had searched the kingdom for three parched years, trying to find this troublemaker. Finally, Elijah sent a messenger to Ahab so they could have it out.

When they met, Ahab and Elijah began their finger-pointing meeting by blaming each other for Israel's problems. This was not your average my-daddy's-bigger-than-your-daddy argument. No, this was much bigger.

At that point in the debate, Elijah issued the divine dare. He invited Ahab's wise guys to a community barbecue and challenged them to a cook off. But listen to the plan: 850 wise guys against one fire-preaching prophet. If Elijah pulled it off, imagine the payoff on those kinds of odds!

Speaking of odd, the people thought this barbecue was a great idea. (I personally would not have wanted to go against a guy who spoke a drought into existence, but then I'm funny that way.)

The rules stated that the wise guys were to prepare an ox, lay it on the altar, and ask their gods to consume it in fire. Elijah would do the same and ask his God to send fire from heaven. The first one to smell fried ox (yuck!) wafting from his grill won.

The Baal and Asherah prophets pranced around the altar (similar to ring-around-the-rosy), trying to ignite a spark of enthusiasm from their gods. When they began to grow weary, Plucky Prophet Elijah taunted them: "I think your gods are out to lunch, nah, nah, nah, nah" (loose translation—very loose).

This brought a fresh surge of rage (you just can't kid with some people) and a renewed effort to kindle their gods' attention. But try as they might, the answer still appeared to be a big fat "Ho-hum."

Elijah was fired up. He positioned stones, prayed, and then watched the power of God consume the ox and everything surrounding it, including the dust. (Do you know how difficult it is to burn dirt?)

The fire-licking flames even lapped up water and sizzled the surroundings bone dry.

Remember the odds? They changed. The barbecue turned into an evangelistic meeting, and no one had even sung 13 choruses of a favorite hymn. The people fell on their faces and acknowledged the one true God. Elijah took it from there and wiped out the wise guys.

Elijah's barbecue was a blazing success. That is, until. . . .

Word arrived, via Ahab, to Queenie. To say Jezebel was not happy to hear she'd missed the big event of the year would be to understate this sinister woman's fury. She faxed her seething sentiments to Elijah, outlining her outrage, and he hotfooted it into the hills.

Excuse me? What happened to our plucky powerhouse who took on a passel of prophets? Surely one wicked woman couldn't douse our fiery prophet's ministry. Could she? Was this another case of "never underestimate the power of a woman"? I think not. Looked more like a slump in emotions following a big event.

Our fading hero ended up knee knocking under a juniper, singing a familiar refrain in the key of "me." He whined so long that he wore himself out and fell fast asleep.

I love the next part of the story. Here was a wayward man, battling self-pity and anguish, headed in the wrong direction, and the Lord sent him company and provision. An angel woke him and offered him a cake. (Wow! Angel food cake, one of my favorites.)

Elijah, a man after my own weakness, ate and fell back asleep. But the Lord of the second chance awakened our friend again, fed him, and allowed him to continue his journey. The heavenly host's cooking was so vitamin-enriched that Elijah went on in the strength of it for 40 days. (I'd sure like that recipe, although I've cooked some meals my family hoped I wouldn't fix again for 40 days. Does that count?)

Even with two chances, Elijah's fears didn't diminish. Instead of turning back, he scampered away. He eventually hid in the side of a mountain. He caved in emotionally. (I wonder if he was agoraphobic.) He trusted in a rocky fortress instead of the Fortress who is our Rock.

Once again, our God pursued the lost, the lonely, the confused, the fearful, the deceived. In a gentle breeze, He whispered His loving direction to our fleeing friend. Elijah heard, returned, and for his grand finale joined the Lord in a blaze of victory.

I don't identify with many of Elijah's strengths, although I once set my dish towel on fire while cooking lamb chops. What I connect with are his weaknesses. I'm reminded how susceptible we are emotionally to the threats of the enemy, especially following spiritual conquest.

I have made some of my worst personal bungles following some of my sweetest spiritual advancements. For me, I think pride edged in, and I tripped over it. But I'm convinced we need more than luck in this life. We also need pluck. And I know of only one reliable Source for that kind of character.

26

Bouquet

I AM A woman who loves getting presents. Fortunately, I'm married to a man who gets a kick out of buying me surprises. He also is famous, in a spontaneous moment, for whisking me off to a mall to shop for a new outfit. It's not unusual for us to go into a dress shop and have Les want to buy more for me than I would for myself. That causes quite a reaction from the sales clerks, since his attitude is not the norm. They all want to know how I trained Les to be that way. Unfortunately, I can't take credit. (I love credit, too.) He just has that kind of giving heart.

I remember our nineteenth wedding anniversary, when Les wrote me a funny, little poem that I still cherish.

Roses are red, violets are blue,
If I had it to do over again,
I'd still marry you!

The poem was especially dear to me because Les and I married when we were 17 and 18, and we had been through some challenging years (financially, physically, and emotionally), including my period of agoraphobia. From time to time, I wondered if he regretted his choice. So even though the poem didn't exactly start off originally, it ended for me like a masterpiece.

Over the years (30), Les has given me gifts that have made me laugh, cry, gasp, and even learn some lessons.

One sunny, spring day, Les came bounding into our home embracing two apricot sweetheart rosebuds for me. I, of course, was delighted.

The flowers had come with a powdered mix to lengthen their blooming time; I stirred it into the water. I gave each rose a fresh cut and then slipped them into one of the many vases collected from Les's continued courting of me. I sat my mini-bouquet in the living room, being careful to protect it from direct sun and yet giving it visibility for my enjoyment.

As the days went by, I was fascinated by what happened. My seemingly identical roses responded very differently to their environment. One began slowly to open, and at each stage of development, she was exquisite. Her unfolding presentation pleased me and added beauty and wonder to the room. Finally, my apricot beauty dropped her petals in a breathtaking farewell performance.

In contrast, the other rose seemed stuck in her beginning. She held tenaciously to her baby form. In the end, the brooding bud turned brown and hung over the edge of the vase like a tragic teardrop.

For days I thought about the contrasting visual. I've always applauded rosebuds as being so romantic. Yet there was something sad and unnatural about seeing a flower begin and end at the same place. The bud that didn't open never reached her potential. She never released the sweet fragrance placed within her to share with others. Her death portrayed regret and sadness.

I could celebrate even the loss of the open rose, knowing she accomplished all she was designed to do. Her fragrance lingered in our home even after the vase was removed.

My friend Vella was a flower in the fullest sense. When she was told she had only a short time to live and that her cancer was the most painful of cancers, instead of closing up, she spread her petals all the way open and bathed us in the fragrance of faith. We would not have blamed her if she had drawn into a bud and died privately in her pain.

But Vella saw this illness as her farewell performance, an opportunity for as long as she had left to fulfill the design God had for her. Vella lived out her remaining days with exquisite grace. Dropping her last petal, her parting words were, "Praise the Lord." Then she fell asleep and was gone.

Family and friends could celebrate her life and her homegoing. At the time of this writing, it has been 11 years since she left us . . . and her fragrance still lingers.

Because there's a great deal of cancer in my family, I sometimes wonder how I would handle it if I were to be diagnosed with the dreaded disease. I'm not a brave person . . . except in my imagination. There I am valiant, noble, and steadfast. In reality, I whine when I get a cold.

Three years ago, I watched my dear, 73-year-old mother endure breast surgery for cancer. She went through her diagnoses, surgery, and radiation not only with courage, but also with sweetness and humor. That gave me hope.

I want, whatever my environment, to be growing and fragrant. I don't want to be closed and unable emotionally to open up to others. I don't want to die holding to myself what I should have given away.

Les's gift of roses, pressed between the pages of my memory, has been a poignant reminder: Openness is a risk, growth is its reward, and His grace makes it all possible.

27

Seasonal Seesaw

I LOVE THE holidays!

I hate the holidays!

I am a Christmas contradiction. I'm up with excitement and then down with disappointment. I'm up with anticipation and then down with depression. I'm up with . . . well, you get the idea. I'm on my seasonal seesaw. My teeter-totter partner is my own Currier-and-Ives expectations.

Ever notice in those Currier and Ives pictures how even in frigid weather the cows are contented? They willingly pose next to the wood for the fireplace, which is neatly stacked next to the house. While Bossy grins, Junior is shown joyfully skipping out to bring Mother dear kindling for the stove.

I don't have a cow, but I do have a dog. Pumpkin refuses to go outside if it's damp. She has an aversion to moist feet. She will sit for days with her paws crossed, waiting for the sun or wind to dry up the ground. No way is she going to pose willingly by a wet wood pile.

Of course, that would be difficult anyway since we don't have any wood—that is, unless I hike five miles to the woods and gnaw off a few branches. Oh, well, our fireplace stays cleaner that way.

I tried to imagine our Junior skipping joyfully toward a task outside in inclement weather. Ha! I think Junior caught Pumpkin's malady.

No matter how I try, I can't seem to cram my family onto the front of one of those cards.

I don't know why I can't remember, from one Christmas season to the next, that Currier and Ives is an unattainable height. Every Christmas, I want my house to be picture perfect. Ha! I can't achieve that in a nonholiday time, much less in a season with so many added demands.

I imagine white birch logs (cut by me in our back 40—feet, that is) snuggled in a handwoven basket (I designed) placed next to the hearth. The blazing fire invites guests to warm in our candle-lit (all hand-dipped by me) dining room. I would serve a gourmet dinner for 30, followed by strolling musicians playing Handel's "Messiah." All this would take place in my 10-by-12 dining area.

When I have such unreasonable goals, I end up with a high frustration level and a frazzled nervous system. Then I find myself in last-minute panic spurts, trying to excuse, hide, and disguise all my unfinished projects.

One year we decided to write Noel in lights on our house. We started late and finished only half the project because of bad weather. That left a multicolored NO flashing on our rooftop. We had fewer guests that year.

Usually, I wait too long to complete my shopping, leaving me victim to jangled nerves from holiday traffic, crowds, and checkout lines. People's personalities are seldom enhanced under pressure. Also, I tend to be more impulsive in my buying when I'm running late. I suffer from bargain whiplash trying to take advantage of all the Christmas markdowns. Too many last-minute purchases leave me holding the bag . . . and it's full of bills. The bills then pile up in my emotions, leaving me feeling spent.

Also, during the holiday hoopla I seem to get bit by the bug. No, not the flu bug; the love bug. I fall into the trap of thinking everyone is going to get along. Give me a break! How unrealistic to believe relatives and friends, some of whom have never hit it off, would suddenly become seasonal sidekicks! I'm learning there are those who believe "Ho, Ho, Ho" is something you do strictly in your garden and has nothing to do with exhibiting a merry heart.

Another habit I have is wanting everyone to love the gifts I give them as much as I did when I selected them. I'm into applause and appreciation. Here's the problem: I live with three guys (one husband and two sons), and they only applaud silly things like grand slam home runs in the World Series, touch-downs in the final seconds of the Super Bowl, or when I fix dinner and they can tell what it is.

They don't show the same enthusiasm for my gifts—like the nifty button extenders, the monogrammed electric socks, or the fuchsia-colored long johns I wrapped for them. I realize my gifts are . . . uh . . . distinctive, but I want them to be memorable. My guys agree they have been.

Well, there it is, my Christmas confession. Maybe some of you can identify with part, if not all, of my seasonal seesaw. Come join me in entering into the holidays without the teeter and totter in our emotions. Here's how:

1. Set more-sane house goals. Better to plan less and accomplish more than to fall short of your ideal and start your holidays feeling disappointed.

2. Shop early, and buy a couple of generic emergency gifts. (Unlike fuchsia underwear, a box of fine chocolates holds general appeal.)

3. Settle on a reasonable budget before going into the stores to prevent falling victim to strong sales tactics (which include Christmas mood music that plays on our nostalgia, sale-sign seduction, and plastic explosives in the form of credit cards).

4. Sow the seeds of goodwill, but don't expect every "Scrooge" in your Christmas circle to embrace your efforts . . . or you, for that matter. Don't snowball your own emotions by expecting love from people who can't give it. (History in a relationship is usually a good benchmark of his or her ability.)

5. Seek some silence. Balance your busyness with moments of meditation. Don't allow all the flashing lights on the outside to distract you from the inner light of His presence. Even a short silence each day will give a greater semblance of order to your emotions and schedule.

Set goals, shop early, settle budget, sow goodwill,
seek silence,
and don't forget to
SIMPLY CELEBRATE!

Ways to celebrate simply:

Make a snow angel, drink eggnog, write a forgotten friend, decorate a snowman, go caroling in your neighborhood, feed the birds, bake apples, watch the movies *Heidi* and *Little Women,* write a poem, cut out cookies, share tea with a friend, frame an old snapshot, hug a child, hug an oldster, read the Christmas story out loud, and sing Happy Birthday to Jesus.

28

Eek!

Y'ALL COME, HEAR," is music to my ears. I love knee-slappin', banjo-pickin', harmonica-playin', good ol' country livin'.

Every summer when I was a youngster, my family would travel south to the Bluegrass State to "sit a spell." We had more relatives in Madisonville and Nebo, Kentucky, than a corncob has kernels.

One of my favorite places to go was my Aunt Pearl's. She was feisty and funny, and she made visiting her memorable.

I remember one visit when I stayed alone with Aunt Pearl. Usually one of her four children was around, but not this time. Even though I was a teenager, when it came time for bed, I didn't want to sleep by myself. She lived out of town, and I was

a city slicker not used to the wide-open, dark countryside.

Aunt Pearl was a down-home girl who knew how
to make people feel welcome and comfortable. She
had me crawl right in bed with her.

We had said good night, and I was listening to the
outside night sounds, about to doze off, when an
inside noise caught my attention.

It sounded as if someone or something was
scratching frantically.

"Aunt Pearl," I whispered.

"Huh?" she groaned from her half-conscious rest.

"What's that noise?" I whimpered.

"I dunno," she slurred.

I realized I was losing her to sleep, and I needed
to know what that frightening sound was. So I gently shook her arm and called, "Aunt Pearl, Aunt
Pearl, listen."

Coming to, she lifted her head, eyes still closed,
and listened. Then, from years of experience, she
stated, "It's okay. It's only a mouse that has fallen
off the kitchen counter into the garbage can."

Only! Only! She might as well have said, "It's
okay, it's only Big Foot." I don't do mice. I was pet-
rified.

Much to my amazement and horror, my aunt laid
her head back on her pillow instead of getting up
and calling 911.

"Aunt Pearl, aren't you going to do something?" I
questioned.

"What do you want me to do?"

"I'm not sure. Call someone maybe."

She laughed, rose up, and headed for the
kitchen. I heard some shuffling around, and the

scratching stopped. Within minutes, she was climbing back into bed.

"What did you do?" I puzzled.

"Oh, I opened the door and dumped him out into the night. Now go to sleep."

"Okay," I responded, trying to imagine anyone so brave as to have deliberately gone close to a monster in a mouse suit.

Within moments, my aunt began to snore. But in between the short and long snoring sounds, I heard something. It sounded like frantic scratching.

"Aunt Pearl, Aunt Pearl, please wake up," I pleaded.

"Now what?" she said groggily.

"Did you close the door before you came to bed? I think that mouse is back."

"Just go to sleep. That mouse ain't botherin' you."

I listened to its attempt to escape its paper prison. Then I told her, "You're wrong. That mouse is bothering me a lot."

She swung her legs out of bed, grabbed her slipper, and left the room. Another minute passed. Then I heard a couple of thuds followed by silence. My aunt hurried back to our room, dropped her slipper next to the bed, and climbed in.

Wide-eyed I said, "What did you do?"

"I killed it," she replied calmly.

"Killed it!" I cringed. "With what?"

"My slipper," she reported as she rolled away from me.

Now I was nauseated. I had wanted the mouse excommunicated, not executed. I could hardly stand the thought that I was sleeping in the same room with the weapon that was probably covered in mouse particles. I wanted to go home.

As I was trying to figure out how to tell my aunt I needed to leave immediately, I heard a now-familiar sound. I wondered if this mouse had swallowed a cat and therefore had nine lives. It scrambled around in the garbage bag and evidently was trying to leap out, as we heard it falling repeatedly.

This time I didn't have to say anything. My aunt marched through the house, determined to put my fears to bed, as well as herself. I heard the back door slam, and then her footsteps as she made a beeline for her bed.

When her head dropped onto the pillow, she announced, "The can, the bag, the slipper, and the mouse are outside, and the door is closed and locked. Good night."

I scooched closer to her and fell sound asleep.

Today I still have fears dressed in Big Foot suits. Often these fears grow larger in the night as I lie awake and hear them vigorously stomping around my house. I sometimes find myself whimpering, but now I cry to the Lord. Again and again, I've found Him faithful to respond, and the closer I move to Him, the safer I feel and the better I rest.

29

TNT

AFTER DINNER ONE night, my friend turned, looked intently at me, and stated gently, "Do you know what I see when I look in your eyes?"

"Blue?" I quipped.

"Anger," she responded.

"Anger!" I exploded with venom. "Anger! You don't see any anger in me! You might see fear, but not anger."

I went home that night ticked! As I stomped through the house, I bellowed out to the heavens, "Who does she think she is?"

At that point, I noticed my clenched fist flailing around in midair. I stood for a moment, staring at this volatile visual. As I opened my fist, I saw imprints deeply etched in my palms by my finger-nails. I asked aloud, "Am I angry, Lord?"

Immediately my mind was catapulted back to years before when I had a panic attack after a spat with Les. The attack was terrifying. I decided it wasn't safe to get angry (an old message that was now reinforced). I had pushed down deeper inside of me some unresolved anger issues, and what came up to take their place was unrelenting guilt and unreasonable fear—I had become one of the "un" generation. That gruesome twosome, guilt and fear, dominated my life for a number of years.

When I began to deal with my guilt and fear through the wise counsel of Scripture and friends, I thought emotionally I was going to be home free. I believed I would finally be normal. Instead, with-out the cover of the gruesome twosome, my now-volcanic anger had begun to erupt toward those around me.

I discovered different kinds of anger. There's the temporarily-ticked kind in which we want to yank a hank of hair off someone's head, but only for a moment. There's the slow sizzle style in which we work overtime on the details of the offense and then revel in our wrath. A favorite of many is the dump-truck approach. This is when we back up to a person and unload all our "stuff" on them. Fol-lowing close is the rage routine, sung to the tune of "I'm going to hate you forever . . . or at least until Jesus returns."

My sister, Elizabeth, saw the dump-truck approach at work in her own home. She had just finished a phone call and found that her three-year-old son, Nicholas, had been making use of his "free" time. He had sprinkled two pounds of flour laced with Kool-Aid powder throughout the living room. After a firm scolding from his mom, Nicholas, indignant that his culinary endeavors had not been appreciated, trucked into the playroom and hit his two-year-old sister, Lindsey.

I can identify. There have been times when I've released a flurry of fury at some unsuspecting soul, surprising, at times, both of us. I've learned that when I haven't dealt with my emotions and they stockpile, I will inappropriately dump them on an unsuspecting bystander—like a checkout clerk, a bank teller, or a waitress.

I remember trucking over to a receptionist for a mistake on a billing. She was calm and kind. I, on the other hand, was spitting words through tight teeth and displaying pulsating purple veins. The good news was that I had more color than I usually do. The bad news was that my faith faded fast in the eyes of this young woman. Even though I returned and apologized, it changed our relationship. She is far more reserved than she once was with me . . . and rightfully so.

The results of dump-trucking on an innocent party are that it leaves them on-guard, and they skirt around any meaningful involvement with us. It takes a lot of time and effort to reestablish a relationship. Even if we don't care to reinstate a connection, that type of dump-'em-and-leave-'em behavior runs over our chances of having any personal integrity.

I wasn't that put out with the receptionist's mistake when I "let her have it." My reaction came following a disagreement with a relative in which I had shoveled my feelings into the back of my dumpster instead of saying how I felt. Then, when the botched-up bill came, I jumped into my rig, backed my truck up to the receptionist's desk, and unloaded my cargo right in her lap.

I'm learning that as long as I misdirect my emotions, I will find myself rationalizing my TNT behavior and limiting my ability to have honest relationships.

30

Overnight Fright

I WAS BOOKED on an early-morning flight out of Detroit on my way to Iowa. Because I was leaving before daybreak, Les and I decided to stay at a hotel near the airport the night before. We had done this on several occasions and found it less stressful. I didn't have to get up early and therefore would be more rested, and Les didn't have to battle the morning rush-hour traffic.

We arrived at the hotel and checked in. Somehow our request to be on the first floor had been mixed up, and instead we had a third-floor room. Les and I decided we could adjust. We wouldn't allow a room change to ruin our evening.

We had an early dinner that was not good enough to recommend and yet not poor enough to send back. After our mediocre meal, we retired to our room to relax.

I kicked off my shoes and began to leaf through a newspaper. Les remembered seeing a pop machine and thought he would buy a few sodas for us. He was gone quite a while, and when he returned he was shaking his head. He had visited three different soda machines, and the change makers were broken on all of them. He then checked at the front desk, and they were unable to provide him with change. So we settled for ice water.

Then we noticed the red message light was flashing on the phone. I buzzed the desk and asked for the message. It was for a Mr. Hudson from a business associate. I assured the gal I was not Mr. Hudson and asked if she would please turn off the red blinker. She said she would.

I organized what I would be wearing on the flight the following day and decided to go to bed. I whipped back the bedspread and top sheet so I could crawl in. Much to my disgust, the sheets were dirty. They looked grungy, and every square inch was wrinkled. I wondered if these were Mr. Hudson's sheets. If so, he had left wisps of his brunette tresses and makeup behind.

I called the desk and reported the need for clean linens. The girl at the desk apologized and said someone would come with fresh bedding. Well, someone came all right . . . the Sheet Inspector.

The (six-foot-five) Sheet Inspector announced he had come to inspect our sheets. (Of course, we should have known.) He approached the bed, looked closely at the sheets, then made his way slowly around to the other side of the bed, still examining. (To have an in-house inspector made me think ours may not have been their first sheet complaint.)

After contemplating for a moment, he announced, "These sheets are dirty."

I wondered how much he got paid for linen appraisal. I'd been thinking about a part-time position. It was obvious I qualified, since we both had come to the same conclusion.

As the inspector left, he took our sheets and promised to return soon. He kept his word. He returned promptly. We opened the door and found out that Sheet Inspectors must be specialists, because he handed us our linens and marched away.

Les and I stood looking at each other in disbelief, then shrugged our shoulders and resigned ourselves to the bed-making task. To expedite this project, we each got on one side of the bed, and Les flung one corner of the sheet over to me. I caught it, and then I gasped. Les looked, and his eyes dropped in disgust. These were the same sheets we had before.

We called the desk, and the girl told us she would lodge a written complaint to housekeeping. Now, not only did I have grungy sheets, but I also had developed an attitude the size of the inspector.

When it registered that they were not planning to bring us clean sheets in the near future, I became creative. I gathered all the clean towels and spread them lengthwise on the bed, giving us a somewhat nappy but clean sleeping surface. Then we climbed in bed, and I fell asleep despite the message light flashing in my face, still beckoning Mr. Hudson.

I woke up off and on throughout the night. I couldn't seem to get the looped threads in the towels to go all in the same direction. I dreamt that the Sheet Inspector came back to our room dressed in red blinking pillowcases and fined us for sleeping on the towels.

Finally morning arrived (Mr. Hudson's light was still flickering), and we could hardly wait to leave. We certainly were not rested. *Tested* would be more like it. I can't tell you how difficult it was to leave, knowing we had paid for this stress-filled night.

I'm sure you're wondering why we didn't demand retribution. We did . . . eventually. When the time was right.

You see, the day before the hotel havoc, Les had gone through a heart catheterization. He had just found out he had had a second heart attack and that one of his bypasses had closed. We checked into the hotel (part of a reputable chain) to protect him from stress while he was recovering. When we ended up in "The Hotel from Hell," we had to weigh which was more important: fighting for what we paid for, or adapting and filing a complaint at a more appropriate time.

Believe me, demanding my rights would have been far easier for my temperament. But when I weighed the battle with the hotel against my husband's well-being, what was one uncomfortable night?

Too many times in my life, I have reacted from my emotions rather than from wisdom. Wisdom says, "There is . . . a time to be silent and a time to speak" (Eccles. 3:1, 7b).

I don't think it's a mistake that silence is listed before speaking. Usually if we wait, we're more likely to handle ourselves and our words with greater dignity.

After returning from my speaking trip, I did call the hotel's headquarters. They were surprised to find they had a Sheet Inspector working for them. They refunded our money and sent us a coupon for a free night at the same hotel. Harrumph! Not in this lifetime.

I sure hope Mr. Hudson received his message.

31

Bedded Bliss

WHEN WE MOVED into our new home, I could
hardly wait to decorate. I started with our bedroom.
It was a generous-size room and showed potential.
All I had to do was coordinate the decor.

Our aging bedspread had served us well but
needed to be relieved of duty. Selecting colors and
a pattern for our new spread was great fun. I chose
a multicolored comforter. The saleswoman pointed
out the matching shams and sheets. Les and I
hadn't thought about an ensemble . . . but it would
be nice.

As we were getting ready to pay for our mound of
goods, the sales gal pulled out a wallpaper book to
show us the paper designed just for our bedding. It
was beautiful. I *had* planned to wallpaper . . . even-

tually. Besides, if I didn't get this now, I might never find another paper that would fit so perfectly.

As Les and I left the store with our arms full of parcels, we were elated, in a heavy sort of way. We comforted and buoyed each other with the thoughts "It's not like we've ever done this before" and "We just won't spend as much for the living room."

When we arrived home, I immediately put the bedding on, and we oohed and ahhed it. Then, after the wallpaper was hung, we were even more pleased with the coordinated look we had achieved. But I had failed to think through the pictures on the walls. They didn't fit in well. I could always bring some in from another room or buy some cheapies.

As I was hanging my newly purchased pictures beside my bed, I noticed how tacky the table cover was on my nightstand. It just didn't fit with everything else. How much could a little cover cost, anyway? Actually, more than I had anticipated.

We had invested a lot, but at least my room was in harmony with itself . . . except for the bath that opened into the bedroom. It seemed visually disruptive. After hanging an antique mirror and lace shower curtains and adding a looped rug, my pocketbook was empty, but my eyes were full of continuity.

As I studied my endeavors, it hit me that I could enhance my efforts with multiple pillows and some flowers. Those two additions are the way a woman places her finishing touches on a room. I added eight pillows and a bouquet of silk roses. Yes, yes, these were like a feminine signature . . . and with a few candles would be complete.

I must have overdone the candles, because Les installed a smoke detector. But the candles seemed necessary to add ambience. Our bedroom would have been a masterpiece, but it seemed to need an injection of character. I dragged in Les's grandfather's trunk and set it at the foot of our bed. That worked. I displayed an antique wicker tray on the top of the trunk. The tray required just a few small, framed photographs, a teapot, a pair of women's gloves, and a man's pocket watch to create a still-life effect.

Funny I could be that far into our bedroom project and only then notice how out of place my lamps looked. Totally the wrong feeling, and even the shape seemed passé. It would be a shame to allow them to rob us of the rewards of all our time and toil. Lamps are small in stature but big in impact. Once you flick on one of those babies, you can't help but notice it.

Speaking of noticing . . . I have worked so intently with this room that I've developed a new problem. I'm tired of the whole thing and wish I could start over.

When is enough . . . enough?

32

Awakening

"Hello, PATSY. THIS is your sister, and I thought you should know that I am very sick."

When I hung up from Elizabeth's call, I immediately prayed on her behalf. Thoughts of her would come to me again and again over the next 24 hours, and I would quietly pray and then go on with my day. Even though I could tell from Elizabeth's weak, quivering voice that she was ill, I was not prepared for the next call.

This time it was my brother-in-law, Bryan. He reported in disbelief that in the night, Elizabeth's fever had gone up and she was shaking uncontrollably, so he had taken her to the hospital. By the time they arrived at the emergency room, she had become disoriented. The nurses helped her into bed, and Elizabeth went into a coma.

The doctors weren't sure what was wrong with her, but her brain was swelling. I was devastated. How could this be?

Seventeen years prior, our 39-year-old brother had died of a brain injury following a car accident. The thought of losing my 33-year-old sister through some sort of brain problem seemed more than I could bear. It just didn't seem normal that our family would have to go through a second tragic loss of this type.

Another call came informing us that Elizabeth had been placed on life support and was now listed in critical condition.

Her voice kept replaying in my ear: "Patsy, I just thought you should know that I am very sick."

Waves of realization would flood in on me, and I would reel from the impact. Then I would busy myself, only to have another wave crash down on me.

Tears came like raindrops that soon built to what felt like tidal waves racking my body. I was over-whelmed.

Bryan called again to report there was no response from Elizabeth, even to pain. "Patsy, I just feel that if you would come, she would be able to hear your voice," he choked out through his tears.

When I hung up, I told Les that Bryan's belief she could hear me was that of a desperate man longing to have his wife and the mother of their three young children back. I knew the days of Elizabeth's life were in God's hands and that I could not add to or subtract from them.

"Yes," Les agreed, "but God often uses people to speak."

I knew that was true because of all the times the Lord has given me insight, counsel, and encouragement through the voices of people. Some of my reluctance to go to her bedside was self-protective. I didn't feel I could handle flying out to Utah to see her die. But Les's tender reminder caused me to make plans to leave as soon as we could.

The closer our plane got to the Salt Lake City airport, the calmer and stronger I felt. Upon arriving, we rented a car and drove immediately to the hospital, half an hour away.

When we got there, we tried to prepare ourselves for what Elizabeth might look like. Much to our surprise, she looked quite well, even with all the life-support equipment. But our hearts and hopes dropped when we touched her. Her skin felt like wax, and her limbs were ice-water cold.

I was heartsick when the intensive care nurse came in with a rounded pair of scissors and pressed them as hard as she could into Elizabeth's cuticles on her fingers and toes. Elizabeth gave no response.

Sleep was skimpy for Les and me that night. We grabbed some breakfast and headed for the hospital at the first light of dawn. Then we took turns talking to Elizabeth and asking her to give us some sign that she could hear us.

At one point, Les was sure she put some pressure on his hand with hers, but it didn't happen again. Several times that day, her eyes seemed to be trying to open, but the nurses said it was an involuntary movement of a comatose patient. We watched the countless machines and computer printouts, trying to analyze what it all meant.

That evening, we went back to our room for another long, fitful night.

The following afternoon, I was alone, sitting next to Elizabeth's bed, and started to talk to her about when she was a little girl. (I was 13 when she was born, and I felt very motherly toward her. Translated, that means I was bossy and protective.) I was telling her about the time she gave her stuffed monkey, JoJo, a bath in the toilet and then threw her moist monkey and our mom's poodle in the dryer. Fortunately, both JoJo and Sassy survived.

All of a sudden, I realized Elizabeth's eyes were darting around under her closed eyelids. There wasn't a nurse around to ask about it, so I leaned in to my sister's ear and said, "Elizabeth, it would really help me to know if you can hear me. If you can hear me, would you please open your eyes?"

I cannot begin to tell you how I felt as I saw her eyes open fully to my request. In that moment, hope surged through me like electricity. Even though I could tell she couldn't see, I now knew she could hear, understand, process, and respond.

I flew out to the nurses' station and excitedly reported what had happened. The nurse looked at me as though I had said, "There is dust on the windowsill."

Realizing my own nervousness, I figured I hadn't spoken clearly. I deliberately slowed down my speech and retold my story. The nurse looked at me and simply stated, "That did not happen. I have been taking care of her for the past ten hours, and she is incapable of responding."

Then her voice softened. "Families tend to over-react to patients' involuntary movements."

"Trust me," I insisted. "She responded on command."

"As far as I'm concerned, that never happened," she stated flatly, then walked away.

I sulked back to my sister's room and stood silently at her bedside, mulling over what had happened and what was said.

About then, the nurse came in to check the equipment. I looked at her and then at Elizabeth.

I moved close to Elizabeth's ear and pleaded, "I know I've been bugging you a lot today, but I need you to leave that quiet place where you're resting, and I need you to open your eyes. I want you to open them wide, and I want you to do it right now!"

As I said "now," the nurse looked nonchalantly over her shoulder toward my sister. Elizabeth's eyes popped open like an owl's. My hope surged! And the nurse? She almost fainted. After catching her breath, she scurried to the phone to alert the doctor.

By the next morning, when I spoke Elizabeth's name, she not only heard me, but she also knew me and almost jumped into my arms.

It took days for all the equipment to be removed and for her vocal cords to heal enough from the trauma of her breathing tubes that she could talk. Then she told us that the first thing she could remember was my voice calling her name and talking to her as though she were a young child.

Weeks later, as I looked back, I began to see how my responses to my sister's illness were like the flowers I harvest from my garden. When a bloom is cut from the plant, the stem seals the severed area to preserve the moisture it contains. This self-protective action prevents the flower from taking in any additional water. So while the sealing is an attempt to preserve life, it also keeps the plant from receiving sustenance from sources such as water in a vase. For this reason, florists instruct buyers to make a fresh cut in the stem and immediately place it in water to extend its life.

When I first received word about Elizabeth, I, like the flower, felt as though I had to seal my resources within myself to survive. I had just come through an emotionally and physically draining season of my life that had left me feeling incapable of dealing with this crisis.

But when Les suggested God could somehow speak through me even though I felt so fragile, it was as if someone had made a fresh cut and placed me in water. Deciding I could go to Utah and sur-vive—whatever the outcome—gave me a quiet strength. That strength grew every day.

I wasn't strong because of any special wisdom or stamina within myself, but because I had been plunged into the water of the Great Sustainer.

It was an important lesson on human nature and divine intervention. All in all, I feel fortunate to have been a part of Elizabeth's awakening and to have learned how He restores us by His living water when we would wilt without Him.

Life often comes at us with TNT force, leaving us emotionally tentative and spiritually bewildered. Our circumstances often don't seem fair and cer-tainly don't appear to be normal.

My quest for normalcy has brought me to the understanding that our commonality is in our abnormality. The good news is that that's okay. We are unique, which beats normal any day. In fact, we are so amazingly designed that God supervised the placement of our inner workings and registered our existence even before we were held for the first time. Then He who formed us takes His involvement a step further and uses our circumstances in our best interests. That leaves us free to embrace the fact that normal . . . is just a setting on your dryer.

Sportin' a 'Tude

To my
antique friend
Carol Porter,
who is full
of `tudes—
all good!

Contents

Acknowledgments

I offer my ongoing appreciation to my family—Les; Marty; Jason; Danya, my brand-new, beautiful, first daughter-in-law; and my spunky, 80-year-old mom, Rebecca. Les, I have loved you since we were children. That has never changed—except to grow deeper and sweeter. Marty, you were invaluable to me as my computer-rescue person. Thank you, thank you. I would have been lost in cyberspace (whatever that is) without you.

Special thanks to my secretary, Jill Scribner, who put up with my book 'tudes yea, these many months. Your warmth, charm, and assistance are a bright spot in my day. Thanks to Debbie Wirwille, who helps to keep my home in order and always takes time to respond to my stories. Lisa Harper, your incredible energy, outrageous sense of humor, and creative friendship were a gift to me during these months of toil. Jan Frank, your calls (filled with chuckles and encouragement) were often the nudge I needed to get back to my computer. How did you know? Virginia Lukei, thank you for continuing to believe in me and for me. Also, Lana Bateman and Donna Alberta, you are two zany friends who add sparkle to any day.

I would be remiss if I didn't thank the following three couples for supporting me with their friendships: Bruce and Carol Porter, Paul and Ann Meredith, and Gene and Ruthann Bell. I will always be grateful.

A big bouquet of thanks to Focus on the Family and its wonderful staff. Al Janssen, you are one kind of great guy; thanks for all you do. Larry Weeden, your professional input and gentle manner are a winning combination.

Janet Kobobel Grant, how I admire you. Your wit, brilliance, and insight are enhanced by your sterling character. How fortunate I am to have you in my life as my editor and friend.

1

'Tude Time
(tŏŏd´ tim) n.

Dictionary's definition:
A manner of carrying oneself.

Patsy's definition:
A 'tude for all seasons.

TAMI, WHO WAS seven, and Mindy, who was four, went to visit their grandma. After a few hours, as can sometimes happen at Grandma's house, the girls grew restless. Big sister began to notice that bored little sister was following her everywhere. In an attempt to lose her sibling shadow, Tami slipped into the bathroom and began to brush her hair—vigorously. Much to her aggravation, Mindy appeared at the bathroom door and gawked at Tami's every move.

"What are you looking at?" spewed Tami.

Insulted by her sister's lack of hospitality, Mindy crossed her arms and asked, "What's wrong with your attitude?"

Tami shook her head in disgust and with hand on hip replied, "You don't even know what an attitude is."

Insulted, lip-quivering Mindy stamped her foot and retorted, "I do, too. It's . . . it's . . . it's something that stinks!"

How true. Stinky attitudes are airborne. They waft around and add to the pollution on planet earth. But we don't have to take a deep breath to detect attitudes; they're as obvious as a new pair of iridescent sneakers. Just as surely as we wear our Liz Claibornes and Ralph Laurens, we can be seen strutting, sneaking, and slumping around in our negative 'tudes. A raised eyebrow, a leer, a sigh, a tilted head, folded arms, and pursed lips are just some of the outward adornments that give away our inner attitudes.

Nell provided her co-worker Sue with an elaborate display of attitude as they wended their way to lunch. Nell talked nonstop about her rough week. She whined and wailed over everything from escalating taxes to her boss's unfair expectations to her unending household duties. When Nell paused to take a breath, Sue, who had obviously had an ear full, shook her head and declared, "Girlfriend, you are really sportin' a 'tude!"

Yep, "sportin' a 'tude" pretty much describes my wardrobe more often than I'd like to admit. At times I've even worn the layered look, simultaneously sporting several 'tudes of questionable taste.

But I'm not alone. A group of young women who had just heard me speak on sportin' a 'tude were chatting among themselves when one of the gals confessed, "My problem is sometimes I have a 'tude on top of a 'tude."

Her friend responded, "Well, I get a 'tude, on top of a 'tude, on top of a 'tude."

The third friend quickly chirped, "Why, that sounds like a multi*tude* to me!"

The dictionary defines an attitude as "a position of the body or manner of carrying oneself, indicative of a mood or condition; a state of mind or feeling with regard to some manner; disposition."

Hmm, sounds like all we have to do to stop sportin' a 'tude is reposition our position, recondition our condition, and dispose of our disposition. Oh, my, this could take time. No, make that surgery.

When my husband, Les, had a heart bypass, I learned that during the operation, the doctor would hold Les's heart in his hand. I said to a friend, "He's going to get fingerprints on it."

Her response was, "Grow up, Patsy, the doctor will wear gloves."

What I was trying to say was that the surgeon's holding Les's heart was so invasive, so personal, so intimate. I think that's the scary part of looking at the condition of our attitudes as well. That kind of examination opens us up to the heart of who we are deep inside ourselves. I suspect that might not be a pretty sight.

The good news is that not all 'tudes have to be eliminated. Some of them benefit us, motivate us, deepen us, and inspire others. Embracing life-giving attitudes more fully will add to our well—being, enhance our relationships, and clothe us in honorable attire.

Consider Daniel: He was a prayer warrior, a lion tamer, a visionary, and a connoisseur of carrots. Huh? Carrots?

No kidding. As a teenager, Daniel was dragged from his homeland and tossed into the clinker. He was then offered tantalizing morsels from the king's menu but chose veggies instead.

That would be like a group of teens ordering ten super-duper pizza supremes, to be washed down with your leading cola, quickly followed by hot fudge sundaes. But one fellow in the group says, "No, thank you. But if you have any eggplant, spinach, and beets, I'd sure be one happy camper. Oh, yes, and if it's not too much trouble, would you mind bringing me a big, icy tumbler of H_2O?" Then he orders the same for his three closest buddies. His food fetish sure would make me think twice before I palled around with ol' dietary Dan. Not that I couldn't benefit from such nutritional nuggets, but for me to choose peas over pepperonis— p-l-e-a-s-e—would be highly unlikely.

Under the circumstances, who would have been shocked if this kidnapped youngster had chosen wine over watercress? A few nips of the king's bubbly could have temporarily eased his pain and helped him forget about home. Besides, who would want to risk upsetting his captors?

What enabled Daniel to show such courage as well as dietary discipline? Daniel 1:8 provides the clue: "*But Daniel made up his mind* that he would not defile himself with the king's choice food or with the wine which he drank" (italics mine).

The "but" tells us the situation was not of Daniel's choosing. Then following that scriptural beeper, we see how Daniel adjusted his attitude when he "made up his mind." The surgery of imprisonment exposed, and perhaps defined, Daniel's attitude to obey God even in life's unexpected disappointments. He was determined not to use his misfortune as an excuse to sin. Daniel didn't allow his imprisoned position to determine his condition or his disposition. The result was that he found favor, as did his buddies, in the king's eyes.

Folks, that's what it's all about, this thing called life—finding favor in the eyes of the King. For it's in the Lord's presence that we find the presence of mind to dress up in godliness and not to spend our lives sportin' stinky 'tudes.

Join me as we playfully—and purposefully—consider our attitudes and more importantly consider the only One who can surgically change our hearts.

> Change my heart, O God,
> Make it ever true,
> Change my heart, O God,
> May I be like You.

2

Rude 'Tude
(rōōd tōōd) n.

Dictionary's definition:
Ill-mannered.

Patsy's definition:
Snit fit.

THE WOMAN WAS definitely out of control. Her face blazed like the noonday sun, and her purple arteries puffed and pulsated in time to her temper tantrum. She leapt repeatedly into the air and, in an earpiercing voice, shrieked loud enough to drown out the airport P.A. system.

Our plane had been delayed not once, not twice, but four times. Then they canceled the flight. This change of plans was evidently more than hot-headed Hannah could handle. While the majority of the disgruntled passengers obediently formed a line to be rebooked on a later flight, Hannah Reeboked to the nearest phone and called the airlines.

When her call connected, her manners discon-nected. She ranted so loudly that she soon gained an audience of about a hundred people. This momentary stardom seemed to add to her head of steam, for she reached over, picked up a second phone, and dialed the airline's number again, this time reaching a different clerk. Then she held the receivers in front of her and verbally let loose into both phones at the same time.

Ms. Hothead gave new definition to the phrase "talking out of both sides of your mouth at the same time." She proved that she was ambidextrous and aerobic as she jumped and juggled her phones and her phonics. She definitely had a two-fisted rude 'tude.

We seem to be a generation suffering from a "be kind to your brother" blight. Rather than "be nice," the slogan "fight, fight, fight for your rights!" rings throughout our land. Curt customers, irksome employees, belligerent bosses, testy teachers, and snarling students are frequently the norm instead of the exception.

My sweet-natured young friend Missy had a customer return an item of clothing to the dress store where Missy worked. The customer called Missy every name in the book (not the Good Book, either) because she was dissatisfied with her purchase. Imagine that we would allow an article of clothing to have greater value and higher priority than the treatment of a human soul!

Yet I, too, have been a rude 'tuder. In an intolerant moment, I have shared not from my heart but from my heat. My rudeness is often a misdirected vent for my anger. And my suppression with one person can lead to my aggression with another. I've found that to keep short accounts with the Lord and others is imperative if I am to soften my reactions to people who cause me inconveniences and disruptions.

Shakespeare penned, "Rude am I in speech, and little blessed with the soft phrase of peace." The "soft phrase of peace" catches my ear and convicts my heart. How sweet the sound of phrases of peace like "Please," "Thank you," "Excuse me," "You go first," "Let me help," and "I'm sorry."

Scripture takes us a step further than Shakespeare and tells us the results of our words. "A soft answer turns away wrath: but grievous words stir up anger" (Prov. 15:1, Amplified).

Imagine how stirred up Job's wife must have been when she lashed out and told him, "Curse God and die!" Not exactly words of comfort. Not that we couldn't understand that Mrs. Job was in emotional turmoil big time. They had just lost everyone and everything most precious to them. But the soft phrase of peace could have offered them both a moment of consolation rather than separation and isolation.

Consolation brings us together in our losses, which helps to make them more bearable. But because we're attracted to opposites, a couple will often process problems in opposite ways. That leaves the door open for additional pain, the pain of misunderstanding.

Maybe Mrs. Job became hostile when she heard her husband worshiping God after the death of their children. She may have considered Job's actions rude in light of their catastrophic losses. The Lord's allowing them to experience severe problems may have stirred her wrath.

Job's reaction was to seek the Lord in worship. Perhaps that was the only way he knew to maintain his grip on sanity. They suffered the same loss, but Mr. and Mrs. Job processed it, at least initially, differently.

Being different isn't the major divider, however. Judging another person's heart is what sparks a rude 'tude. When I decide to measure and determine the contents of your heart, I set myself up as judge. Often I'm wrong in my finite assessments, basing them on my limited experiences and my fluctuating personality. Along with my high percentage of error in evaluating someone's inner thoughts, when I judge I bring judgment on myself (see Matt. 7:1-2). When I play judge, I add heat to my own already volatile condition. That's when the sparks really begin to fly.

Ever notice how sparks fly in the New Testament every time we approach an account of the Pharisees? Talk about rude 'tuders! Seems those pompous puppets of the law preferred traditions to truth, judgment to justice, and malice to manners. The Pharisees' headiness got in the way of their hearts, and they chose to embrace a lie instead of the Liberator. Again and again the Lord warned them against their rude and unrighteous behavior: "Woe to you . . ."

Woe is a word like *alas,* with a hefty helping of indictment uttered in grief and (or) indignation. For it saddens and offends God's heart when our words and our ways don't line up with His will. The Lord isn't looking for perfection in our lives, but I do believe He expects progress.

Peter the impulsive disciple had problems with things like sandals, swords, and seaweed. I'm sure he wondered if he would ever get his walk of faith right. But it was hard for him to walk when his sandal kept getting stuck to the roof of his mouth.

Speaking of sandals, within moments of stepping onto the water to walk to the Lord, Peter's sandals began to take on water, and he started to sink. Treading water in a robe is tricky, and somewhere between Peter's spitting kelp and yelling "Help!" Jesus came to his rescue.

Then there was the incident in which Peter lopped off the guard's ear. No doubt about it, Peter proved he could be presumptuous and rude. Yet the Lord saw within Peter the potential, with progress, to become a foundational man of faith.

We hear and see one of Peter's personal steps of progress when Jesus asked the disciples, "But who do you say that I am?" and Peter responded, "Thou art the Christ, the Son of the living God" (Matt. 16:15-16, KJV).

Now, that's a soft (and powerful) phrase of peace: "Thou art the Christ, the Son of the living God." If we will fully embrace this truth, it will caution us in our words and cushion our actions toward others. When we're aware of Christ's living presence in our lives, we will then have the presence of mind to draw from His reserve, that we might become peaceable people instead of contentious ones.

Remember hotheaded Hannah? How different her impact on those around her could have been had she understood Someone bigger than the airlines ultimately controls the disappointments and destinations of our lives. Hannah was not wrong to feel frustrated. Even registering a complaint could have been warranted. But she paid an inner price—her peace—when she allowed her fury to dictate her behavior. And she left others verbally whiplashed by her rudeness.

We'll need more than a refresher course from Ms. Manners to help with our behavior. If we're to be truly gentle women and gentle men, it will take a work within us by our gentle Lord Jesus.

3

Plenitude
(plen´ i tōod) n.

Dictionary's definition:
Abundance.

Patsy's definition:
Lots and lots of stuff.

I HAVE THE delightful privilege of being part of a speaking tour with three gifted women. We laugh a lot both on and off the platform, which makes the experience fun and memorable. Along with the laughter, I find I lean in to glean from their wisdom, I dab at tears of empathy, and I nod in agreement at the been-there-done-that segments.

One of those times is when Luci Swindoll talks about her "stuff." It's all I can do not to fall on the floor in a tantrum of guffaws as she explains her desire to have her own row on airplanes so she'll have enough space for her stuff. That tickles me because of my own obsession with stuff.

On a recent flight home, Les and I were in the center of a wide body (airplane, of course). The plane seemed to be designed so that each time we moved, we could puncture each other with our elbows. In this restricted space, I then had the challenge of gaining access to my stuff. And believe me, I had brought plenty of stuff. I had crosswords, magazines, snacks, manuscript, newspaper, planner, and my Bible. You can only imagine how Les on one side of me and a woman on the other loved being jabbed and disrupted by my aerobic shenanigans as I wrestled my stuff in and out of my briefcase. Call it a short attention span, but I find it difficult to go anywhere without carrying enough paraphernalia to see me through, say, a hijacking.

My house is full of stuff, too. Our home is small, but I've filled it as though it were large. I call it cozy, but there are those who would call it claustrophobic. My wall-to-wall decorating has reduced our floor space to the point that one might feel, on entering my living room, that he or she were wearing it rather than sitting in it. But one needs plenty of stuff . . . doesn't one?

What is this romance that America, the land of plenty, has with stuff, anyway? Does it make us smarter? (Duh, I don't think so.) Does it save us time? (Are you kidding? It takes up our time to maintain it.) Does it make us more popular? (Sure, to freeloaders, salespeople, and tax collectors.) Does it improve our looks? (It adds worry lines as we work to protect our stuff from "stuff" thieves; they're everywhere, you know.) There must be some reason many of us have a fetish for belongings. Do you think it fills a need? (Evidently not for long, as we scurry to the nearest stuff store to repair and replace—what else?—our stuff.)

Guess what Les and I did? We rented a storage building for our extra stuff. Imagine a monthly bill to pay for a roomful of unused stuff. Of course, one never knows when one might need a felt skirt with a pink poodle on it; a now-somewhat-oval, glow-in-the-dark hula hoop; a 1989 license plate; or a pair of (egads) chartreuse living room lamps.

One day, my neighbor Alicia placed an office chair at the curb in front of her home and put a "free" sign on it. I couldn't sprint over fast enough. A freebie—that's my idea of a quick fix for my need for stuff. I rolled that chair down the sidewalk, up our driveway, and right into my crowded office.

To make room for the office chair, we moved the couch into the garage. To make room for the couch in the garage, we moved the pinball machines into my son's apartment. To make room for the pinball machines, my son gave a dresser to some friends. To make room for the dresser . . . well, you get the idea. We'll go to great lengths to make room for our stuff.

My friends Ann and Linda own a stuff store—a classy one. Sometimes they let me play store. I help them select new stuff and arrange displays, and occasionally they even allow me to be head of the stuff and watch the store—for a couple of minutes. You can never leave a stuff person in a stuff store for long unchaperoned.

Sometimes I tire of my stuff. Then I have a stuff sale with my friend Carol. Well, actually what happens is I buy her old stuff, and she buys mine. That way we maintain our plenitude, but we somehow deceive ourselves into believing we've pared down. The added advantage is we can visit our stuff at each other's homes, sort of like joint custody.

Sometimes I'll even repossess some stuff if I've really missed it.

Carol and I believe stuff people naturally gravitate to each other. We think that's because we, well, like each other's stuff. But Carol's house doesn't appear as stuffed as mine. That's because she not only has more floor space, but she also has a stuffer's dream, a two-story barn to hold her overflow, which is far better than renting a shed. You can access the barn easier, it gives you more latitude, and you don't feel as guilty because no monthly storage charge crosses your already-paper-laden desk.

Occasionally Carol and I have a stuff-arranging party. That's where we take turns telling each other different ways to display our you-know-what so that the you-know-what appears to be new. And if we're truly creative in our placement, we can even carve out space for another trunk load of stuff. (I had to say it.)

I once heard a friend say she wouldn't need another dish as long as she lived. I couldn't imagine that . . . until now. My bulging cupboards can barely hold all my dishes, and that's after I've given away three sets. And worse yet, I don't even cook. Who has time to cook? I'm too busy taking care of my . . . my . . . items.

Stuff has to be polished, buffed, waxed, stripped, sized, primed, oiled, shook, dusted, watered, washed (yawn), pressed, bleached, stretched, dyed, scrubbed, trimmed, hemmed, hung, hammered, leveled, sprayed, shampooed (z-z-z), adjusted, wired, glued, swept, painted, lacquered, and fluffed, to name just a few of our exercises (in futility). No wonder we're a weary nation; we've worn

ourselves down to the nubbins preserving our_ _
_ff.

Then, of course, there's the concern of who to
leave our stuff to. Families don't always value some
of our best stuff. I have an old, wooden toolbox that
I treasure. I have it laden with things on my covered porch. Yes, it's worn, faded, and marred, but I
think it's charming. My sons, though, on more
than one occasion have announced that at my
demise, they're going to use the box as (shudder)
firewood. I've since decided that I would bequeath
this prize to a friend who respectfully wants to fill it
with some of her prime stuff. Now, that's a buddy
and a more worthy use of one of my best pieces of
stuff. It will comfort me, somehow, to know my
stuff will be full of her stuff.

I wonder if it would be wrong to ask my loved
ones to, instead of burying me—yeah, you guessed
it—stuff me. (Roy Rogers did Trigger.) But instead
of displaying me in a museum (neigh), they could
just lean me in the corner and surround me with
my stuff. (Yea!) Not that it will matter to me then,
because, for the first time, I won't need, want, or
require any more stuff—free at last, free at last!

4

Mood `Tude
(mo͞od´ to͞od) n.

Dictionary's definition:
Shifting disposition.

Patsy's definition:
Inner tantrum.

IF YOU WERE to integrate the Little Rascals into one personality, you would have my six-year-old nephew, Nicholas. He has the hugability of Porky, the rascality of Butch, the determination of Spanky, the innocence of Buckwheat, the charm of Darla, and the singing ability of Alfalfa.

The latter we found out recently when my sister, Elizabeth, went to pick him up from school. Seems Elizabeth was frustrated from a hectic day, and when Nicholas had an agenda different from hers, they ended up at odds with each other. Nicholas could see his mom was in a bad mood and that he wasn't going to get his way. He then developed his own mood. After silent moments of heavy air had hung between them, he began to sing the song

Alfalfa had sung to Darla in the Little Rascals movie. Alfalfa had crooned, "You are so beau-ti-ful to me." Nicholas, though, made a slight editorial adjustment. While looking out the window, as if singing to no one in particular, he trilled, "You are so pit-i-ful to me."

Mom didn't find the humor in his lyrics until later . . . much later. Then she chuckled to herself, realizing Nicholas had found the safest way he could think of to circumvent her mood and vent his.

Moods can hang between us like heavy draperies. They can separate us, isolate us, and even violate us. Moods can be signs of unresolved issues: damage, anger, depression, immaturity, grief, hormones, health, and a loss of or need for control.

As a little girl, when I pouted, it brought about desired results. So I carried that into my adult life. I used quiet hostility (often unconsciously) to manipulate people, especially my husband. Les frequently experienced the chilling effects of my emotional distance and my silent temper tantrum. Years of childish actions passed before I realized how selfish and destructive my moody behavior was. It wasn't easy to break my old response patterns, but it was liberating. I gradually learned not to give in to swings in my emotions but to give up my need to be in control. Occasionally I feel myself sinking into an old mood, but I'm more open and honest now, two responses that can help free us from unhealthy behavior.

King Ahab obviously had experienced that sinking feeling in his life. Seems the king was in a downer over dirt. He was, if you'll excuse the phrase, filthy rich. He owned plenty of land, but he wanted his neighbor Naboth's vineyard in which to plant a vegetable garden because it backed up to the king's palace. Naboth wasn't willing to give up this land for any price. It was an inheritance from his father. So what did the High Muck-a-Muck do? The pitiful potentate pouted.

Scripture tells us, "He lay down on his bed and turned away his face and ate no food" (1 Kings 21:4b). The king did some big-time boo-hooing on his bed over his broccoli's future bed until Queen Jezebel came to his rescue. She took one look at Ol' Sad Sack and asked, "How is it that your spirit is so sullen that you are not eating food?" (He was hoping she had noticed.) I can just imagine Ahab's lower lip hanging and shaking slightly when he told her, "Naboth said, 'I will not give you my vineyard.'" Sniff, sniff.

The queen's first response sounded as if she told him, "Grow a brain!" Well, actually what she said was, "Do you now reign over Israel?" In other words, "Use your power to get what you want, Bozo." (She didn't realize it, but he just had.)

Before Ahab could respond, his codependent cohort, the Queen Bee, injected her deadly venom in the form of a plot. And we're not talking garden plot; we're talking burial. She set up Naboth to be killed.

When Naboth was down and (six feet) under, Ahab "arose to go down to the vineyard of Naboth the Jezreelite, to take possession of it" (1 Kings 21:16). My, my, what a transformation occurred in the royal rascal. Once he got what he wanted, Ahab leapt out of his "grave" clothes and into his bib overalls. Seems his appetite had returned, and he was hankering for some homegrown vittles. There's

something about a mood `tude that causes a pow-
erful appetite. (I wonder if it's all the effort it takes
to work one up?)

But the king's hunger pangs ceased when the
prophet Elijah announced Ahab was about to "go to
the dogs" for his part in Naboth's demise. Nibbles—
I mean Kibbles—and Bits takes on new meaning
when it's you the dogs are nibbling and biting. The
king traded in his bibs for sackcloth, humbled himself before the Lord, and asked the Lord for what
Ahab hadn't given Naboth—mercy.

We seem to be quick to yell judgment toward others while crying mercy for ourselves. Isn't that
right, Jonah?

Now, there was a moody guy if ever I met one. Mr.
Doom & Gloom called down judgment on Nineveh
and then sat ringside to watch the people perish.
But when God extended the city mercy, Jonah was
miffed. A megamood (about the size of a large fish)
swallowed the pitiful prophet. Jonah confessed he
would rather die than not have things turn out the
way he wanted.

He actually complained because God was too gracious and too compassionate. And worst of all, from
Jonah's perspective, God is "one who relents con-
cerning calamity" (Jonah 4:2).

The Lord decided to let Jonah cool his jets under
the shade of an appointed plant. Some believe it
was a castor oil plant. It certainly had a medicinal
effect. In fact, the experience was a bitter pill for
Jonah to swallow, because just about the time he
was joyfully basking in the plant's shade, the worm
turned. The only thing that had brought him relief
and pleasure from the pressures of life was taken
from him.

Isn't that how it goes for mood-tuders? They often feel picked on and plotted against. It seems to them that when life starts to take a turn for the best, they can count on some intruder to come along and eat holes in their happiness. Their favorite line is "I knew it was too good to be true." (Don't ask me how I know this.)

Jonah's joy went as deep as the roots of the plant, which overnight withered and died. Hot from the searing sun and from his scorching temper, he once again asked God to take his life. I guess Jonah forgot that God is in charge of the decision on the length of our lives; we're in charge of what we make of it. And the quality of our lives remains shallow or deep depending on what we're rooted in—our will or His.

From a little boy who couldn't get his mom to do what he wanted, to Ahab who couldn't get Naboth to do what he wanted, to Jonah who couldn't get God to do what he wanted, we begin to see a pattern. A pit-i-ful pattern of our moody struggle to be in control of the uncontrollable—life and others.

The book of Jonah closes with questions. That left me pondering. Twice the Lord asked His melancholy messenger, "Do you have good reason to be angry? Do you have good reason to be angry?"

5

Finitude
(fǐ´ ni tōōd) n.

Dictionary's definition:
Condition of being limited.

Patsy's definition:
A sizable deference.

I AM LIMITED. I can exist in this life for only a measured amount of time. As hard as I persist, a day will come when my persistence won't matter. I was designed to endure many things, but my endurance has boundaries I didn't set. I am finite.

The issue of our finitude is the most difficult of life's restrictions to embrace. But if we don't embrace it, we'll have no choice except to go out screaming and kicking. And isn't that the way we came in? Surely those of us who have journeyed for some years on this earth would hope we had grown enough in grace to accept our limitedness, to have made peace not only with our past, but also with our destiny. Yet I struggle at times.

A young friend, Julia, passed me in a gift store and headed for the card racks. We greeted each other, and she mentioned she was looking for an anniversary card for her husband. "How many years?" I inquired casually.

"Three," she cooed with a smile of newlywed delight.

Three? I said to myself. *Three?* The number was a jolt to my menopausal brain. Les and I have been married 33 years at the time I'm writing this. Whoa, count them—33 big ones. Where, oh where did all those years go? I'd like to kick and scream over their quick passage, but I'm too worn out.

I've noticed since turning 50 and being smack-dab in the middle of my change of life that I sometimes feel frantic, as if I'm charging to the finish line—and I'm not finished! The older I become, the more I want to do, see, and experience, and yet the days aren't long enough, nor my energy sufficient, for me to attain all my desires.

Fifty is heralded as the youth of old age, but it's also the beginning of the end of our age. What did God promise us at most in this life? Psalm 90:10 tells us, "As for the days of our life, they contain seventy years, or if due to strength, eighty years."

Let's see, that tells me that I possibly have 30 years left. That's not bad, except that unlike news flashes that bring information, my hot flashes have erased everything I've ever known or thought I knew. My brain is now the consistency of ABC gum (Already Been Chewed). That leaves me at times grappling to find two thoughts that are even distant relatives to one another, which means I'll finish out my years on a mental dimmer switch. Talk about learning to live with limits!

Not only am I a few wires short of a mental connection, but my body parts are also getting shoddy. I can no longer touch my toes. In fact, I can't even see them. Between my unfocused vision and my overblown midsection, checking out the shine on my shoes is no longer a convenient option. My increased weight and my decreased metabolism have left me heavy in the saddlebags and slowed my trot to a totter.

I wonder if all this disintegration has to do with John the Baptist's statement, "I must decrease and He must increase."

How can the infinite increase? Perhaps what John was saying was that his ministry and life would have an end, but there is One who is endless. Death puts us up close and personal with our finitude and His infinitude.

When I was growing up, whenever I acted as though I had all the answers, my southern-bred momma would remind me, "Young lady, you are getting a little too big for your britches." Little big britches—yep, that was me. I still have that problem when little ol' finite me thinks I know more than I actually do.

I think the scribes needed a momma to remind them about their bigness. *Haughty* certainly described those men of the cloth who were bound up in self-importance. They tried repeatedly to trap Jesus in word or deed, only to have their verbiage expose their own filthy hearts. They flaunted memorized portions of Scripture, trying to incriminate Jesus to the multitudes and diminish His influence. He, in turn, spoke unadulterated truth. And like a straight arrow, the truth punctured the scribes' inflated egos, sending them scurrying into dark corners to mend their big britches and plot their next vicious attack.

It's scary to think the scribes regularly handled the Scriptures and missed the point. They memorized but never internalized. Instead they became heady and haughty. Talk about not recognizing your limits! The scribes saw themselves as superior, when in truth they were spiritual slugs. They grew fat feeding on their own arrogance and vanity.

King Solomon said, "Vanity of vanities! All is vanity." Sol started out the wisest man and ended up the most disillusioned. What happened to the wise guy, anyway? Do you think being so smart caused him to get too big for his britches?

Scripture tells us to have a sane estimate of our value (see Rom. 12:3). We actually have dynamic (restricted) potential. We can be more than we realize but not so big that we can alter our certain end.

Talk about big . . . Goliath knew that the young boy David had outgrown his shepherd's britches when the youth challenged the giant bully to a free-for-all. What Goliath didn't understand was that little David came in the big strength of the Lord. The shepherd slung his sling and slew the sarcastic sap with his sack of smooth stones. Goliath, felled like an oak, never knew what hit him.

Talk about heady . . . check out David's trophy (see 1 Sam. 17:57). Goliath saw *himself* as big (too big for his mammoth trousers), whereas David saw *God* as big.

Joshua, our five-year-old great-nephew, had a mammoth trouser episode. Josh believes no task is beyond his ability. So, with his daddy's saw in hand, he made an architectural adjustment to their home. Now, why Josh decided the stair railing should be removed is beyond us. But the repeated notches and gashes in the railing did prove he had a good working grip on his equipment. He felt quite satisfied with his penetrating progress until the foreman, Joshua's mom, walked onto his work site. Later the building inspector, his dad, clearly expressed his feelings to Josh regarding his future in the construction field. Seems Joshua was forced into early retirement—at least until he was bigger.

I thought I was bigger at 12 because I could look eye to eye with my mom. When I turned 13, I soared past her four-foot-10-inch frame. Okay, okay, *soared* may be a stretch, but I did inch past her. By 15, I was a lumbering five feet tall. I thought I was so cool because I was taller than my mom. She used to tell me, "One day you'll learn that being bigger than me doesn't mean much." Sure enough, talk about discovering your limits!

The truth is we're all little (from Patsy Clairmont to Goliath), and God is big. We're small, and He's great. He's wise; at best, we're wise guys. We're finite, and He is infinite.

6

Habitude
(hab´ e tōōd) n.

Dictionary's definition:
Customary behavior.

Patsy's definition:
Knee-jerk quirk.

LIFE IS HABIT-forming, and habits help to give life form. Without habits, we would be like scared rabbits, running hither and yon, exhausted from our efforts while not making any progress. (Hmm, sounds vaguely convicting.) That's not to say that all habits lend themselves to progress. In fact, some are downright aggravating, dumbfounding, and unproductive.

For instance, my friend Paul collects dead car batteries. That drives his wife, Ann, wacko. "Why, Paul? Just tell me why," she insisted one day.

He confessed that years ago, a person could sell defunct batteries for five dollars, and he just fell into the habit of hanging on to them. ("I've always done it this way.") Ann reached inside her purse and extracted a $20 bill, quipping, "Here, Paul. Now get rid of them."

Paul's dead batteries remind me of a habit at our home. Les always rises first in the morning, followed, in t-i-m-e, by his sputtering, half-charged wife. On that rare occasion when I speed out of bed ahead of him, it seems to drain the charge out of his battery. My appearing in a vertical position while he's still horizontal is not only shocking, but it also breaks the pattern of Les's morning. He will then linger longer than his norm between the sheets, and upon arising, he'll wander aimlessly for a while before he can get back into a routine that feels right.

We are creatures with patterns, and those patterns help us to define our direction. When someone changes the game plan, it takes time to find our rhythm again.

Speaking of rhythm, my parents were both finger thumpers. They would thump out mystery tunes on the table in time to their stress level, which increased ours as their kids. We would gladly have paid them big time to tune down or turn off their nervous music-makers.

My dad was also a change jiggler. He would shake his pants pocket of change while he talked. Maybe this habit came out of the Great Depression, when money was scarce and that left him enamored with the jingle of coins. Whatever caused him to develop the habit, it was music to my ears. I knew the sound meant I could hit him up for jukebox money. With a quarter, I could play five songs. Often I would play the same song for all five selections: "This Old House," sung by Teresa

Brewer. By the third time Teresa was belting out her song, people in the restaurant seemed slightly amused. The fourth time, they would roll their eyes and glance around to try to figure out who the obsessive nitwit was. And by the fifth replay, people were downright annoyed, especially the financier, my dad.

Yep, I guess we all have habits that make others jumpy and grumpy. My son Jason and his wife, Danya, love to crunch ice. As far as I'm concerned, they might as well drag their fingernails down a chalk-board. They've learned that if they must crunch when I'm around, they should go to another floor of the house—or another house.

I, on the other hand, am a fanatical picker-upper. I have the aggravating tendency to pluck up pop glasses or coffee cups before people are finished. In fact, I move so rapidly that I have them washed and back in the cupboard before people realize their drink is missing. I don't mean to sabotage their thirst; it's, well . . . just a habit.

Some habits are obvious, like gum popping, nail biting, or hair twirling. Then there are the *other* habits. A friend confessed that when she's in conversation with someone, she writes that person's name with her tongue on the back of her teeth. (Honest, I didn't make that up!) Another gal then admitted she has a habit of writing her name over and over with her toes as though she's using a typewriter. I then 'fessed up that I make words out of the letters on people's license plates. (My habit seemed so sane next to theirs.) Of course, I didn't mention that every time I get into the shower, I burst into my rendition of "The Hawaiian Wedding

Song." We who inhabit planet earth are a weird—I mean, a unique—lot.

Speaking of Lot, he allotted a lot for his lot in life. He gave up his extended family and moved his immediate family into jeopardy. Even after a hand-delivered, divine telegram warned Lot of danger, he still hesitated to make the right choice. He evidently had become comfy in his habit of making bad—no, let's make that *destructive*—choices.

After Lot was willing to compromise his daughters' virtue and had been resistant to holy shoves from heavenly messengers to escape, he finally fled sin city with his family. And they all lived happily ever after. Not! As is usually the case, indulging in indiscretions had its repercussions. Suffice it to say that Lot had salt added to his wounds.

Lot's life is an example of sin patterns begetting sin patterns. He's a reminder to us that destructive choices (like greed, ambivalence, and procrastination) can become habits as easily as knuckle cracking, lip biting, or spitting. (Yuck!)

Lot evidently didn't learn a lot. Even after he escaped disaster, he tried to drown his sorrows in booze and ended up committing acts of incest. Lot lost a lot.

What a contrast to the life of Daniel, who initially lost everything (family, home, freedom), only to eventually become the righteous ruler over many. Both men suffered loss, yet one became weak and one became wise. What made the difference? Let's take a peek back in time to see. . . .

We find Daniel on his knees, living out his faith via his habit of prayer. Three times a day, he knelt before an open window to gain a view larger than his own. Three times a day, he acknowledged to himself and others the importance of the Almighty in his life. Three times a day, he opened his character to the character of God.

We hear the results of Daniel's determination to hold himself accountable before the Lord when the saps, I mean satraps, tried to find a reason to indict his behavior. "But they could find no ground of accusation or evidence of corruption, inasmuch as he was faithful, and no negligence or corruption was to be found in him" (Dan. 6:4).

Imagine having that kind of character scrutiny— and passing. Daniel's walk of faith was consistent whether times were tough (see Dan. 1:8), threatening (see Dan. 2:13), or thriving (see Dan. 6:28). Daniel was faithful to God even with his habits (see Dan. 6:10), and God was more than faithful to him (see Dan. 6:26-27).

Healthy habits (e.g., prayer life, pure thoughts, good manners) can assist us toward soulish ways by helping us draw boundaries on our behavior. Then, instead of being a loathsome Lot with a weak-kneed approach to life, we can be an esteemed Daniel, disciplined and dedicated. We can charge our batteries by changing our habitudes and thereby deepening our character and commitment.

7

Hebetude
(heb´e tōōd) n.

Dictionary's definition:
Mental lethargy.

Patsy's definition:
Duh.

THEY (DON'T ASK me who, but a bunch of some-ones) say Einstein used only 10 percent of his brain. Yikes! Where does that leave the rest of us?

I guess it means mine has not yet been activated. I do remember, however, that when I was young, I used my mental agility to conjure up excuses not to learn. Now that I've grown older and long to be enlightened, I find my faculties are sluggish. When I study, it takes me longer to "get it," and in no time at all I "forget it." I think, *I'll never forget this profound thought.* Then, as I move through the house to tell Les, it begins to seep out. By the time I get to him, I not only don't remember the thought, but I also can't remember why I was even looking for him.

Many of us regret not paying better attention when we were young, when all our brain cells were still speaking to each other. I guess we thought there was plenty of time to learn, and besides, we were pretty smart cookies. But when the cookie starts to crumble, we find life and faith are not as sweet without needed information.

For some of us, a crisis sparks our interest in further education, whether that's formal, emotional, relational, or faith education. Even though we have to work twice as hard to learn half as much as when we were young, the effort is worth it. The verse comes to mind, "My people are destroyed for lack of knowledge" (Hosea 4:6).

Of course, we also are cautioned that "knowledge makes arrogant, but love edifies" (1 Cor. 8:1b). That says to me we need to learn, but we need to do it while growing in grace. Grace allows us to serve up to others with kindness and respect what we have mentally digested.

Mental lethargy is a crime against ourselves, others, and the Lord. What we don't know can hurt us, which is probably why Peter said, "Wherefore gird up the loins of your mind" (1 Pet. 1:13, KJV). To gird up the loins of our mind means to strengthen, fortify, brace, steel, harden, and prepare our thoughts. We need to know what we believe and then believe what we know. Mental prowess is strengthened by being decisive (cut to the chase), discerning (cut to the quick), and disciplined (cut it out!).

Years ago, I saw a poster that made me giggle and groan. It read, "Some come to the fountain of knowledge to drink; I just came to gargle." I found that funny in an uncomfortable way. For I know at times that I've sloshed a valuable insight around in my head and then quickly spewed (women don't spit) it out, when what I really needed to do was swallow it.

Consider the apostle Paul, however, who swallowed volumes and knew tons of stuff. In fact, his stuffin's not only filled his head, but they also temporarily blocked his heart. It was after Paul was struck dumb that he got smart. His education took a turn from sharpening his opinions based on his faculties to deepening his understanding based on his faith. We need head smarts, but if that's all we have, we become like a forgotten book on a high shelf. Others know the volume has a lot in it, but it sits unconsulted and unread. Those who are smart and exhibit a heart, on the other hand, are approachable and desirable as companions, especially to those who long for truth.

I think Jonathan saw David as a man of wisdom and a whole lot of heart—so much so that Jonathan risked his life, his family, and his position in the kingdom to secure David's friendship. It was Jonathan's daddy, King Saul, who had the hebetude—big time. He evidently became so enamored with himself as king that he put his brain into neutral and then filled up with jealous rage. The emotion of jealousy and the action of rage must have annihilated his rational thoughts and therefore his judgment.

Saul knew the Lord had appointed him as the chosen king, yet he felt threatened by the young shepherd boy David, who honored Saul and loved God. As the king's senses dulled, his defenses were quickened. Saul didn't sharpen his wits but instead strapped on his serrated sword and came out swishing. Saul's fencing brawl ended in his own pratfall. If Saul had only used the smarts the good Lord had blessed him with, he probably would have retained his throne, aged gracefully, and had a faithful companion and successor in David. Instead, he died violently and left the latter a legacy of lunacy.

Later, when David was king, he, too, had a lull in his thinking. When his men went to war, David didn't lead them into battle, as good kings do, but instead hung out at the palace. Bored, the king went onto his porch to check out his kingdom. That's when his brain cells really went bonkers. He allowed his gray matter not to matter when he let his eyes and his hormones betray his good judgment. David and his neighbor, Bathsheba, became a little too neighborly—correction: a lot too neighborly—which resulted in duplicity, deception, and death. David had been an honorable king until he traded in his brain cells for body thrills. King David allowed Bathsheba's bath to turn into her husband's bloodshed. It's obvious the king wasn't thinking.

But we don't have to be a king or queen to be dull of mind. Or should I say "duh" of mind? Have you ever had a duh day, a day in which you should have known better about something? Like the time I backed my husband's newly purchased car over the enormous boulder at the end of my mom's driveway. It wasn't as if some boogie man had planted the rock in the driveway under cover of night. I knew the stone monument was there. I'd been in and out of her driveway hundreds of times, but, duh, I wasn't thinking. I also recall the time I sprayed on my deodorant, only to discover I had used my, duh, hair spray instead of my antiperspirant. It didn't help my perspiration problem, but it sure kept my arms in place. Then there was the time I used the can of room deodorizer for hair spray. It not only didn't hold my hair very well, but I also smelled like a pine tree for a week. Or how about the time we moved, and it took me two days to find where I had put our frozen turkey, which was now, duh, no longer frozen? When I become dull in my thinking, I get duh in my behavior.

What causes the d.t.'s (dull thinking)? Too much to do (taxes me), too little to do (spoils me), complacency (dims me), depression (numbs me), unhealthy behavior (splinters me), rebellion (indicts me), and health issues (deplete me). When we have imbalances in our behavior, it uses up our vitality, draining us of the strength to be bright. Then we pay in other areas by having duh days, which can add up to duh years, until, alas, we've led a duh life. An overused but often accurate saying is that "the light's on, but (duh) nobody's home." I'm reminded by the author of *Disciples Are Made, Not Born* that "there can be no outward shining without an inward burning."

I don't want to leave a legacy of lunacy or a heritage of hebetude. I want to will my family a history of mental clarity, competence, and compassion. For that to happen, I need to purpose to be mentally vigilant, emotionally disciplined, and spiritually attuned. Now, I'm no Einstein, but it's clear to me that I won't be able to do that on my own.

8

`Tude-ometer
(tōod äm´ e ter) n.

Dictionary's definition:
Measured reactions.

Patsy's definition:
Too hot to handle.

I F YOUR BACK suddenly straightens, your neck lengthens, and you find your arms plastered squarely across your bosom, uh-oh, it could be a `tude coming on. If your eye twitches and your hands slip past your waist to gain a death grip on your hips as you plant your feet deeper than your rosebushes, evidence is mounting. If your lips purse, your eyes fade into slits, and your forehead is drawn into a roller coaster of wrinkles . . . well, you get the idea. It's `tude time. `Tudes can definitely be seen.

If your pulse multiplies and your thoughts divide while your senses subtract, it all adds up . . . to an attitude. When your blood pressure percolates and your head throbs in time to the bubbles bursting in your digestive tract, it could be a you-know-what developing. 'Tudes can definitely be felt.

When I'm into a full-blown 'tude, my words fly faster than the Concorde. At times, though, I'm as silent as the eye of a hurricane with the threat of major devastation looming. When you notice my voice rising and falling more often than the president's popularity, and my s's sounding like a hissing snake, there's a good chance I'm ticked. 'Tudes can definitely be heard.

I'm aware that, on any number of occasions, I've caught a 'tude at our local grocery store—often from one of its work-worn employees. I'm also cognizant that just as often I have left one of my 'tudes with them, which they probably have passed on to the next customer. The ambushed customer then takes the 'tude into traffic, honking and harping at anyone who crosses his path. The honked-at drivers rush home and bark at their kids, who in turn do the Heimlich maneuver on the neighbor's cat. 'Tudes can definitely be shed abroad.

When 'tudes can be seen, felt, heard, and shared, you would think we would not be so easily taken captive by them. Unless we're just not in touch with ourselves. Or we've allowed too many things to stockpile inside us. Or we're feeling justified in our reactions. Out of touch, too much stuff, fuss, fuss, fuss.

That reminds me of the time I was out east, in the mountains. I had just finished speaking at a ladies' event, and a young woman was waiting in the wings to take me to the airport. My schedule had been especially demanding that season, and I found myself crisscrossing the country to try to fulfill my crammed calendar.

The driver whisked me into her pickup truck and made two unforgettable statements. Statement #1: She had 30 minutes to get me to an airport that was 50 minutes away. But (statement #2) I shouldn't be concerned because she had once been an ambulance driver. With that information, she plunged the accelerator through the floorboard and sped down the mountain. We passed several logging trucks (one on a curve), not to mention assorted other vehicles. We careened precariously close to the unfenced edges (giving me glimpses into glory). We dropped in elevation so rapidly that my eyebrows became permanently arched. I'm not certain I breathed until our tires were on level ground.

When we arrived at the airport (in the nick of time), we ran, bags in hand, to the gate. I was then rushed outside to board a microscopic airplane. How small was it? It was slightly larger than a model plane and definitely smaller than a real one. It held only a couple of passengers, including lucky, white-knuckled, nauseated me.

I hid behind my briefcase, fussing and fuming during the flight. Finally I asked myself, *How did I ever end up ridge-running with Wile E. Coyote's sister, much less find myself booked on a plane-ette that is flailing about in the jet stream?*

The answer was all too obvious. I hadn't faced my physical and personality limitations. I had taken on more than I could handle sanely, sensibly, and sweetly. Then, when it got to be too much for me, I wanted to blame others for the unwanted challenges I was facing. I was sportin' a 'tude because I hadn't stopped long enough to check my 'tude-ometer.

If we would listen to our body's responses, our mind's conversations, and our verbal intonations, we could begin to nip destructive attitudes in the bud. Of course, it takes more than just spotting them to overcome them. To give up an attitude takes a commitment to change, ownership of our behavior, a willingness to die to self, and a reliance on the Lord to do for us what we can't do for ourselves.

Change can be a threat, a relief, a necessity, an inconvenience, and (usually) a laborious process. Many times, personal pain has been the motivation I've needed to make critical changes in my life. When my life-temperature rises high enough, I find I'm more willing to do whatever it takes to be well again. There's nothing worse than withering in feverish agony emotionally, relationally, or spiritually. But I've also noticed that after I've made important attitudinal adjustments, the mercury begins to fall as my fever breaks, and I'm restored to good (mental, social, and spiritual) health. In other words, change is worth the effort and the cost.

I live in a delightful town with a personality problem—not enough parking. Unfortunately, this deficiency doesn't improve my personality. Recently, after circling the parking lot in town several times, I spotted a car leaving. I picked up speed and raced around to position my vehicle to take its slot when, lo and behold, another car approached from another entrance and pulled toward the space before I could get there. The driver didn't know I had already circled the lot more times than Joshua did Jericho. But she got the idea when I sped around the corner honking like a flock of Canadian geese. She stopped her car, checked her mirror, and then politely drove away. I then zoomed into *my* spot and screeched to a halt, bumping the curb.

My friend Jill, who had witnessed my noisy maneuvering from the passenger seat of my car, looked at me in surprise and said, "I am so embarrassed." Then she speculated, "What if she knows you? What if she has read your books?"

Startled by my own behavior and sobered by the thought that I had allowed my poor attitude to turn into bad manners, I got out of the car and looked for the woman. She had just found a vacated space and was pulling her car into it. I headed in her direction. I knew I needed to apologize. I prayed she wouldn't know me; anonymity would make this confession less painful. When she slipped out of the car and turned toward me, however, I realized I *did* know her. And yes, she had read my books. My overdone aggression had turned into humble pie, and now that I was recognized, I found it even more difficult to swallow my failure.

I could have saved myself (and Jill) an embarrassing episode, and the gracious woman a jolting experience, if I had checked my 'tude-ometer instead of my speedometer. In fact, let's do that now. Let's see if we're reasonable people or if it's time to change because we're attitudinally too hot to handle.

Are you often aware of having a larger response to a situation than it calls for—for example, screaming at someone for an innocent mistake, passing severe judgments against others, or outbursts that surprise even you (honk, honk)?

Do you frequently feel deficient? defective? defensive?

Do you often feel misunderstood?

Is self-pity a regular party you throw for yourself?

Do you wish you were someone else—somewhere else?

Do you overwhelm others? Are you often overwhelmed by others? by life?

Do you talk too much? too little? too loud?

Are you often uptight and in a fight-or-flight mode?

If we find ourselves identifying with more of these questions than we would like, we need to look under our attitude to the hole in our heart. If we'll take truth as far as we can on our own behalf, the Lord will begin to heal the places we can't reach, and He will expose the sin we haven't faced. That will then give us the opportunity to experience growth at a deep, life-changing level. Remember, if your `tude-ometer's needle is stuck on the hot side, park yourself in His presence until you cool down and wise up. Take it from a former Indy 500 wannabe.

9

Exactitude
(ig zak´ te tōōd) n.

Dictionary's definition:
Being exact.

Patsy's definition:
Picky, picky, picky.

M Y DELIGHTFUL NEIGHBOR Alicia alphabet-izes her spices. My friend Jill is filing all her recipes in the computer. An acquaintance, Linda, dates her groceries before she puts them away. These girls have been bitten by the exactitude. But they're not alone.

For years, my mom has crocheted the most exquisite floor-length tablecloths. If she finds she missed a stitch 22 rows back, she'll rip out all the perfect rows to correct the one imperfection that no one in the world would have noticed. It hurts to watch her unravel row after row of her beautiful work in search of a mistake. But she's into exacti-tude. And when she completes her work, it's lovely . . . and exact.

When I was growing up, we would go on vacation every summer, usually to my parents' home state of Kentucky. My mom would start to pack days before the trip, and by the time we left, we could have entered our suitcases in a *Good Housekeeping* contest—and won. They were truly works of art. Mom would iron every item before packing and then carefully fold it and secure the corners with straight pins. Once the clothing was pinned, she would smooth it one last time with the iron. All my pj's were on the right side of the suitcase, and my pedal pushers were on the left, pinned to their matching tops. My dresses were hung and wrapped in sheets and then carefully stretched across the top of the suitcases in the trunk.

I admire people who are exacting—evidently not enough to follow in their footsteps, though, at least not in packing. If I can close my suitcase once it's packed, I consider that a worthy accomplishment. I have still more problems when I repack for my trip home. Even if I haven't purchased anything additional, once I wear my clothes, they gain weight. Those fat things refuse to fit back in the suitcase, leaving my luggage obese and overwhelmed from carrying such a hefty load.

My nightmare is that one day, what I once witnessed at the Detroit Metro Airport will happen to me. Les and I were waiting for my cases and had been almost lulled to sleep by the monotonous circling of luggage on the conveyor belt. A woman who had obviously not ironed or pinned her clothing before packing and must have been on the return segment of her trip had overtaxed her suitcase. Dangling big-time from her partially opened, circling luggage were her huge Hanes (and we're not talking socks). Her husband spotted the case, saw her unmentionables exposed and fluttering at half-mast, and had the audacity to mention them. The brute picked up the suitcase in one hand and her bloomers in the other. Holding them in the air like a sail on a schooner, he walked through the crowd, chirping, "Are these yours, Honey?"

I was mad at Les all the way home. Poor guy, of course he had nothing to do with that woman's embarrassing fiasco, but he was the only one around for me to be upset with. Besides, I wanted him to understand exactly what I would do to him if he ever embarrassed me like that.

So I guess I can be exacting on things like threats, opinions, and knickknacks. Knickknacks? Yep! I'm fanatical about the arrangement of my pretties around the house. When my friend Debbie helps me clean, I drive her crazy as I shadow her around the premises, resituating items after she dusts them.

Being an exacting person has its benefits and its detriments. For instance, I want my surgeon, my dentist, and my accountant to sport an exactitude. That's beneficial for everyone concerned. But when I nitpick about incidentals like the placement of a teacup and whether the handle should be turned to the right instead of the left, that can become detrimental. Nitpicky people are seldom sought after as good company.

I guess, though, that we all have some areas of our lives in which we're more exacting than others. What are yours?

I love a well-made bed. I don't like the sheets to be lopsided or lumpy but smoothed out and tucked tightly. I like my bed full of fluffed pillows in varying sizes, and I like the spread draped evenly. But I've learned that if I don't have time to do it exactly the way I like it, that's okay. Time won't stop, the stock market won't crash, and a bed cop won't suddenly appear and write me up for loose bedding.

My friend Lana learned some lessons about exactitude when her son's girlfriend invited her over for a birthday dinner. It turns out this gal was a gourmet cook, and Lana said it was one of the best meals she had ever eaten. Everything had been prepared exactly as it should have been.

Lana's only disappointment was that some of her good friends didn't get to sample this excellent fare. She felt her words fell short of describing something that only experience could define.

So Lana was elated when a second invitation arrived to attend an open house and to bring guests of her choice—exactly what Lana had hoped for, gourmet goodies and all. Lana regaled her friends about this dream-come-true cook.

When they arrived, Lana and her now-excited friends gathered in the living room and selected cozy seats around a tray of lovely appetizers. Eager to try them, Lana's guest Beverly selected an item and dipped it into the candle-heated sauce. She took a bite, chewed, swallowed, and then began to spit. She tried to dispose of the rest of her gourmet treat into her napkin while shaking her head in disgust.

Lana was aghast. "What's wrong?" she whispered to her friend.

"It's terrible," Beverly choked out quietly.

"Don't be silly," Lana replied, beginning to feel defensive. Then Lana, to prove her friend wrong, picked up the identical item, dipped it into the sauce, and popped it into her mouth. Her eyes began to grow larger, and she looked for a place to get rid of the disgusting stuff in her burning mouth. Her now-experienced friend handed her some napkins. Lana was confused, embarrassed, and nauseated.

She decided the offending culprit was something in the raspberry sauce. When one of the kitchen helpers walked through the room, Lana meekly asked about the sauce's contents.

"Sauce?" said the woman. "Why, that's liquid pot-pourri!"

Later, Lana had to admit the evening had not gone exactly as she had thought it would. The good news was that Lana and Beverly had the sweetest breath for weeks afterward.

Isn't that just like life? Seldom does it go exactly as we anticipate.

When my husband's niece Carmen had an operation as a young girl, we became concerned because she was in surgery much longer than the doctor had predicted. When the surgeons emerged, they were shaking their heads in amazement. Carmen had a lot of extra parts, they said, and they had needed to figure out exactly how she was knit together before they could accomplish their task. The operation was a success, but the doctors were still scratching their heads at her puzzling design as we left the hospital.

There is One, however, who isn't surprised by our inner workings. He understands exactly how we're put together, every stitch, for He was there when we were formed. He isn't surprised by the unexpected happenings in our lives, either, for He knew exactly what would occur. He knows even our nitpicky ways and loves us exactly the way we are. He is "the Father of lights, with whom there is no variation, or shifting shadow" (James 1:17). How grateful I am that in this fluctuating, unsure, compulsive world, a Point of Reference holds steady! Jesus is the perfect exactitude example, for He is exactly the same yesterday, today, and forever.

10

Fortitude
(fôr´ te tood) n.

Dictionary's definition:
Strength of mind.

Patsy's definition:
Heads up.

IN *THE FAMILY Book of Christian Values*, Stuart and Jill Briscoe quote a poem titled "Courage." The last two lines read, "Courage is fear that has said its prayers." Those words say to me that courage doesn't always start off strong, but it can find the needed strength in spite of weakness—even in the midst of it. That means little knee-knocking me can qualify as potentially courageous.

I used to believe I had to feel brave before I could take steps in a scary direction. I have since learned bravery is not what you feel but what you make up your mind to do. The challenge is to "set [our] face like flint" (Isa. 50:7) in the right direction, then take the first steps onto an unsure and sometimes intimidating path, with the willingness to see it through. The result? Voila! Fortitude.

Fortitude is like buying a lifetime membership to an exercise club and then actually showing up for each session. Whoa, think about it: This isn't a word, it's an aerobics course! What an exhausting thought, a lifetime of courage! Admirable, enviable, yet it seems unattainable.

Remember Daniel in the pen, though, accused unfairly by the men and then thrown into the den (not to be confused with the study). He never gave up (his faith), he never gave in (to their demands), he never gave over (to their ways), but he walked through each difficulty one courageous step at a time.

Or consider a more reluctant fortitude candidate: edgy Esther. Talk about having to walk a knee-knocking line—between royalty and relatives, Esther's queenly position was precarious at best. A pretty maiden, she was chosen as queen following a beauty pageant of sorts. But unbeknownst to the king, Esther came incognito. She had conveniently withheld her Jewish origin so as to avoid unnecessary pressure and to respect her uncle's counsel.

Then an enemy in the kingdom, Haman, devised a treacherous scheme to eradicate the Jews, thus threatening Esther's and her people's lives. She was alerted to the rascal's plot, thereby placing the future of her people in her trembling hands. Esther reluctantly, after big-time nudges from her honorable uncle, proceeded with a daring dinner. Between drinks and dessert, Esther served hard-boiled Haman to the king. The king gratefully couldn't digest this sneaky snake in the grass but had Haman hung out to dry. (See Esther 7.)

Esther didn't find it easy to put her life (she was young and beautiful) and lifestyle (cushy, spa city) in jeopardy for her people, especially since the last queen was banished forever for her unwillingness to be at King Ahasuerus's beck and call. Young Queen Esther was hesitant to do anything that might vex his highness. But Esther pushed past her feelings of fear and intimidation and became a female of fortitude. She spoke the truth, spared her people, and exposed a sinister plot.

Then there's the apostle Paul, a man of sagacity and tenacity. After his conversion, however, he didn't see himself that way, which was probably a key to his ongoing courage. Paul faced shipwrecks, floggings, stoning, and imprisonment with strength and, of all things, joy.

Excuse me, but if I have to wait more than a few minutes in the checkout line at the store, I'm offended and think I'm really suffering for Jesus. I don't mean to be flippant, but honestly, we in the western world seem to see simple inconveniences as indignations and hardships as unfair atrocities. Paul, on the other hand, saw danger as an opportunity to trust the Lord and hardship as a way to identify with the Savior. What a 'tude! I sure hope courageous is contagious.

Actually, instead of waiting to perchance "catch" fortitude, we can prepare ourselves for the times when we'll need strength beyond our own and courage to replace our fear. On close examination, we see the fortitude tactics implemented in the lives of Daniel, Esther, and Paul.

Repeatedly, Daniel presented himself to the Lord. Repeatedly, he made his requests known and then leaned in to listen to God, who hears our words and sees our heart. Repeatedly, amidst the demands of his influential position and threats to his life, Daniel stopped his activities to acknowledge and worship God.

No wonder enemies couldn't intimidate this mighty man of faith. No wonder lions slept peacefully in his presence. No wonder the king rejoiced at the miraculous deliverance of his esteemed counselor, Daniel the lion-hearted.

A willingness to repeatedly bend our knee to the Lord prepares us to rise up clothed in His dignity and strength. Daniel had learned through his life of exile to talk to God. Daniel had years of prayer practice by the time he faced the lions.

But Esther was a different story. She was young and inexperienced in life-threatening dilemmas. She appears to have been a cautious woman, an easy-does-it lady, a let's-not-make-any-waves kind of gal. Along came her uncle and asked her to risk her throne and possibly her life by being a bearer of bad tidings. The king had already eliminated one lippy queen, and Esther didn't want to further rile his royalty. But knowing she must do what she must do, Esther asked that her people fast, as would she and her maidens, before she chatted with his hasty highness.

What a wise young woman to entreat her extended family of faith to fast, because witnesses in humble agreement before the Lord are a powerful force. Esther feared that if she proceeded and exposed the enemy to the king, she would perish. Instead, she prospered even more than before. Now Esther was secure not only in her position with the king, but also in her position with the King of kings.

The apostle Paul knew the importance of both prayer and fasting, and he added a third cord to our rope of hope that will pull us out of our fear and into courage—Scripture.

In 2 Timothy, Paul wrote to his beloved son in the Lord and reminded him of the importance of the Word of God. It seems that those surrounding Paul had grown weary of prisons, punishments, and ongoing persecution, so they deserted him. Paul reminded Timothy that difficult times (and people) would come into his life, and he must stand firm and be courageous (whether others were or not). To prepare him for hardships, Papa Paul told Timothy to remain faithful to the Sacred Writings, for they would profit him, reprove him, correct him, and train him.

God breathed the Scriptures knowing we would need guidelines, encouragement, enlightenment, comfort, and courage.

When I read that Daniel faced lions, it strengthens me to face the growling beasts in my life. There was the time, for instance, when I was commissioned by my husband to pick up auto parts on his behalf. When I arrived at the store, I felt like a china cup in a bull ring. But I assured myself I'd be all right. All I had to do was give Les's name, and they would hand me his order.

I wonder why I live under the delusion that life is going to be simple?

The man behind the desk began to bark questions at me about the order. I think my blank stare reminded him of his mother-in-law, whom he obviously didn't care for. He began to speak louder. Yelling at me doesn't make me smarter . . . or him, either. I thought about yelling back, but he wasn't who I wanted to be like. Instead, calmly (a rare moment) and quietly (a semiprecious moment), I left. After I got home, I was so glad I hadn't joined the man in his growling behavior. It was one of those times when I faced a lion and didn't flinch or give up my personal dignity. Thanks, Daniel.

Then when I see Esther tiptoeing toward truth, I'm encouraged to continue my walk, even if, at times, I'm only taking baby steps. I'm amazed and sometimes discouraged to realize I'm still asking the Lord to help me in some of the same areas where I was asking for help years ago . . . like discipline. I still don't eat as well as I should, and my desktop looks like the leftovers from a ticker tape parade. I also tend to slump while sitting at the table. There's something so tacky about a woman who rests her chin on her plate.

Yet I have finally reduced and organized my purse. I no longer strap a trunk over my shoulder, and the contents no longer become dangerous projectiles hurling in all directions when my treasure chest is opened. I now have a petite pouch with just the necessities tucked neatly inside. Mind you, it wouldn't see me through a stint on a deserted island, as my former one could have, but my condensed system is simpler and therefore saner (not to mention lighter).

Also, even though I'm not jostling my cellulite at a gym, I did move my closet upstairs, forcing myself to climb up and down the steps many times a day. My thighs are still flapping in the breeze, but I can now reach the top step without turning greenish blue.

As for my eating habits, I'm far better informed, and I now purpose to read fat and sugar contents before purchasing. I've learned how to make my own vegetable juices, and sometimes I even drink them. I give up dessert more often than I accept it, with the exception of pumpkin pie. (I've been known to consume an entire pie without assistance.)

So, like Esther, I may not be racing to the finish line, but I am headed in the right direction. And given enough time, I may even learn how to sit up straight. Thanks, Queen Esther, for making the right choices . . . eventually.

Now when I follow Paul's journeys and jog in and out of prison with him as I read the epistles, I'm prompted to be courageous and to endure faithfully to the end. Some of the scariest steps I took in my prison (agoraphobia) days were down the steps outside my front door. I mentally held onto my rope of hope as I tentatively inched my way toward freedom. I had prayed, and I had sought the prayers of others. I did some fasting, and I was gradually becoming a student of the Scriptures. Yet even with my rope of hope, my freedom wasn't easy or fast, but it was definite and sure. I sometimes felt as if I were emotionally dangling off the edge of a cliff, but I found the rope held. In time, I regained my footing and then scrambled my way up onto a ledge. What a relief! But I knew it was just a matter of time before I would have to take another step out of my safety zone if I was ever to be well mentally, emotionally, relationally, and spiritually.

One of my first excursions out of my agoraphobia was to attend a Bible study for nervous folks. My concern was that it might be more like a babble study if the others were in as bad a shape as myself. Gratefully, the gals attending were better acquainted with the Scriptures than I was, and they were helpful in directing me to verses that encouraged me to be courageous. One of the gals introduced me to 2 Timothy 1:7: "For God hath not given us the spirit of fear; but of power, and of love, and of a sound mind" (KJV).

After years of being housebound, I learned to face my fears, trust the Lord, and experience His power, love, and a sound mind. I learned to drive a car again and to ride with others. (Today I travel extensively and continually.) Once I made it to the car, I began to attend church, and eventually I even risked sitting in the front row. Then one day, I found myself as the speaker on the platform. Wow, that's some rope!

Lost hope? There is a rope (prayer, fasting, and the Scriptures), and "a cord of three strands is not quickly torn apart" (Eccles. 4:12b). Remember, we're not born with fortitude, but we can develop into courageous people. And it also helps me to remember Who holds the other end of our rope—the One who will never let go.

11

Senectitude
(si nek´ te tŏŏd) n.

Dictionary's definition:
Old age.

Patsy's definition:
What, like 50 or something?

M Y 80-YEAR-OLD mother is a kick. Mom loves to dress up every day and go somewhere. She doesn't care where as long as she can be out and about. Les and I took her out for her birthday dinner just recently. When the young waiter came to lead us to a table, she pointed her tiny finger at him and said in her biggest voice, "Give me the best table in the house; I'm 80."

Mom has gone through a number of health challenges: a dramatic loss of hearing, breast cancer, glaucoma, cataracts, a fractured hip, and the most frustrating of all, Parkinson's. Yet even with the fading of available information, she continues to have a delightful, if at times disconcerting, sense of humor. Mom called one day and asked me to take her to the doctor. When we arrived, the office was full of waiting patients. We sat down in chairs that were linked to the chairs next to them, putting us elbow to elbow with those on each side. As is usually the case in a waiting room, the only sounds were an occasional wheeze and the ripple of magazine pages being turned. We were all aware that even if we whispered, because of the tight proximity, everyone would be privy to our conversation.

I was innocently skimming through a *Time* magazine when my mom decided it was her time to make an announcement. As clear as a clapper striking a bell, she proclaimed, "Yep, guess I'm going to grow a mustache."

To say I was taken aback would be mild since it had never occurred to me that Mom was even considering such an undertaking. Not knowing for sure what to do with this now-public information, and feeling an obligation to respond, I asked weakly, "And why is that?"

In her inimitable way, she declared, "Because yours is getting so much longer than mine!"

Senectitude must mean the freedom to say whatever comes to your mind. Yikes! Sounds as if this latter season of our lives could be the most revealing. I think Mom is getting back at me for every labor pain she endured at my birth. The good news is that I, in my senectitude, can do the same to my children.

At a retreat I attended, I met a lovely older woman who had never married. In a conversation we had regarding funerals, she told me all her pallbearers were going to be women.

"Really?" I replied, surprised and fascinated.

"Yes," she said. "Since the men didn't want to take me out when I was living, I'm not going to let them take me out when I'm dead."

She made me giggle, as did this senectitude poem about grandmothers:

In the dim and distant past when life's tempo
    wasn't fast,
Grandma used to rock and knit, crochet, tat,
    and baby-sit.
When the kids were in a jam, they could always
    count on Gram,
In an age of gracious living, Grandma was the
    gal for giving.
Grandma now is at the gym exercising to keep
    slim,
She's off touring with the bunch, taking clients
    out to lunch,
Driving north to ski or curl, all her days are in a
    whirl,
Nothing seems to stop or block her now that
    Grandma's off her rocker!

My mother did recognize in a public way this truth: I'm getting older. Not only am I "off my rocker," but I've also noticed my physical resilience is becoming sluggish. Still, I was surprised last week when even my muscles went awry. I was on a drug run (we had left my husband's medicines in the trunk of a woman's departing vehicle), and as I sprinted (okay, okay, sauntered rapidly) to catch her, it seemed someone threw a hardball into the back of my leg. Later, I found out that the gripping wad in my calf was ripped muscles.

A compassionate athletic therapist came to my aid and packed my leg in ice. He was attentive, helpful, and young. He proceeded to tell me that "at your age," I shouldn't rub my leg in case of blood clots. As beneficial as that insight was, actually, at my age, I don't want anyone to bring up my age. If you know I'm old and I know I'm old, isn't it kind of redundant? Instead of "at your age," I would have liked him to say, "Winter's winds have weakened your willows, and the sap's lodged in your limbs." There now, doesn't that sound better?

I find the aging process full of surprises. Oh, I don't mean just the negative physical changes, but the positive emotional and relational liberation as well. I've become wiser in my responses and therefore don't feel the same unhealthy obligations to individuals I once did. I've learned that I'm not responsible for the happiness of others (hallelujah!), although I always want to be a giver, a nurturer, and a true friend.

That description reminds me of Edith Gelaude and Eleanor Barzler, two seasoned pros who give me courage to keep on keeping on. They are amazing women full of joy and zeal. Their individual trees have stood through a myriad of seasons. They've gone through great losses and have braved them with humor and heart. And they both continue to stretch out their fruitful branches to offer others sustenance and comfort.

Isn't that what enhances life, our willingness to invest wisely in others and to continue to be productive? Consider Elizabeth, the mother of John the Baptist. She had the surprising opportunity to bear fruit in her old age. No, I'm not speaking of when she gave birth to John but of her visitation from Mary.

Mary ran to Elizabeth for comfort and direction, and Elizabeth received her with humility and honor. Then Elizabeth opened her arms and her home to Mary for three months. *Months?* Yes, months. Two pregnant women in one house—that's a lot of hormones.

I am taken aback not only by the generous length of Mary's stay, but also by Elizabeth's greeting of homage. The aging Elizabeth showed the young maiden deference. Now, that's admirable. Elizabeth could have felt resentment that she wasn't chosen to bear the Christ child. She could have been judgmental toward Mary since she wasn't married. Elizabeth could have felt a spirit of rivalry between herself and Mary and between their firstborn sons. Instead, Elizabeth was joyous and used by God to affirm Mary's womanhood and the fruit of her womb.

Then there's 84-year-old Anna, widowed prophetess who served faithfully in the temple, awaiting the coming of the Lord. And when He came, she recognized Him, even as a mere babe in arms.

I just did a retreat in Florida. I was excited about going, because that meant I would have the added benefit of seeing my sister, Elizabeth, and her family. But we hadn't arranged a time when we would get together. So when Elizabeth came up at the end of my first talk, I didn't recognize her. She looked like herself, but I was caught up in the activity of the moment and didn't focus, even though I was looking right at her. When Elizabeth began to talk to me, her voice clicked my brain into gear, and I, embarrassed, jumped up to greet her. My one and only sister—and I didn't recognize her!

Anna, on the other hand, not only anticipated the Lord's arrival (she served night and day, fasting and praying), but she also hadn't allowed her long wait for Him to dishearten or distract her. When the Lord was finally brought to the temple, Anna instantly recognized Him and heralded His arrival. Her 84-year-old physical light may have been dimming, but Anna's mind and heart were full of the light of redemption. Anna, unlike me, wasn't embarrassed; she was emancipated. Her Redeemer had come.

When I grow up, I want to be like my mom, Edith, and Eleanor. Despite difficulties, dark days, and diseases, they carry on with verve.

When I grow up, I want to be like Elizabeth and Anna, tenderhearted toward others and sensitive to the presence of the Lord. Those are 'tudes I would sport proudly.

Beatitude
(bé at´ e tōōd) n.

Dictionary's definition:
Blessed truth.

Patsy's definition:
Insight for living.

"BLESSED ARE THOSE who mourn, for they shall be comforted."

My friend Sheila Hamman teaches at an elementary school. One day, she gave her third-grade students an assignment to compose a letter to someone in history.

One young boy decided to write to Joan of Arc. He wrote, "Joan, I'm sorry you had to go through so many bad things, but I'm glad your husband was able to get all the animals to safety."

Even though this young student had his stories crossed, I'd still give him an A+ for searching out a redeeming factor in the midst of tragedy. Children have a way of reminding us of what's really important.

Joshua, Les's nephew's son, certainly has done that for us. Joshua and his mom and dad, Mike and Michelle, live 600 miles away. We became instantly and intimately acquainted when a family crisis arose. Joshua, at age three, had to be airlifted to a hospital near our home when he was diagnosed with leukemia. He required regular treatments at the clinic in Ann Arbor. Because we were close to the hospital, Mike, Michelle, and Joshua stayed in our home before and during treatments over a two-and-a-half-year period. This allowed us the privilege of getting to know our geographically distant kin.

Joshua is his own little man. He's feisty and fidgety, and I'm almost sure he's full of rocket fuel. Joshua keeps us all on our toes.

At one point in his treatments, he received heavy doses of chemotherapy, causing him to lose his thick, red hair. We adults were sad but thought it a small price to pay if it meant Joshua would eventually be well. But Josh was devastated by his new, slick image. He couldn't comprehend, at three and a half, our concern about his future welfare; he was concerned with right now. Josh had a wardrobe of nifty hats, but they didn't make up for his lost hair. He was in mourning.

When Christmas came around, he announced to his mom that he wanted Santa to bring him hair. As a family, we would have bought Joshua anything he requested, but hair was outside our jurisdiction. We made suggestions of other gifts that would be great fun, but try as we might, we couldn't budge his decision. Michelle considered cutting her hair and weaving it into a "do" for him, although she knew a wig wouldn't satisfy her little guy's heart, much less fit his head.

As Christmas arrived, we all hoped the excitement of gift giving and receiving would distract Josh and keep him from feeling devastated when he didn't get his hair. At the first break of light, Joshua came bounding down the steps. As he circled the tree, Michelle noticed he had already been into something and had gotten dirty. She went into the kitchen, dampened a washcloth, and proceeded to wash off Joshua's dirty head. Then Michelle noticed it wasn't washing off . . . and it wasn't dirt . . . but a soft down of new hair.

After the initial excitement over his hair had settled down, Josh set about unwrapping his gifts. When he opened the last one, he once again remembered his best gift of all. He ran his hand across his head, and his eyes grew large with fresh realization. "Mom," he whispered in awe, "I have hair."

Talk about rejoicing! All other gifts paled. One of Joshua's aunts, examining his soft wisps of hair, exclaimed, "Wow! Makes me want to believe in Santa."

But Joshua's Grandma Diane wisely added, "It's somebody bigger than Santa."

Later, as they recounted the story to me, I said, "Yes, it's Someone who hears the prayers of a child."

Les and I went to visit Joshua at his northern Michigan home. His hair had grown in and was more beautiful than before. After we had been there for a while, Josh suddenly disappeared and then returned carrying a comb. He presented it to me, as a knight might his sword, so I could have the joy of combing through his lovely, bronze hair.

Joshua is under the constant threat of losing his hair again, because his treatments continue. But I don't think it will be as difficult next time, even for Josh. His miracle hair on Christmas served as a reminder to us that there is One who cares for and comforts a hurting child in ways we never could . . . and understanding that comforts us, his mourning family.

"Blessed are the peacemakers, for they shall be called sons of God."

When we decided to name our second son Jason, I didn't realize his name meant "peacemaker." Nor could I have realized how accurate that description would be. My grandmother told me you get babies through the Sears catalog, and I've wondered sometimes if that's where we acquired Jason. Then I remember my labor pains and that we look so much alike, and I realize Sears had nothing to do with this transaction. But in our family, Les, Marty, and I are far more feisty than Jason.

When he was in elementary school, the teachers would tell me that if they had a hot spot in the room, where students just couldn't get along, they would move Jason in the middle of it, and soon the squabbles would stop.

My friend Lana tells me that's because Jason is a phlegmatic personality, and phlegmatics are natural peacemakers. In fact, she says they're the human tranquilizers of society. Just having someone of that temperament enter a room can change an intense climate to a more hospitable one. Perhaps we should take a few notes on what these peacemaking personalities do, that we might become less volatile and more peaceable.

When Jason was in middle school, I wanted to teach him the importance of forgiveness. (Middle-school days seem to be such a hormonally and atti-tudinally disruptive period.) I asked him to think of someone he didn't like. Jason thought and thought and finally said he couldn't think of anyone. I found that amazing. Well, actually, I found that ridiculous. I could think of *tons* of people I wasn't terribly fond of; surely he could come up with *one*. Finally, in frus-tration I said, "Okay, okay, then think of someone who doesn't like you." Again Jason couldn't come up with a name. (My own list, for myself, was lengthy.) Now, how was I to teach this boy how to forgive when he didn't have hostile conflicts with others?

In Jason's senior year of high school, he took a trip to Florida and brought back a wardrobe of new T-shirts. He was proud, sportin' his collection of "awesome finds." Then one day he called me into his room and asked if I had washed his T-shirts. I told him I hadn't had time. So he pulled a basket-ful of his new shirts from the closet to show me that someone had washed them with a pair of bright pink shorts. The shorts had run all over every shirt. He asked if I thought the blotches would come out, and I said I didn't think so. They appeared to be ruined.

I snapped up one of the shirts to go find out who the culprit was, but Jason stopped me. "Don't say anything, Mom," he protested.

Confused, I replied, "Why not?"

"You might hurt their feelings," he said.

Maybe I did get him from Sears. Honestly, if someone had just ruined my new clothes, I would want to hurt the person's feelings, at least a little. Know what I mean? Jason, though, valued his family's feelings over the cost of the shirts, and he felt the incident should be overlooked.

His brother, Marty, came along and discovered the gaudy, pink pile of stained shirts. He quietly disappeared downstairs with the basket tucked under his arm. Some time later, he reappeared carrying Jason's restored shirts. Marty had treated, soaked, washed, and dried the T-shirts. They looked spanking new. Hmm, if I remember correctly, I believe we ordered Marty from Spiegels.

I wonder if peacemakers are called the sons of God because peace is more important to them than their pride?

"Blessed are those who hunger and thirst for righteousness, for they shall be satisfied."

As a young, newly expectant mother, I experienced a rush of hormones and emotions that kept my inexperienced husband guessing what my next outrageous request might be. I had heard of cravings and even had some strong longings for certain foods at times, but I had never experienced such intense desires as I did when I was pregnant.

I remember one evening when I suddenly needed, DO YOU HEAR ME? NEEDED! some chocolate pop and lobster tails. My devoted hubby traversed the countryside and, believe it or not, found me chocolate pop. The lobster tails took an extra day to locate. Then I needed fresh coconuts, which weren't easy to obtain in Michigan during the winter, but Les once again triumphed. My cravings gradually lessened. Actually, I should say they "expanded," because I went from wanting select items to just wanting more of everything, which left me exiting the hospital, after giving birth, the same weight as when I checked in. *Moan.*

When my office manager, Jill, was with child, she sent her bewildered husband, Greg, out at midnight in search of liverwurst and oranges. By the time he found a place open and returned with offerings in hand, her desire for oranges had left as unexpectedly as it had come, while her passion for liverwurst had doubled. Then Jill decided that instead of oranges, she needed orange juice (a drink she had scorned in the past).

During her last pregnancy, my friend Carol went on a Snickers toot. She couldn't seem to get enough chocolate. Trick or treat time was fast approaching, so she stocked up on bags of small candy bars for the neighborhood children. But on Halloween Day, she had to make an emergency run for more candy, because during an intense chocolate frenzy, she had eaten every single piece. Her squishy, brown, chubby fingerprints were all over every empty bag and wrapper.

Wouldn't it be wonderful if we suddenly became deliriously desirous of the Lord? If we developed a ravenous appetite for righteousness? If we craved His ways? If we feasted on His Word? If we thirsted for His will? Then—just think of it—instead of being satiated, we could be satisfied.

"Blessed are the merciful, for they shall receive mercy."

I thought I was a merciful person until I compared my behavior with that of real mercy-givers. Then my mercy paled into niceness. Although appreciated in a cordial way, nice is shallow like a puddle, whereas mercy is deep like a well. Its value cannot be measured in words, for mercy in action is a verb of the richest, highest, and purest kind. Allow me to share with you some "mercy drops" in hopes that some of the mercy might splash over on the rest of us "nice" folks.

When my friend Rose heard of unkind words that had been said against me by a vindictive woman, she wept. Her tears did more for my pain than a thousand condolences could have. Rose extended mercy to me.

My Aunt Pearl, in her late seventies, traveled 600 miles to help our family. She took the all-night shift for weeks, sitting at my mother's beside in the hospital. Aunt Pearl extended mercy to my mom.

When Carol's son died, her new friend Ruth Manus came to the funeral home and sat quietly for the better part of the day. Her silent vigil was for Carol a strong mercy.

Virginia and Lauren, close friends, gave birth to daughters a short time apart. Lauren became ill, and Virginia became the wet nurse to Lauren's baby. Virginia offered more than her milk to a baby; she extended mercy to a concerned mother.

My friend Lana guided her mother-in-law through the healing of broken relationships before her death to cancer. That was more than being supportive; Lana extended tender mercy.

Don, a friend, was recovering from back surgery and was sitting on the beach, too weak and unsteady to join his friends in the water. One friend noticed Don sitting alone and offered to assist him to the water. Once at the water, the friend held onto Don, steadying him so the waves wouldn't knock him down. Then he helped him back to his towel. This friend extended to Don a hand of mercy.

We lived at a youth camp for several years. One summer, a camper was to receive a three-whack discipline by the camp supervisor for disruptive and disrespectful behavior. But just before the swats were administered, a junior counselor stepped in, took the shaking camper's place, and bore his pain. The young counselor extended to that rebellious boy Christlike mercy.

The "mercy drops" I've listed remind us that mercy goes beyond common courtesy to compassion in action. Mercy extends tender regard to those who are suffering, just as Jesus administered mercy when He freed a frenzied man; wrote a love letter in the sand; spoke to the wanton woman at the well; wept over Jerusalem; consigned His mother's care to John; and then—unselfishly, compassionately, and mercifully—died for us on Calvary's cross.

13

Amplitude
(am´ple tōōd) n.

Dictionary's definition:
Fullness.

Patsy's definition:
Plenty good.

HAVE YOU EVER wished you could be a mouse in the house of someone with a great mind, perhaps Oswald Chambers, Hannah Whitall Smith, or Louisa May Alcott? I actually have had the benefit of traveling and speaking with an exceptional individual, Florence Littauer.

Florence does incredible things with her mind. She uses it, which is what I thought I did with mine until I joined the staff of her Christian Leaders and Speakers Seminars (CLASS), where I served for 10 years. Then I discovered my brain was operating on only one cell . . . sporadically. The rest of my brain cells were evidently out to recess. Florence's cells were not only sitting at their desks paying attention, but they were also prolific.

Florence demonstrated by example the importance of mental agility. She would quiz us, challenge us, and stimulate our interest with visuals, articles, and books. She regaled her staff with her wit and wisdom and had a presence about her that drew the attention and interest of total strangers. She moved through a room with confidence and charisma. Her striking appearance and flamboyant style were only transcended by her wellspring of creativity.

After one particularly exhausting speakers class, we, the staff, stayed on at the hotel for a Christmas party. We all pictured ourselves camping out around the pool and soaking in the Jacuzzi until we shriveled up. Our first morning off we met for breakfast, and then we planned to kick back and relax.

Florence, the Energizer Bunny, had other ideas. She handed out job descriptions to each of us for the party that evening. Job descriptions? We had just planned to show up and eat. Instead, however, she sent us off to the mall with partners to collect all the items necessary for our part in the Christmas celebration.

Francine Jackson and I were assigned to give out awards to each staff person. "Awards? For what?" we asked Florence. She smiled and, with a twinkle in her eye, said, "That's up to the two of you." Puzzled and frazzled, we grumbled our way over to the mall.

At first, Francine and I were like two walking blanks. But when we started to move out of our tired 'tude and into our assignment, our creativity began to flow. With the ideas came something else unexpected—energy and excitement. We laughed at our award choices and giggled over how we would present them. Soon we were buzzing around the stores, having a grand time. Once we completed our scavenger hunt, we had just enough time to hurry back to our room, wrap the awards, and dress for dinner.

When we entered our private dining quarters for the evening, our mouths fell open at the splendor of the room. The candles on the tables illuminated the golden apple sitting on each plate; wrapped gifts glittered; and we had our very own chef. It was obvious Florence had put a great deal of thought into this event.

After a fabulous, flaming meal, the program began. We laughed until we cried at the poems, titles, awards, and especially the music. Lana Bateman and Barbara Bueler, two classmates, selected old songs to portray personality temperaments and then acted them out. They were hilarious, and we saw a side of Lana and Barbara we had never seen before. I think they surprised even themselves.

By the time the evening was over, I was so relaxed and renewed that I was sorry to see it end. It was truly one of the most delightful parties I had ever attended, and all because Florence had challenged us to think and act creatively. She put stretch marks on our brains and left imprints on our hearts. I learned that the more effort I'm willing to invest, the greater the result and the sweeter the memory.

During the years I was involved in CLASS, each seminar day we would break into small groups. As a group leader, I had the joy of watching men and women develop their communication skills. One way we mentally stretched the groups was to give each participant an ad from a magazine and to challenge the student to develop a speech around the ad, including an example from his or her life. Often the class would look at us wide-eyed, certain they couldn't do this. We only gave them five minutes to prepare, and they had to speak for three minutes.

Again and again, however, as the group participants risked thinking in ways they hadn't experienced before, they were thrilled with the results. Many times they would ask to keep their ads to show others and as a reminder for themselves that they were capable of spontaneous mental creativity and clarity, if not downright brilliance.

Our brains can think more, retain more, and process more than we realize. But just as our bodies get flimsy without exercise, so do our minds. Let's try some mental gymnastics to see if we can't firm up and use the ol' cranial for something other than a hat rack (as my dad would say).

How long has it been since you've read a classic? What about taking a course at your local night school? Have you added any new words to your vocabulary lately? (*Samovar* is my newest.) Try some difficult crossword puzzles. Do a study on the life of the apostle Paul. (Did you know Paul was stout, bald, and bowlegged?) Memorize Psalm 100, the Ten Commandments, and the Sermon on the Mount. Teach a Sunday school class. Learn the basics of a new language. Read a book a month for six months. Then write reviews of them and pass on the positive reviews to encourage others to read. (Keep a copy of your reviews. A good book, like a good friend, is worth remembering.)

Visit a museum or an art gallery. Attend a ballet, an opera, or a play, and don't forget to take in a symphony. (A symphony is a bubble bath for the brain.) Have a brainstorming session with someone you respect about a stuck place in your life or a new endeavor. Write a poem, a song, your will, a book (everyone has at least one book in him or her—just ask Florence). Plan a trip on paper, and then take it. Talk to an elderly person; visit with a child; hold an infant. Then write down what you learned from the experience. Invest what you know in an eager recipient. Let someone younger teach you something. Write a children's story, and then find a child to read it to. Allow him or her to critique it.

There really is no end to amplitude opportunities. In fact, why don't you make your own list and act on it? Perhaps one day someone will want to be a mouse in your house!

14

Certitude
(sur´ té tōōd) n.

Dictionary's definition:
Complete assurance.

Patsy's definition:
"I told you so."

HAVE YOU EVER been certain about something or someone, only to be surprised later by a change of heart, a turn of events, or a new revelation? As a young girl, I believed birds stayed dry in the rain by standing in between the drops. My daddy told me that. He also said I could catch a bird if I put salt on its tail. It didn't take long, about one box of Morton's, before I realized my dad was spoofing me. It has taken me much longer to sort out other misconceptions.

My husband and his siblings grew up in a poor and difficult environment. Their childhood lifestyle was very different from the ease of mine. Often I sat spellbound as I listened to them describe their family adventures. One time, Les mentioned that they were so poor (How poor were they?) that their dad rubbed bacon grease on their faces before they left for school so people would think they had eaten breakfast. Just call me gullible, but I believed it for years.

I believed getting married would end all my problems. A week after the wedding, fact turned into fallacy when I realized Les expected me to cook. Then I was sure children were the solution for marital bliss and personal harmony. Six weeks of our baby's colic cured that certainty. I knew owning a car would bring us a sense of well-being. Two weeks later, our new-used car blew an engine, and I blew a gasket. Certainty was fast becoming uncertain.

I know I'm not the only one who has felt this way. Ask little Anne Wallis. She went to her first day of kindergarten certain of what to expect. Things went her way until the end of the day. Then her teacher announced it was time to pick up all the toys. A frown fell over Anne's face as she headed for the teacher. "Miss Ruth," Anne said with her southern drawl and an air of five-year-old authority, "I'm Anne Wallis, and I don't do pick-up."

Well, Miss Ruth and little Miss Anne Wallis had a heart-to-heart discussion regarding Anne's `tude, wherein she was assured by her teacher that her kindergarten future *would* include "pick-up."

I'm on Anne's side. In fact, there are a lot of "up" phrases that feel down: pick up, give up, time's up, get up, throw up, grow up, and shut up. Yet I can say with certainty I've done them all. (Well, I'm still working on one of them. Okay, maybe two.) Anyway, just about the time we think we're certain about "things," somebody changes the script.

My niece Susan assisted with a singing group at her church. Called the Music Sprouts, the singers were three- and four-year-olds. The song they learned was "Praise Ye the Lord." Gratefully, it was a song of few words and constant repetition, making it easier for everyone to memorize. After practice one evening, Susan heard a little sprout practicing her lines as she left the church. In her clearest voice she sang, "Crazy the Lord, hallelujah! Crazy the Lord, hallelujah!"

Sometimes when I'm not certain what the Lord is doing, I sing that same song. The Lord is unpredictable; you can almost predict it. I remember the time I developed a mysterious cough. I sounded like a wounded seal in labor with triplets. My cough registered a 7.2 on the Richter scale. It became so debilitating that I couldn't even lie down to sleep but had to be propped up with pillows. All night, as I tried to snooze in an upright position, my head bobbed around as if I were dunking for apples.

This bobbing and barking had been going on for about three months (Les was ready to mount me on his dashboard) when a lady in a restaurant heard my cough, came up, and told me she was certain she could help me. She then insisted I come by her place and try a natural remedy she had.

I nodded my head in consent on the outside, but I shook my head "no" on the inside. I had already tried more weird concoctions than I had previously known existed. Besides, she wasn't a believer, so how could she help me? I was certain that if the Lord wanted to help me, He would use one of His own—thank you.

But somehow we ended up at her doorstep. She handed me a bottle of teensy Ping-Pong-ball pills to be held under my tongue. I envisioned slam-dunking them into the garbage when I got home. Then, as if she had read my mind, she opened the bottle and spilled several into my hand to take in front of her. I hadn't counted on that. I reluctantly ingested them, took the bottle, and left murmuring.

I was certain iridescent flowers would sprout from my ears in reaction to the strange medication. Instead, however, within a few hours, Les noticed I wasn't coughing as much and suggested I take more of the pills. I did.

In two days, I was well. I was breathing normally, sleeping horizontally, and finally free of my hacking cough. Who would have thunk it: a nonbeliever used by the Lord for one of His own. "Crazy the Lord, hallelujah!"

Come to think of it, wasn't that the theme song of the Israelites, the Pharisees, and some others who couldn't figure out what unpredictable God was up to? Why, take a look at poor, baffled Gideon. He was a young man who learned he was God's choice to lead his people into battle. Shaken at having been selected for this post, Gideon whipped out a current résumé to prove how unqualified he was.

The angel, undaunted, commanded Gideon to stand tall in his own strength.

Gideon then asked the angel for *his* résumé. Gideon was certain one of them was crazy. After all, he knew for certain that he had been sneaking around to hide from the enemy, so why had the angel of the Lord referred to him as a valiant soldier? (I think the confusion here was that Gideon looked back on what *was,* while the angel looked forward to what *would be.*)

The angel of God responded to Gideon's need for proof by creating a consuming fire on a rock. Then he disappeared and spoke without a human form to Gideon.

Now, I don't know about you, but that would have been enough proof for me. In fact, forget the fire. One flick of that angel's Bic and I would have signed on the dotted line. Actually Gideon did, for a while. But then he lapsed into uncertainty—I think he wanted to be sure no one was pulling the fleece over his eyes—and made extreme requests of the Lord. (Check out Gideon's wet-wool/dry-wool tangent in Judges 6:36-40.)

The Lord not only answered Gideon's requests, but He also responded with a few unusual requests of His own. You might say the angel asked Gideon to take potshots at the enemy, for his soldiers were armed not with Uzis but with trumpets, empty pots, and torches to place inside the pots (pitchers). If ever there was a time to sing "Crazy the Lord," that would seem to have been it. (I know I'd have been humming a few bars.)

But surprisingly, once Gideon took his place as leader, the men followed him into battle. They honked their horns, flashed their lights, and sang, "For the Lord and Gideon." They caused such a ruckus that the enemy created its own deadly traffic jam.

My, my, the Lord certainly has His ways. And I've noticed they certainly don't seem to be our ways. I guess it's not so important for us to be certain of what or how the Lord will perform His will, but just to be certain He will.

I do understand Gideon's reluctance to believe the best when he felt he was the worst. In my twenties, I was not only an agoraphobic, but I was also addicted to tranquilizers, caffeine, and nicotine. I smoked two packs of cigarettes a day for years. After becoming a believer, I wanted to quit, but my addiction was strong, and I was weak. I repeatedly asked the Lord to deliver me, but it wasn't happening.

Then there came a voice from heaven. No, it wasn't the angel of the Lord, but it was nonetheless an angel (unaware). My Jewish friend Louie said to me, "You're using all your strength to give up smoking. Don't worry about the cigarettes. Instead, take that strength and use it to fall more deeply in love with Jesus, and one day the cigarettes will give *you* up."

Following my talk with Louie, I attended Bible studies, church, and women's retreats, nurturing my love for Jesus. Then it happened . . . I was certain it was time.

I was at a friend's house, and I told Rose the cigarettes were ready to give me up. She called to Daryl, another friend, to join us in the kitchen. Rose then announced that we would pray, but first we would anoint me with oil. She checked her cupboard and found she was out of oil. "Not to worry," Rose said, because she had a can of Crisco. She scooped out a dollop on her finger and splatted it onto my forehead. (Do you know what happens when Crisco meets body heat?) I felt like a french fry. Rose then offered to lead the prayer. My thought was, *Good. While she prays, I'll dab the Crisco from my drippy eyebrows*. Then she and Daryl placed their hands on my shoulders and prayed. And I never smoked again.

What a strange service! But I guess that if the Lord could use pots and trumpets for Gideon's victory, He could certainly use a kitchen and Crisco for giddy me. Praise ye the Lord!

The next time you discover certitude has turned into uncertainty, you might try humming a few bars of "Crazy the Lord." It will remind you that what at first crazes us can turn into praises to Him. Of that you can be certain.

15

Longitude

(län´ je to͞od) n.

Dictionary's definition:
Measurable distance.

Patsy's definition:
The long and lonely distance between
two hearts.

I LIVE IN A small but fast-growing community. Our house is close to downtown on a lovely, tree-lined street. Our modest home sits nestled among similar houses. My immediate neighbors are warm and friendly. We often chat over our fences about the weather, our flowers, and our families. My loving husband is usually at my side, and our grown sons are, gratefully, a constant part of our lives. My phone rings endlessly, and I've been blessed with many friends. My mailbox is often plump with thoughtful cards and notes. So how, with wonderful people surrounding me, could I ever feel a long, lonely distance between myself and others? Yet at times I do.

Loneliness for me is like a dull ache, a sadness, a feeling of being forgotten. It feels as if I'm calling for help down a long, empty hall. When I'm lonely, I feel misunderstood, neglected, and separate. I'm then a prime candidate for self-pity to come visiting. Actually, it's more than a visit, for self-pity brings her endless supply of tissues and becomes a sniveling houseguest, uninvited yet indulged.

How is it that so many people (6 billion) live on earth, and yet longitudes are one of our greatest emotional and relational battles? It's certainly not a new battle, but it seems that as time goes by and our population enlarges, the distance between us only increases. You would think that the more people who inhabit the world, the less loneliness there would be. *Unless loneliness isn't caused or resolved by people.* Hmm.

Could it be that loneliness began when Adam and Eve opted to go their own way? I wonder if the ache within could be a call to our hearts to turn toward Home? Perhaps loneliness is a scary siren to remind us that people are unable, try as they might, to move close enough to ease our deep discomfort and disconnection. If that's so, is it possible that loneliness is actually an evangelist, a teacher, even a friend?

The evangelistic side of loneliness reminds us that only One hears our unspoken words, and that our unformed thoughts are in His conscious awareness. The teacher part of loneliness points out our inability to draw sufficient comfort from others or ourselves in these forlorn moments. The friend in loneliness might try to convince us that in and of ourselves we're insufficient, but our sufficiency is in Christ.

Loneliness has the potential to guide us to the friend who is able to stick closer than a brother. But potential can turn to poison when, instead of responding to truth, we indulge our loneliness until it becomes a melancholy mind-set, a distorted way of thinking, seeing, and feeling. At times we entertain our sadness and become dependent on our despondency to extent to us a sick sort of comfort.

I took a spontaneous poll at our local eatery, Lynn's Cafe, this afternoon. I asked the owner and her family, workers, and patrons when they were most aware of being lonely. They all agreed the pangs were greatest when they were with others rather than when they were by themselves.

One of the customers said, "There's no type of loneliness more painful than when you're married and feel alone while in the presence of your mate."

To that one gal replied, "I was talking with a single friend, and she was saying she felt lonely. I told her that when you're alone you expect at times to feel that way. But when you're married, you anticipate your mate will fill that empty place. When he can't or won't, it's more devastating than being by yourself."

What I heard them say is that a deafening distance can exist between two people even in the same house, the same room, the same bed. Also, people are limited, by desire and design, in what they can do to relieve each other's inner emptiness.

I wonder if that's how David felt (empty) when he had been deserted by friends turned foe. David cried out to the Lord, "Turn to me" (Ps. 25:16). It sounds as if David felt not only a long distance away from God, but also that God had turned His attention elsewhere and was unaware of David's dilemma. David continued, "For I am lonely and afflicted." I guess we all feel abandoned when we're under attack, especially when we're persecuted unfairly.

Paul knew about persecution and loneliness from both sides of the fence. For he (Saul) not only persecuted others for their faith, but he (Paul—new name) also suffered at the hands of others for his faith. Perhaps it was in lonely moments that he wrote, "For our citizenship is in heaven, from which also we eagerly wait for a Savior, the Lord Jesus Christ" (Phil. 3:20), and "We . . . prefer rather to be absent from the body and to be at home with the Lord" (2 Cor. 5:8).

At some point in his dramatic life, Paul realized we weren't going to be at home totally (even with ourselves) until we stepped on heaven's shore. Then the disturbing distance between us and others would disappear. Any disconnected feeling between us and the Lord would be over, and our inner and outer struggles with loneliness would be eternally resolved.

Until then, we need to keep on keeping on. It's not easy to carry on when you're feeling alone, which is why it's important to expect to feel separation at times (from God, others, and ourselves) as part of our fallen condition. That way, the long-distance times can't sneak up on us and leave us distraught, but we can lean into our loneliness and learn.

Jesus promised never to leave us, and He is a promise keeper. Our times of loneliness don't testify to His absence in our lives, but rather the loneliness allows us to feel our human dilemma (of limitations) from which only He can rescue us. The Lord didn't say He would shelter us from the full range of human emotions, from joy to devastation and from sweet fellowship to acute loneliness. Our emotions don't alter God's constancy in our lives. Instead, negative emotions often prompt us to search out the positive principles of His unfailing presence.

One of the tender artistic portrayals of Christ as shepherd that stands out in my mind is entitled "Lost Lamb." The artist shows Christ as He leans over the side of a cliff and extends His shepherd's crook around a bewildered lamb on a ledge. You know He will then draw the lonely creature into the safety of His arms.

The next time you feel lost and lonely, remember there is One who longs for you to know you're not alone. The good Shepherd knows you by name, and He will travel the long distance on your behalf. He will search the widest pasture, the steepest highlands, the deepest valley, and even the most desolate desert to help you find your way, so intense is His love for you.

16

Ineptitude
(in ept´ e tood) n.

Dictionary's definition:
Unsuitable.

Patsy's definition:
Oops!

AFTER REPEATED EPISODES of Marvin's garbage being ripped apart by some varmint, Marvin just wanted the vandalism to stop. Then one evening, he took the garbage out, and—aha—a raccoon was hot-footing it for the big maple out front. Marv, being a hunter from way back, instinctively grabbed his bow and arrows with the thought of ending the mania of this midnight marauder.

Marv took aim, and the arrow took flight. It hit the masked scavenger but didn't finish him off. Marv, who was usually an accurate marksman, was concerned because he didn't want the scamp to suffer needlessly. He shot a couple more times, but now his target darted higher into the tree, and Marv had trouble seeing through the leaves. The

neighbors weren't having any trouble seeing, however, and what they saw they didn't like. Evidently
they thought Marv was the Big Bad Wolf and the
raccoon was Little Red Riding Hood. The neighbors
called in reinforcements.

When the police arrived, no one was more surprised than Marv, who thought he was ridding the
neighborhood of a rascal. Well, the policeman must
have had a soft spot for raccoons, because he
thought Marv was the rascal. Within a short time,
the animal protection people were on the scene, as
well as the fire department, which had arrived with
a ladder rig to assist in the rescue of Little Red Riding Hood. A crowd from the surrounding homes
formed. People took turns pointing at the Big Bad
Wolf, who was now seated in the back of the patrol
car.

After repeated attempts to rescue the raccoon
failed (the coon had climbed beyond the reach of
the ladder), a cherry picker from the city was called
in. And the woman from the animal protection
group set up a tent under the tree to spend the
night in case they couldn't reach the raccoon before
morning.

Marv felt stuck in a bad dream. But he woke up
when the police slapped him with a ticket. It was
now midnight, and a police car, a fire truck, an animal rights vehicle, a cherry picker, and a disgruntled crowd stood in front of his home. Finally, the
coon was caught and Marv was released.

But Marv's story didn't end there. No, he still had
to go to court and pay fines and the city's cost in
sending out vehicles. Then there was the newspaper article informing the community of his mis-
deed.

Oh, by the way, the Big Bad Wolf turned out to be a sheep in wolf's clothing. Marv was the pastor of the church I attend. You can only imagine what kind of complications this brought him ("a man of the cloth caught cooning"). Marvin contritely went before the church and apologized for any embarrassment he had brought on the congregation. He said that in retrospect, he realized he hadn't thought through his action and hadn't imagined the uproar it would cause. His choice to pursue the raccoon, he confessed, was inept.

Marvin is one of the dearest, sincerest, and funniest men you would ever want to meet. He handled his humiliation with appropriate regret and then took a tremendous amount of ribbing from the congregation. In time, the scandal settled down (yes, we live in a small town). But have you ever noticed that the thing you wish people would forget is what seems to linger in their minds?

Some months later, it was Marv's fiftieth birthday, and the church put on a surprise shindig for him. At one point during the hoopla, we blindfolded Marv, and my husband, Les, came out in a raccoon suit carrying a bow and arrow. The group guffawed, stomped the floor, and beat on the tables until everyone was almost sick. Marv was still blindfolded and chuckling as he tried to imagine what riotous thing was occurring.

Finally, we uncovered his eyes just as Super Coon drew back his bow and pointed it in Marv's direction. Good-natured Marv spotted the 200-pound raccoon and bent over to give the raccoon an ample target. What fun we had that night as we let our pastor know he was loved and that we realized we're all inept at times!

Marv wore his mistake well. He wasn't defensive, he didn't deny his actions, and he took responsibility in court and in church. After years of chiding, he has kept up his chin but not his back.

My back was up so high recently that I was five inches taller than usual. Les and I had just parked our car in a mall parking area. Because of my husband's severe health issues, we have a handicap permit, but Les doesn't *look* handicapped. As we stepped out of our car, a woman walking toward the store suddenly turned around and said, "Did you know that's a handicap spot?"

Immediately my hackles went up, and I responded, "We certainly do."

"Well, I don't see your permit," she said accusingly.

"Well, it's there," I snapped, and then added, "and we've had it for years."

The woman took a couple of steps toward the door and then turned back and said, "You know, you really shouldn't get angry. You should be grateful I'm checking."

"I do understand your concern," I replied, "but I felt your tone was accusatory."

She and I continued to walk toward the store, and then she turned and said, "If you'd hang your handicap tag from your mirror instead of laying it on your dash, people wouldn't have to challenge you."

Certain I should have the last word, I shot back, "I think it's up to my husband where he places his tag." With that I marched away, and she headed in a huff in another direction.

I hadn't taken five steps when I stopped, realizing I had just experienced a major ineptitude episode, and I needed to do something pronto. I knew if I waited even a few minutes, I would lose that woman and possibly never have the chance to take responsibility for my behavior. I spotted her and started down an aisle in her direction. She saw me coming and seemed to grow taller in preparation. When I reached her I said, "You were right, and I shouldn't have been so defensive. There was no reason for that. And we'll take your suggestion under consideration."

As I started to walk away, I heard her say quietly, "Thank you."

What a brouhaha I had created! All I needed to say when she asked if we had a permit was "Yes, we do." Then I could have reminded Les to hang up his permit. "A soft answer turneth away wrath, but grievous words stir up anger" (Prov. 15:1, KJV).

I doubt that woman has had half as much trouble forgiving me as I've had forgiving myself. I'm 50, not 15. I know better than to behave so ineptly.

Perhaps my trigger personality is why I've always had compassion for the disciple Peter. I feel as if I've walked in his hyper-sandals. Talk about inept! Peter couldn't take two steps without tripping over his tongue. His words and actions often slipped out past his better judgment. He either said too much or not enough. Or worse yet, in a fit of fury, he would rearrange people's anatomies, like the time he lopped off the Roman soldier's ear.

I'm reminded of Alexander Pope's description, "a brain of feathers and a heart of lead." Gratefully, Peter had a lot of heart—no lead there. I'd like to think I have a big heart, too. But about the other, well, I guess if the feathers fit, we have to wear them—at least until we purpose to think before we speak and act. That's not to say that even thinking will always keep us from being, looking, or sounding inept. Sometimes our information is just plain faulty.

Greta Propps waited eagerly for the principal to call her name for her junior high school diploma and outstanding student award. This was an exciting moment as she looked forward to entering high school. The long line in front of her at the commencement services slowly diminished until finally, it was her moment to rise and shine. The principal cleared his throat and succinctly announced her name into the microphone: "Gurta Poops." Well, the audience loved it. The principal was stymied by the crowd's response. And "Gurta" almost lived up to her name. But the principal had read correctly. Somebody, ineptly, had typed Greta's name wrong not only on the list of graduating students, but also on her trophy. Imagine displaying that *faux pas* for future generations.

Making an honest mistake with a name is one thing, but trying to make a raccoon into a pincushion (like Marv), a stranger into an enemy (like Patsy), or a guard into a hearing aid candidate (like Peter) are more deliberate and blatant forms of ineptitude. It becomes harder for others to forgive our foolishness and extremely difficult for us to forgive ourselves.

I love the picture of Jesus when He looked back at Peter after he had betrayed Him. I believe it was not a look of condemnation but one of deep compassion. Peter left the Lord's gaze devastated by his own ineptitude. After the resurrection, however, Jesus sent back a special message to Peter so that he might be assured of his place in the Savior's heart.

I'm grateful Peter wasn't perfect, because I identify with his flighty, forceful personality. Peter is like a message of hope from the Savior for all of us who experience ineptitude. We are loved, 'tudes and all.

17

Similitude
(sim´ e le to͞od) n.

Dictionary's definition:
Resemblance.

Patsy's definition:
Mirror, mirror on the wall.

MY FRIEND CAROL and I have similar interests. We're both antique buffs (not to mention we're both antiques), and we enjoy our collections of teapots and cookbooks, our artistic endeavors, entertaining children, and eating Finnish pastries. But if you were to compare our physical similarities, there aren't any. Carol is a skyscraper, and I'm a scanty shanty. Carol has enormous eyes; they're about the size of coconut pies. My eyes are slim slits similar to those of a cat-napping Siamese. Carol has an elongated, casual stride. I take short, snappy steps. We also are dissimilar in our personalities. Carol is reticent. I'm loquacious. Carol looks for others to take the lead. I could have been a dictator. So even though we share a similitude in some areas, we're very different.

My son Jason and I look like tic and tac. My son Marty and my husband, Les, look like bric and brac. Jason and I are fair-skinned, blue-eyed blonds. Marty and Les are darker-skinned, with brown hair and brown-and-hazel eyes. In our family pictures, we look like two sets of bookends.

When Jason was in high school, I went with him to attend a program for parents. I was concerned it would embarrass him if I walked at his side, so I offered to trail in after him. He said, "It won't matter, Mom; one look at you and everyone will know we belong together anyway." It was true; we're that similar.

But a closer examination would tell you how opposite we are. Jason has a hammock mind (slow and easy), whereas I'm more of a blender brain (lots of thoughts spinning around, all mixed together). Jason avoids conflict, and I'm challenged by it. He's naturally cautious, while I'm given to spontaneity. His favorite word is *chill.* Mine is *thrill.* We're similar; yet we're different.

I like being my own unique person, although I long to be similar and to connect with others. It's often a relief when someone else admits to a fault that I have but haven't admitted (like overdosing on Godiva chocolates). It sounds as if misery loves company, but it's more, because relating, even in a fault, gives a sense of belonging and normality. Yet as much as we need to identify closely with others, we fight to maintain our distinctiveness. Aren't we a peculiar lot?

When Carol and I were growing up, we would often wear matching outfits, except we would buy them in different colors. (There's that struggle again; we want to be like others . . . sorta.) One summer, we both bought beach hats, and even though we couldn't stand for the other to have a hat unless we did, too, we couldn't bring ourselves to buy identical hats. Carol's looked like a spaceship, while mine looked like the landing pad. Similar, yet, well, you know . . . different.

My friend Ann tells of being at the mall with her husband, Paul. It was crowded, and they were moving through the crowds, window-gazing as they walked. Ann glanced into a store and then turned back and took Paul's hand. As she did, she looked up at Paul, only to find she was holding the hand of a stranger! Shocked and embarrassed, she tossed the startled man's hand as if it were a hot coal and turned to find Paul casually strolling behind her. Hands can look so similar.

My mom, Rebecca, had three sisters, Elvira, Hazel, and Pearl. Not surprisingly, because they were sisters, their hands looked alike, with plump fingers. They were hands that knew work, hard work as well as healing work. Those eight hands touched many lives—not only their families', but also friends', neighbors', coworkers', and patients'. Each was her own dynamic person, but they all connected with other at an important level, the level of human need. Those sisters shared a similitude by the way they extended their hands to help those less fortunate.

At a weekend retreat I attended in the South, I was aware of a small cluster of women as they entered. Three of the gals were similar in appearance. They interacted freely and extended themselves warmly to others. But the fourth woman in the group didn't resemble the others and stood off to the side, uninvolved.

The oldest woman was a hands-on gal, a real hugger. She enthusiastically worked her way around the room, hugging everyone as she went. She seemed to sincerely care for others, and I looked forward to meeting her. Sure enough, when I did, I received a hug, too. It was one of those big-momma hugs, the kind that says you're loved and prayed for, the kind that makes you want to behave.

I found not later that the two similar young women were her daughters. The hesitant gal was her daughter-in-law. The energetic mom continued through the retreat to reach out compassionately to those around her, as did her delightful daughters. The daughter-in-law stayed physically near to her family while maintaining an emotional distance from everyone.

After my closing session, the mother came to me in tears. She said that as she had stood up to leave the retreat, she had turned to retrieve her sweater off the back of her chair and had noticed her daughter-in-law seated behind her, crying. "Now," she said to me, "you may not think that's a big deal, but this girl has been in our family for eight years, and we've never seen her shed a tear. When she married my son, I was excited, because she was an orphan and I was a mother with more love than I knew what to do with. I was certain the Lord had brought us together so that I might give her the mother's love she had never known. But she wasn't interested in my affection or my willingness to nurture her. Year after year I've reached out to her, and she has resisted all my attempts.

"When I saw her crying today, I found myself risking another rejection as I moved toward her to comfort her. I was certain that once again she would push me away. But instead, as I encircled her with my arms, she fell into them and sobbed. I held her and rocked her. When her sobbing eased into teardrops, she looked up at me and said, 'Oh, Momma, I love you.'"

What a sweet time of rejoicing we had as we celebrated this loving breakthrough! Their differences had separated them, love connected them, and for the first time, the mother-in-law and daughter-in-law became family emotionally.

Since that day, I have often thought of the tenaciousness of that little mother-in-law who didn't give up on her daughter-in-law but hung in for the long haul. No one would have blamed her if she had thrown up her hands in frustration after eight years of rejection and walked away from the relationship. But instead, she waited out her daughter-in-law, then extended her hands, not to push away her daughter-in-law, but to draw her in, close to that big mother's heart. The wall of differences was broken down by the power of love.

It was interesting to me that, as the mother and daughter-in-love walked away, they now looked so, so . . . similar. Somehow the new beginning in their relationship had brought about a transformation even in their appearances.

When my son Jason was seven, I noticed one day that he was studying me closely. "Mom," he said, "do you know who I think of when I look at you?"

Amused and interested, I asked, "No, who?"

"Me," he quickly responded.

Wouldn't it be glorious if one day our heavenly Father told us we had become so conformed, so similar to His Son that when He looked at us, He was reminded of Himself?

18

Vicissitude
(vi sis´ e tōōd) n.

Dictionary's definition:
Change.

Patsy's definition:
Discombobulate.

Change jobs, change tires, change diapers, change doctors, change directions, change addresses, change underwear, change hair color—change, change, change. The world is in flux—just ask my dog, Pumpkin. Pumpkin is in menopause, which means exactly that, men-oh-pause. She's very touchy. Just ask my nephew Nicholas. He made the mistake of kissing her when she wasn't in the mood. Warning! Warning! Do not, I repeat, do not do that to a woman in flux. Nicholas now wears a small memento of that occasion on his cheek, and it's not lipstick.

I know Pumpkin is in her change, because she has little growling spells even when no one is near her. She also insists on going outside far more frequently than before. Once on the lawn, she can't seem to remember why she's out there. The other day, she turned around in circles 22 times before she found an acceptable blade of grass to receive her offering—definitely a sign of menopausal indecision. Also, hair is sprouting out of her ears, the skin on her tummy has funny things growing on it, her coat has thinned, her skin has thickened, she has gained weight, and she's always tired. Yep, as I said, this dog's going through her change.

I wonder why change always seems to come with a price tag. I know I find it costly when I change locations as frequently as I do. I often fly back and forth across the country changing time zones, weather conditions, water supplies, and types of food. These variations keep my body and mind topsy-turvy, not to mention my stomach.

One day last spring, I rose early to take a flight to Dallas. I was feeling strange. By the time I left for the airport, Les and I were both aware I had the flu. We grabbed a Hefty bag for any emergency that might arise on the drive. We arrived at Detroit Metro, and halfway through the airport, everyone around me became aware I was not well. We were all grateful I had come equipped for an emergency.

I should have gone home and straight to bed, but for some reason I can't explain, I thought if I could just get to my destination, I'd be fine. I didn't want to change my plans if I could help it. Les reluctantly watched me stagger onto the plane as I embraced a new Hefty.

Ten minutes into the flight, I realized it would be in everyone's best interest if I took up residence in the rest room. Which I did. Knowing I couldn't stay indefinitely, however, after a lengthy visit, I stepped out and found myself face to face with a flight attendant. She took one look at me and insisted I take her jump seat next to the bathroom. Which I did. (Maybe she was hoping I'd jump.)

Now, either flyers were distributed on the plane telling of the sickee aboard, or my pasty-white skin fringed in vivid green was the giveaway. Whatever the reason, every passenger who wanted to use the rest room would look at me for consent before entering. I would lower my eyelids once for yes or knock them back three aisles (as I bolted for the cubicle) for no.

At one point, a male attendant knelt next to me and told me he had talked with my son before the flight had left Detroit. I muttered, "How nice, but that was my husband." Then the attendant looked kind of green. I was so ill I didn't even mind his flub . . . although I did breathe on him before disembarking.

By the time I arrived at the hotel, I had one goal—go to bed and never get up. I was too sick to speak that night or the next morning. I could have helped my situation if I had just stayed home. Then I at least could have taken care of myself and not risked spreading my affliction. But the last-minute change would have inconvenienced many people, and I didn't want to pay the price of disappointing anyone. So instead I showed up looking and feeling as if I had the bubonic plague and ultimately disappointed people anyway.

Change is difficult, whether it's changing locations or changing our minds.

We've often heard it said, "These are changing times." Actually, times have always been changing. Times are different for my adult children than they were for me, just as my times were different from my mom's, whose were different from her mom's.

My Mamaw (grandmother), Thanie Elizabeth Griffin McEuen, walked on this earth's turf for more than 97 years. She was born in the horse-and-buggy days and lived to see men on the moon. Even though her world saw radical changes, Thanie still found personal change difficult.

I remember family members had to do a heap of talkin' to get Mamaw to give up her icebox and buy a refrigerator. Those newfangled things didn't seem that necessary to her. And that was her approach toward most new things that would alter what she was used to. I never did succeed in getting her to wear a pair of slacks. Her spindly little legs were always freezing, and I thought slacks would warm her right up. But she had never worn a pair in her life and didn't plan to start at this late date, "thank ye kindly."

Thanie stuck to her ways a bit too emphatically one time when she was going to stay at my parents' home for an extended visit. She came out of her house carrying her chamber jar. My mom is hospitable, but not that hospitable. Mamaw and my dad had quite a debate over that piece of porcelain before he finally convinced her we had a sufficient water closet to meet her needs.

I guess vicissitude can be scary, because change does have an uncertain (I don't know what's going to happen) element to it. Our younger son, Jason, was married last September to a beautiful young woman named Danya. We were excited and happy for the newlyweds, but in the back of my mind, I knew I would be faced for the first time in 30 years with an empty nest. No doubt about it, an empty nest is different—not bad, but different. I confess, though, that I did have a couple of misty moments as the long-term reality settled in.

My friend Nancy was a big promoter of the notion that when a young person graduates from high school, you should present him or her with a sack lunch and a road map. She had been telling me for years: When kids are old enough, let them experience life. Nudge (or shove) them out of the nest, and let them fly.

Then it came time for her only son, Matt, to graduate from high school, and he chose to attend a college in the East. Nancy was delighted. The change didn't bother her in the least . . . until she was walking through the grocery store a couple of days after he had left and she spotted his favorite cereal. Then she lost it.

Nancy's husband, David, came home from work that day and found Nancy slumped over her son's bed, weeping. The change in change caught her off guard.

Nancy and I have since giggled about how easy it is to theorize, but theory is a long emotional distance from reality. And the reality is, change often comes with a painful transitional period.

Dorcas was trying to help her 11-year-old son, Jacob, transition from childish actions to responsible behavior. He was a delightful boy, but Dorcas was having trouble getting him to turn off the light in his room before leaving for school. In her attempts to convince him to change, she tried a number of creative tactics, but repeatedly when she passed his room, he would be gone, and the light would be on.

One day, she had had it. Dorcas let Jacob know he would suffer some nasty consequences if his light wasn't turned off before he left that day. Satisfied she had made her point, she busied herself until she heard him leave. Once he was out the door, she made a beeline upstairs to see if he had finally responded to her demands. To her relief and amazement, the light was off. And then she began to giggle. Jacob had turned out his *overhead* light, but he had left on his closet light, the hall light, the night light, and the bathroom light. Dorcas said, "Jacob obeyed the letter of the law while totally destroying the spirit."

I've been there, Jacob. I, too, have done what I felt forced to do, but not in the most honorable way. I've apologized in a snarling fashion because I felt I had to and not because I wanted to take responsibility. I've done a good deed because it was expected rather than from a caring heart. I've acted sweet while sportin' an acidic 'tude. More times than I'd like to believe, I've done the right thing in the wrong way.

That brings us to the most important change of all—the change of the human heart.

We can change a number of things in this life, but many we can't. Our heart is a can't. Try as we might to be good and do right, we fall miserably short of wholeness or holiness without Jesus. The wonderful news is He will not only change our hearts at our invitation, but He will also help us through unavoidable changes. He will assist us with the cost of change, the uncertainty of change, and the adjustments necessary during change, whether that be the ticking of our biological clocks, unexpected health issues, or feeling the pangs of watching our last little chicks sprout wings and fly. That's good news for a change, don't you think?

19

Loony 'Tudes

(loo´ ne toods) n.

Dictionary's definition:
Strange and unusual.

Patsy's definition:
My kooky comrades.

I'M CONVINCED THAT the Lord, who created us in His own image, laughs. And I'm certain He meant for us to laugh until we cry as an emotional safety valve. He knew life would pile up inside us, and a sense of humor would help us to shovel our way out of our serious circumstances. At times, laughter must be as sweet an offering to Him as tears and even prayers.

My mom and her sisters didn't believe in foolishness, but they sure believed in a good time. They worked hard and laughed hard. I always looked forward to being with them, even as a child. The smell of down-home cooking and the sound of goodhearted laughter were an unforgettable combination.

I have been blessed to have not only a heritage and a husband of humor, but also a passel of loony 'tude friends. They've helped me survive when life knocked the humor out of me or when I took myself too seriously. Laughter puts life back in its temporal position, lest we think our earthly stint is all there is to this journey. Also, shared laughter leads to an emotional connection with others.

I remember attending a large conference where I noticed a couple of my long-lost friends seated in a row near the front. I decided to join them, which meant I would have to climb over several of them to reach the empty seat. That didn't seem to be a problem—and probably wouldn't have been had I not gained weight.

Forgetting I would need more clearance than in my slim past, I began to slide my body across their laps in an attempt to reach the vacant chair. Well, I made it past Marita, but when I crossed over Becky's lap, the space narrowed, and I didn't. I ended up stuck. Or more accurately, my backside was stuck. And I do mean stuck! Becky had papers, program, and purse in her lap, and somehow I became entangled and Becky became ensnared. The straps of our purses were looped around each other and the chair, tying us securely. We couldn't pull apart the straps or us. I couldn't move sideways or up, and she couldn't move over or back. The more I pulled and tugged, the tighter we became cinched together.

I was now perched on Becky's aerobically thin lap. Both of us were restricted in movement, and to add to our dilemma, we became tickled. The enormous room was fairly dark. That was good. But we were surrounded by thousands of people, and we didn't want to distract them or cause a ruckus. But honestly, we couldn't help ourselves. Becky was laughing so hard she was gasping for air. (That or my added tonnage had knocked the breath right out of her.) I, confused about how I had become permanently affixed to my friend, began to titter. My tittering turned to jostling as my repressed giggles transformed my cellulite body into a human vibrator. I shook so vigorously that I dislodged Becky's papers that had been between us, and they fluttered to the floor. That minute space gave us a little leeway, and with a mighty jerk, I rolled into the empty seat next to my mushed buddy.

We looked at each other, our outfits now askew from our tug-of-war, and we lost it. Tears cascaded down our faces while the arteries in our necks grew alarmingly swollen. Marita looked at us, baffled. She wondered what could possibly have been that funny about our scuffle.

It was one of those times when you not only had to be there, but you also had to be actively involved to understand our reaction. It was unexplainable, but gratefully it was expressible through laughter. Becky and I did gain a wisp of composure but found it necessary to avoid eye contact until after we left the arena, lest we set each other off. Because Becky and I shared deeply an emotion, it added a fun memory to our friendship, enhancing it.

Recently our friends David and Nancy joined Les and me for a northern Michigan, cottage-on-the-lake adventure. They flew in from California for a time of relaxation and fellowship. What we hadn't anticipated was that when the summer residents had moved out of the cottage we were to stay in,

Mickey, Minnie, and several namesakes had moved in.

Signs of their intrusion were, *eek,* everywhere. The invading troops had shredded sugar packets, powdered-cream packets, and tea bags for nesting material. They had set up housekeeping in the pots and pans, and one resident was building a condo in a stove burner. She must have decided on a Southwest decor, because she had dragged in a five-inch feather to enhance her surroundings. And of course a profusion of mouse confetti (if you know what I mean) was sprinkled throughout the premises to announce their ownership of the establishment. It was their little way of claiming squatters' rights, and it was obvious they had been doing that very thing.

Well, it's like this, folks: I don't do mice. No how, no way. I was on my way out the door, headed for higher ground, when the others convinced me we could win against these little varmints. Les and David started the cleanup campaign, while Nancy diverted my attention with the beauty of our surroundings. Then we went to town and bought traps. Lots of traps. Scads of traps. And we placed them all around the house.

That evening we were playing Jenga, a nerve-racking game of building a tower one log at a time, when a trap went off. I almost ate my log. The guys yelled, "All right!" Then they gave each other a high-five victory slap, acting as if they had just struck oil. Nancy and I cried, "Oh, no! Yuck!" Then the big-game hunters went to examine their prize. We heard one say to the other, "Oh, cool. Look at how squished he is. Hey, girls, wanna see?"

What is it about guys and guts, anyway? And why do they love to gross out girls? Talk about loony 'tudes!

The trap snapping continued throughout our four-night stay. The guys were thrilled at the sound of each snared tenant, and we girls were nauseated. In the mornings, Les would say to David, "We'd better check our trap lines." You would have thought they were snaring bear. Afterward, David and Les were sorry they hadn't taken a picture with all their prey dangling between them from a clothesline. They really are a couple of Mouseketeers.

Despite my passionate dislike for those little fur balls with feet (the mice, not the guys), we had great fun. In fact, I'm almost certain that without the little creature-feature, we wouldn't have had such a hilarious adventure. Although. . . .

David, Nancy, Les, and I took a trip out east two years ago, staying at bed and breakfasts, seeing the breathtaking autumn scenery and eating ourselves silly. The farther east we traveled, the more signs we noticed alerting us to moose traffic. Other than Bullwinkle, I'd never seen a moose up close and personal. We were all vigilant in hopes of being the first to spot a moose. Then one day David suddenly let out a yelp. "A moose! A moose!" he repeated in his excitement. His flailing arms pointed back to a road we had passed.

Les, who's always up for an adventure, did a dramatic U-turn and headed pell-mell for the sighting. He careened the van head-long into the road, and there, facing us, was the biggest, fattest barrel you'd ever want to see. Did we ever laugh! Oh, my, all our sides were splitting. Well, David wasn't laughing quite as hard as the rest of us. So for the remainder of the trip, we took turns yelping at barrel sightings just to make David feel better.

Now that I think about it, it wasn't the mice or the moose that added to our vacations. Instead, it was our loony `tude friends who make fun a part of their everyday lives.

Have you ever noticed how some people seem to have a greater capacity for fun and laughter than others? Do you think it's in the genes? Or do you think they purpose to find the good, the positive, and the humorous? Hmm, it might be worth a try.

20

Gratitude
(grat´ e tōōd) n.

Dictionary's definition:
Thankfulness.

Patsy's definition:
Upward tilt of the heart.

THE TOP FOUR things mentioned when you ask folks what they're most thankful for are faith, family, health, and friends. I say "Amen" to that list. And I would add another favorite that causes me to sport a ʼtude of gratitude: seasons.

My senses are activated in autumn. I love the visual splendor of the landscape, the crunchy sound of leaves underfoot, and the crackle of the fireplace dancing in amber delight. Every fall, I drown my innards in fresh apple cider and then fill my face with homemade pumpkin pie. Yum. My cotton gauzes and seersuckers are replaced by my corduroys and cable knits as I prepare for frosty mornings and chilly evenings. My energy level is at its peak during this exhilarating time of the year.

My heart is renewed in spring. I take great delight when, through the lingering snow, the daffodils press their bright yellow faces of anticipation. The gardens are quickened, as is my hope. Just as the frozen soil is warmed by the sun for productivity, so my resistant heart softens in the Son's light for fruitfulness. Spring is winds, wildflowers, wonderment, and whispered promises. My vision is expanded in spring as I watch the warmed earth unfold its fragrant bouquet.

My stress is soothed in summer. The pace of the days allows sanity to seep back into my crowded life. Porch swings, lemonade, baskets of daisies, and strolls through town are some of the casual dividends of this gentle season. Chats over fences, songbirds' serenades, open windows, a nap in the sun—all bring strength back to my weary soul. My mind is mended in this mellow season.

My spirit celebrates in winter. A snowy-white carpet covers my backyard, showcasing silhouetted trees with barren limbs raised in praises. I, too, have little to offer the Bethlehem Child besides my arms raised in gratitude as I think about our world, a frigid land thawed by heaven's Light. The frozen sleep of this season prepares us for spring's revival. My life is instructed by winter's necessity as death gives way to resurrection.

The dailyness of life is filled with seasons, too. We feel winter's blast when relationships seem biting and cold. A mom told me her son had become dependent on cocaine, and with the addiction, their weak relationship withered. Her heart ached with grief over the icy year and a half until her son's destructive journey changed seasons. Through his recovery, his brokenness melted his heart and made room for tenderness, gentleness, and gratitude. Like a spring revival, their mom-and-son relationship moved past their winter of adversity. But the mom is quick to point out that without the bitter winter, there could not have been a blessed spring.

My friend Lana was deserted by her husband and left to figure out a solitary future. During the painful process of establishing her life alone, she would take long walks. Every day, she passed a home with a fence full of cascading roses. One day, the roses' sweet fragrance and beauty captured her undivided attention. As she continued her walk, Lana whispered to the Lord that she wished she could have roses like those. She knew that was unlikely since now she had no one to bring her flowers and she wasn't a gardener.

Weeks passed. Then Lana's friend Penny called and offered her a slip from her great-aunt's flower beds. Lana resisted the offer, knowing how unsuccessful she had been at growing flowers in the past, but Penny came anyway and planted the cutting. In the busyness of all the changes in her life, Lana forgot about the new planting. Spring turned into summer before she walked into her walled-in backyard and discovered that the cutting had flourished. The plant had produced trailing fragrant roses just like the ones for which she had longed. Lana was filled with gratitude for the visual expression of the Gardener's care. Spring unfolded the first signs of hope in a rosebush, which was followed by a summer profusion of His provision.

One year brought a different kind of summer to Michigan, a summer of drought. I remember the country road we lived on formed great walls of dust with every passing vehicle. Flowers were stunted and struggled to open against the searing sun. Bluebirds encircled our birdbath, while flocks of other birds waited on nearby telephone lines for their turn to drink and splash away the heat. Water was restricted to indoor use only, which caused the parched grass to brown underfoot. It was the driest summer I had ever experienced.

The first signs of fall brought relief in the form of nippy breezes and moisture-laden clouds. The thirsty land drank deeply of the cool rains and then responded with brilliant autumn colors. Even the grass greened, enhancing the display.

One friend likened it to a drought in her life when she had suffered a miscarriage. She had waited so long in hopes of conceiving and then lost the child of her heart. She was devastated. Following her loss, her relationship with the Lord felt like a desert, barren like her now-vacant womb. Parched by her depression, she felt alone and lost.

After a long season of wandering in her pain, she began to voice her anger and deep disappointment toward the Lord and herself. That was when she noticed the first signs of change. She felt within her a stirring, not in her womb but in her heart. Color began to return slowly to her life. Relationships mattered to her again. Her energy level improved. And seeing other people's babies no longer caused her such piercing pain. She eventually became aware of the Lord's gentle hand guiding her out of the dry land of loss into an autumn of acceptance.

As her pain level decreased, her understanding increased. She realized the Lord had never left her; like a parent with a sick child, He had remained at her side, waiting for the fever to break. She told me her grief eventually colored her life with compassion and her lips with counsel. She no longer offered easy answers to the hard questions of those who suffered. And most of all, she became thankful for a God who waits with us and walks with us throughout our changing lives.

Rain, sleet, snow, hurricanes, or floods, our Season Maker remains consistent, steadfast, faithful, and available. How grateful I am for the changes of all the seasons!

21

Inner `Tude
(in´ er tōōd) n.

Dictionary's definition:
Secret chambers.

Patsy's definition:
Undisclosed contents.

A YOUNG WOMAN APPROACHED me with a little, black box in her hand when I finished a presentation at a conference. "You've made me laugh," she said, "and now I want to give you something to make you laugh." She handed me the box and instructed me to push a series of buttons.

Each button I pressed had a high-pitched woman's voice screeching out some parental instruction: "Stop it!" "I said, stop it!" "You're going to poke somebody's eye out with that thing!" "You broke it; are you happy now?" When you pushed a master button, the woman proclaimed all four statements in a row like an irritating recital. The woman's cantankerous attitude and her nails-on-chalkboard voice bored a hole right through one's nervous system.

I played the box for the hotel clerk and the waitresses, and I even held it next to the microphone and pushed the buttons for the conference audience. Everyone laughed. I had a great time playing it throughout the airport and for the flight attendants on my trip home. Once home, I played it for my son and his girlfriend. She tittered and said, "Why, she sounds just like you."

Funny thing—I stopped laughing. "Oh, really?" I said at a pitch one tone short of shattering glass.

Suddenly the box didn't seem so entertaining. Up to that point, I had chuckled every time that cranky mom with her shrill voice had given a command. Now it had become, well, personal.

Isn't it enlightening to see yourself through someone else's eyes? Sometimes I've been blessed and encouraged by the perspective of others, and sometimes I've been startled and even temporarily shattered. I find I don't always see myself as I actually am but instead how I wish I were or how I mean to be.

My friend Lana, while shopping at an antique store, picked up an old book on graveyard humor, *Chuckles in the Cemetery,* by William Pellowe. It was full of old quotes from tombstones written by people who knew the deceased and who had left their evaluations of the individuals carved on the headstones for future generations. Whoa, now that's scary! Can you imagine what some people might say about you?

Look at what someone wrote on poor George Hotten's gravestone:

Hotten
Rotten
Forgotten

Certainly succinct. Either George didn't make a lot of points with people in this life or his mother-in-law wrote the comments during a gall bladder attack.

Evidently this next inscription was written by someone who lived close enough to Obadiah and Ruth to have experienced the dynamics of their relationship, for that person wrote:

Here lies the body of
Obadiah Wilkinson and
Of Ruth his wife.
"Their warfare is accomplished."

In 1714, Ann Marr, the wife of the parish clerk, passed away, and someone (the clerk perhaps?) had this engraved on her stone:

The children of Israel wanted bread,
And the Lord he sent them manna
Old Clark Marr wanted a wife,
And the devil he sent him Anna.
But then Sarah didn't fare much better:
This stone was raised by Sarah's lord,
Not Sarah's virtues to record,
For they're well known to all the town,
But it was raised to keep her down.

I guess Sarah's hubby had wearied of hearing her rehearse her own inner goodness. Well, perchance

Anna and Sarah can commiserate one day with this man's wife:

> Within this grave do lie,
> Back to back my wife and I;
> When the last trumpet the air shall fill
> If she gets up, I'll lie still.

To see how others see us is to risk obtaining more information than we may want. Sometimes I find the Lord will send someone into my life to be a mirror, to help me face what I'm really like. Have you ever been aggravated by traits in another person, only to find out you had those same qualities? I hate when that happens.

There was the time I was scheduled to speak at a conference in the Southwest. I had been ill the night before, and I was still weak and limited to a diet of soda crackers. I was met at the airport by a woman, Isabelle, from the staff of the retreat center. She was carefully dressed in a three-piece, pin-striped suit and wore her long, red hair in a neat braid. While her appearance was orderly, she seemed preoccupied and in a big rush.

As we hurried to her car, Belle informed me we would need to stop at her home to pick up her luggage for the weekend. I was surprised she hadn't brought it with her, since we still had a long drive ahead of us. On the way to her home, Belle told me she would first need to stop at the bank where she worked to take care of an unfinished transaction. At that point, I started to feel a little concerned about our timing, but I was too weak to say anything.

We were in the fast lane on the freeway, traveling at the speed of light, when Belle said, "Uh-oh, there's our exit." Having released that abbreviated traffic bulletin, she then swerved across three lanes of traffic, darted down the exit ramp, and squealed to a halt at the stop sign. I thought I was going to lose my crackers.

After stopping at the bank, we finally made it to her house. There she announced she had to go grocery shopping so her family would have food while she was away. She invited me to go along, but, funny thing, I didn't feel up to the ride. I reminded her of our timetable, but she assured me we would make it to the conference without a hitch.

When Belle returned from the store, she put away the groceries, and then she admitted she hadn't packed yet and disappeared down the hall. Finally she reappeared, suitcases in hand, and we headed for the car. I climbed in the front seat, and in a few minutes she slid in under the steering wheel and stared straight ahead. She didn't start the car; she just stared. After several silent moments, I asked, "What's wrong?"

Still looking straight ahead, Belle stoically replied, "I just locked the car keys in the trunk." We went back into the house and waited an hour and a half for her teenage daughter to bring us another set of keys. By the time the keys arrived, we were too late to make it for my first speaking session.

Belle's daughter's parting words to us were, "Don't rush, Mom, you're already too late to make the session. Just enjoy the drive." Belle smiled as if agreeing with her daughter and then put the pedal to the metal. I was plastered to the seat as we sped down the highway in the inside lane. She was obviously trying to make up for lost time.

Suddenly she uttered, "Uh-oh," just as the car began to lurch as though it had the hiccups. Belle cut across two lanes of traffic, and the car hiccuped to a halt. We had run out of gas. She spotted a service station, but it was on the other side of the six-lane highway. Belle took off running across the lanes and made it safely to the center, where she then had to get down on all fours to slip under a fence. That was quite a sight, since she had accomplished all this while wearing high heels.

I watched from the car as her suit and heels squeezed under the fence. I couldn't decide if I wanted to laugh or cry. I'm certain I was in my physically weakened state so I wouldn't be tempted to commandeer this frenzied woman's car.

She returned with a young man who poured five teaspoons of gas into the tank, allowing us to sputter our way down the road to another station, where we filled up. Once back on the highway (uh-oh), it began to rain. Belle turned on her wipers, and the wiper on the driver's side took one swish across the windshield and flopped down on the side of the car, dangling like a hangnail. She pulled off the road, and we inched our way several miles through the downpour to a gas station where they had . . . no tools. The young man who worked there did, however, run over to a restaurant, borrow an array of knives, and tighten the flyaway wiper.

We returned to the road and headed lickety-split to who knows where—certainly not the driver, who now confessed she was lost. Folks, this definitely was not, I repeat, *not* her day . . . or mine. We did, however, finally arrive—nine hours late. I stumbled into my room that night mumbling unpleasantries.

The following day, I found out that the woman, a widow, had many extenuating circumstances complicating her life, and I was one of them. In the midst of a multitude of things demanding her attention, I was an (unwanted) addition. She was never supposed to be my driver, but at the last minute, the retreat staff had dumped me into her already overwhelmed schedule. Not wanting to abandon me at the airport, she had tried to fit me into her basket of duties. The problem was she only had a three-egg basket, and she already had 22 eggs precariously piled in it. Then, sure enough, the inevitable happened—the eggs began to topple. Splat. Splat. (Uh-oh.) Splat.

But the real problem with Belle and her egg basket was that I saw myself too clearly reflected. I find that when life gets ahead of me, if I don't make some immediate adjustments, I end up running around like a chicken with her head off.

Now, if you've never seen a headless chicken, trust me, it's not a pretty sight. I watched my farm-raised momma separate a chicken's head from its body with half a dozen circular swings. That was one split chick. The feathered body ran wild, while her head nonchalantly observed from a fence post.

I've had to ask myself why it is that I constantly take on more than I can handle, which leaves me feeling detached and frantic. I'm sure the Lord must grow weary of hearing my emergency, please-get-me-through-this prayers.

I observed Belle's outward behavior, but what I ended up seeing was my own inner condition. I'm grateful the Lord lets us learn from each other and lets us know we're not the only one struggling. That woman was trying to meet everyone's needs, only to encounter one calamity after another. Now, who did that remind me of? It was easier for me to see what she should have done than it is for me to prescribe solutions for myself when I'm in the midst of my own overbooked dilemma—which is more frequent than I care to admit. I, too, take on more than I should and hesitate to use the grown-up word *no* when people try to give me opportunities I just can't afford.

When I met Belle, I thought she was a real Mickey Mouse. Instead, I found out she was a mega-mirror. Had I written her epitaph, I would have simply put, "Uh-oh!" But I realize mine could read, "Uh-oh, too!"

The next time we feel tempted to critique some-one's behavior, perhaps we should first ask the Lord if the criticism is just about them or indicative of us. We must own our crankiness, frantic pat-terns, lack of good judgment, or other fitting insights mirrored by those around us if we're to experience inner growth. I find that when my atti-tude is supple and I'm willing to learn, He will give me an inner view (sometimes via an outer source) to help me know deep change from the inside out. Then, hopefully, my "Uh-oh's" will become "Oh, I see."

22

Think-a-Tude
(think´ a tōod) n.

Dictionary's definition:
Headed in the right direction.

Patsy's definition:
Mental agility.

THOUGHTS CAN BE powerful. Just observe the little train who fueled his tank with "I think I can's." Or consider Barron Lyton, who believed a written thought to be mightier than a wielded sword. Then there's King Solomon, who proclaimed, "As [a person] thinketh in his heart, so is he" (Prov. 23:7, KJV).

Oh, brother, am I in trouble! At this stage of my life, I'm given to spells of seesawing from the negativity of narrow-mindedness to the negativity of being a tad morose. And a tad of morosity is like a bad perfume; no matter how little you put on, it still stinks.

It's like the mystery smell in our house. It doesn't arise often, but when it does, it's powerful.

We believe it may come from the city sewer lines. (At first we were all suspiciously eyeing each other.) It's almost as if the sewer belches, and we get a backdraft. We spray, use disinfectants, and open windows. But after a while, we don't notice it as much unless we leave, get a breath of fresh air, and come back in.

My negativity (or yours, for that matter) is like the mystery smell in that everyone notices it right off, but no one appreciates it. And the more we're negative, the easier it becomes to adjust to our smelly thoughts, until we don't even realize how bad they stink or how far they've permeated. Negativity is a habit-forming choice and can, unchecked, become a lifestyle. When God's guidelines for our thoughts are followed (see Phil. 4:8), on the other hand, it's like opening a window and allowing a heavenly breeze to waft through.

My six-year-old nephew Nicholas was riding in the car with his mom when he made a dreary announcement: "I hate my life."

My sister was startled but tried not to show it. Calmly she asked, "Well, Nicholas, why do you hate your life?"

He seemed relieved she had asked so he could get it off his chest. He took a breath and sadly reported, "Because of sharks, alligators, and caterpillars."

Cheered to hear it wasn't her, his dad, or his siblings, she probed on. It seems that Nicholas had been fond of sharks, alligators, and caterpillars. But one by one, he had found out they could be dangerous. In fact, just that morning his dad had innocently mentioned that caterpillars can carry germs. Little did he realize the caterpillar was

Nicholas's final straw. How much can a fellow take, anyway?

I giggled over Nicholas's mental ruler for hardships. But then I realized I've had similar thoughts—like when my hair acts hysterical, my panty hose generate a run the width of the freeway, or a cold sore the size and shape of Texas sprouts on my upper lip. Then I mentally mumble, *I hate my life.* Yet when my hair settles down, my panty hose are flawless, and my cold sore dissipates, life seems great. My, it sure doesn't take much to throw some of us off, does it?

Here's a list of some of the things that can push my mental dimmer switch: products at the store that aren't priced or are marked, but in the most obscure places. People who write checks in the cash-only checkout lane. Cars that stall in the middle of lefthand turns (especially when I'm driving them). Lids that have obviously been sealed with Super Glue. Stick-on price tags that take off three layers of the product when removed. Window shades that fall off the window every tenth pull. Pens that skip, making our letters look like Morse code. People who bump into me and aren't sorry. Shopping carts with wobbly wheels. Parallel parking. Somebody's gum stuck on my shoe. The parents of impolite children. Boots that leak.

I feel negative just thinking about those things. Oh, that's the point, isn't it? Our mind-set determines our ability to overcome difficulties, and if we can't get past the inconsequential areas of life (like my list), how will we ever deal with the real life-and-death sticklers?

Perhaps we need to think of the irritants of life as our thought aerobics. That would allow us practice opportunities so we'll be mentally strong when the tough stuff hits. Then, instead of clouding over mentally when I see a line at the checkout lane, I could see it as a chance to exercise patient thoughts. If I did that regularly, the next time a heavy-duty issue visited me for an extended time, I'd be more mentally fit and able to handle the hardship with maturity and maybe even grace.

Changing our thoughts to a more positive vein helps improve not only relationships, but also our health. I learned this when I had to go for a series of x-rays because of discomfort in my chest and upper abdomen. I stretched out on an ice-cold examining table with large, looming equipment overhead. I was strapped onto the table. Suddenly, it began to move up and forward until the table and I were standing upright. I was handed two glasses of fluid to drink rapidly. One was, I'm pretty sure, crushed Styrofoam mixed in liquid cement. The other was like cod-liver oil over fizzing pop rocks. I guzzled and prayed it would stay down so I would only have to do this once.

Then the table tipped back and forth, moving me from standing on my feet to almost standing on my head—similar to rides at an amusement park . . . minus the amusement.

Next a doctor came in and asked me what my favorite food was. I found that irritating, since I hadn't had anything to eat except their x-ray cocktail, which would probably require a Roto-Rooter to remove from my system. But to hurry things along, I said, "Banana cream pie."

He looked away and then looked back at me and inquired, "Would you like it with whipping cream?"

For the life of me, I couldn't see the point in his culinary questionnaire. I guess he heard my exasperation as I flippantly said "Sure" to the whipping cream, because he replied, "Mrs. Clairmont, look over your shoulder at the monitor. Those are your insides." He was pointing to the screen, and he continued, "We need to move the fluid you drank from here to here." He moved his finger across the screen to indicate the desired route. "You can cause that to happen if you'll think about a food you enjoy," he concluded.

Fascinated by the idea, I concentrated on banana cream pie (with whipping cream) while watching the screen. To my amazement, the fluid immediately spilled from one area of my anatomy down into another. Then the x-ray technicians finished their filming.

Afterward, it hit me how just thinking about food can create a physical response. That made me wonder what happens inside me when I think resentful thoughts: churning stomach fluids, tightened jaw, pounding temples, strained neck muscles. Does that also mean that when we think up a good 'tude, we could bring peace to our digestive tracts, relaxation to our muscles, and a smooth flow to our circulation? Now, those would be benefits worth working for.

But I find overseeing my thought life far more difficult than observing fluids in my digestive tract. I'm constantly deluged with thoughts both worthwhile and destructive (in the sense that they don't promote goodwill or good health). It's a full-time job to sort through one's thoughts, a challenge with which I need assistance. The good news is we are offered that support via the Scriptures and the monitoring and strengthening ministry of the Holy Spirit.

Our minds, much like television screens, are constantly receiving broadcasts—from others, ourselves, and the Lord. It's our choice which channels we tune into and which we turn off. The more time we spend considering the Lord and His ways, the healthier it is for our bodies (see Prov. 4:22), our minds (see Ps. 119:165), and our character (see Prov. 2:7).

Now, let's see if I understand what I've just said: With the enabling power of the Lord, we can think ourselves into or out of a 'tude. The healthier the 'tude we choose, the healthier we become, allowing us to affect our world in wholesome ways.

I want to think up a 'tude like a little train that takes on a towering mountain; I want to wield a pen that influences minds for good; and I want to have a mind that reflects its Designer in content and conscience. To do those things, it's obvious to me that I'll need to get busy and more conscientiously turn the channel on my screen from majoring in the minors (inconsequentials) to focusing on what matters. *I think I can. I think I can.*

23

Family 'Tudes

(fam´ e lē tōōds) n.

Dictionary's definition:
Reproducing after our own kind.

Patsy's definition:
Help! I'm my relatives!

MY FAVORITE REFRIGERATOR magnet reads, "Mom, I'll always love you, but I'll never forgive you for washing my face with spit on your hanky." That statement is funny and effective because most of us have experienced ye ol' spit shine. It's part of our family heritage.

My mom often resorted to the lick-and-rub method to remove smudges from a face or make a cowlick submit. I, too, used the technique with my boys when lack of time or facilities necessitated such an earthy approach. In fact, I think this liquid shine solution should be bottled and sold as an all-purpose cleaning fluid. It removes everything from grease to rust, to chocolate, to smartaleck smirks. (It's real hard for a kid to think he's clever or cute when his mom is rubbing her spit on his face . . . in public . . . in front of his friends.) We could start a cottage business with this product and call it "Spew and You, a Little Bit of Homemade Happiness." And to think it all began with Momma.

Isn't it amazing what we learn from our families? When I was a kid, I thought that when I grew up, I'd never talk to my kids the way my mom talked to me. Then I grew up, married, had children, opened my mouth, and out came my mother. But I thought she sounded a lot smarter through my lips.

It seems that if we live long enough, we finally understand what our elders were trying to tell us all along. The only problem is now we're the elders trying to give insights to the next generation, and they're looking at us as if we're six slices short of a full loaf. But any way they slice their bread, we know that one day our words will finally become food for thought.

My dad used to tell me, especially when I would ask him for money, that I talked like a woman with a paper head. Recently I related this statement to a friend, and she couldn't stop laughing. When she settled down, I asked her what was so amusing. She said a picture passed through her mind of a woman's head made out of the funny papers. I had heard that statement all my growing-up years, but I never thought it was funny. I realize today what a comical dad I had, but at the time he was, well, just my dad.

One thing he did do that tickled me and my friends was his condensed version of the jitterbug. Because he was slightly knockkneed and bowlegged, it added to the delight of his little jig. At any given moment, he might, in a 12-inch space, offer his rendition of the Charleston or the old soft-shoe. He was usually dressed in his bib overalls, which added to the comedy. The change in his pockets would jingle, and the toothpick he always held between his teeth would bounce. His dance recital never lasted more than 30 seconds, but that was enough to get us all giggling.

If there was one family `tude Dad exhibited to me, it was his attitude toward life. He didn't require much to be satisfied: a simple home, a car that ran, some meat and potatoes, and an easy chair. He enjoyed a fishing pole, a water hole, a pocket knife, a harmonica, a crossword puzzle, and Kate Smith singing "When the Moon Comes Over the Mountain."

Simplicity, that's one family `tude I wish I had caught from him. My life often seems so rushed and complex, with computers, faxes, portable phones, and answering machines all demanding my time. I think my dad would have been fascinated with today's technology. I can just see him wagging his head in amazement and disbelief. Then he would have gone outside, found a chair in the shade, and whittled a while before he took a nap. Dad was a "Life of Riley" (a hammock between two trees and a soft breeze) kind of guy.

I guess I'm more like my mom in that we're both movers and shakers. And one thing we love to move is furniture. I'm forever changing my house around. I not only move Les's easy chair from one side of the room to the other, but I also sporadically move all the living room furniture into the dining room and vice versa. Les is never sure when he sits down if he should dine or recline.

I definitely inherited my furniture fetish from my mom. Her furniture didn't wear out from being sat on but from being moved about so frequently. She moved her furnishings not only from room to room and floor to floor, but also from house to house. Throughout her adult years, Mom has moved 20 times. It would have been more, but my dad stepped on her apron strings in an attempt to slow her down. Today Mom (who is 80) lives in a senior citizens' apartment building, and guess what . . . she would really like to move (old people get on her nerves), but now I have hold of her apron strings.

Speaking of apron strings, my mom always wore an apron when she was preparing meals. I loved it. There's something down-home about that look to me. It smacked of being on duty and being delighted to be there. It was more my mom's attitude than her aproned image, because she genuinely loved to keep a home and care for her family. She always sang as she worked and took time for the smallest details to enhance our home's environment with her special touches.

I'd carry on the tradition and wear an apron today, but my family is concerned it might inspire me to cook. So rather than cause them premature indigestion, I have hung a crocheted apron on our baker's rack. That way, it's a sweet reminder of Mom without being a direct threat to my family that I might go on one of my Betty Crocker capers.

My friend Ann, when she first married, emulated her mom's baking savvy as she rolled out a crust and then filled the pie shell with fruit. She crimped the edges of her crust as she had seen her mom do so many times. She even remembered to preheat the oven, just like her mom.

Well, *almost* like her mom. Ann had failed to check in the oven before preheating it. She had stored a large bag of chips inside.

When she opened the oven door, flames shot out at her like a cannon. Ann grabbed a five-pound bag of flour and, in her panic, dumped the entire contents onto the flames. At first the flames appeared to be smothered. She stood relieved and gazed down at the fluffy, white mountain she had created. Suddenly, like Mount St. Helens, there was a big poof. It frightened Ann, so she dropped the empty bag on top of the eruption, where it immediately burst into flames.

Ann bolted from her apartment and ran to her neighbor's. She almost beat his door down as she screamed, "Fire!" Her neighbor worked the late shift and was sound asleep when Ann accosted his door. Half-awake, he dashed into her apartment and soon had the situation under control. He then pointed out to Ann that had she closed the oven door to begin with, the flames would have been contained and would have put themselves out. (She hadn't had an occasion to learn that from her mom.) As he headed back to his apartment, Ann heard him mutter that he was going to switch to the day shift.

Ann's experience could have convinced her to give up the kitchen and take up croquet, but she had learned more from her mom than how to bake a pie. Her mom had taught Ann not to be easily discouraged, and that experience is an important step to achievement. Ann's mom was a cheerleader for her family. And Ann mirrors her mom's lively spirit and tenacity.

I believe the purpose for families is multifaceted. And one of those sparkling facets is that we might proudly display our positive family 'tudes, which we observed and absorbed. Another is that we might remember all the worthwhile ways our first family influenced us so we can "pass them on" in our own homes.

24

Megatude
(meg´ e tōōd) n.

Dictionary's definition:
Greatness.

Patsy's definition:
Big deal.

MEGA-EVENTS ARE exciting to plan for and anticipate, although many times the planning is more fun than the actual event—sort of like the child you buy the new toy for, and after he opens it, you discover he prefers the box. Think of the money we could save if we had just found assorted boxes and wrapped them up to begin with! The kids would be thrilled, we wouldn't be disappointed in their lack of elation at the costly investment, and with the bucks we saved, we could all go to Disney World. Of course, then we would be back to planning an other big event, which, in fact, our family did.

A few years ago, Les, Jason, and I went to Disney World on our first vacation in years. We had high expectations for a time filled with laughter and fun.

But the day was steamy hot, the park was packed, lines were long, tempers were short, and halfway through the day, a mega-thunderstorm dumped on us. Within minutes, the storm left us ankle-deep in rain as we waded our way to safety and, as a park precaution, the rides were shut down. It certainly was not the day we had dreamed about.

These types of upsets to carefully laid plans tempt us to sport a megatude. We tend to think, *After all our planning, efforts, and financial outlay, this is the big payoff?* We begin to believe we may be better off not having a plan and just letting life unfold in its own quirky way, or to stay home alone and not risk the headache.

Now, I've lived long enough to know high expectations are like hot air balloons. They're beautiful to behold if the elements are cooperative. Otherwise, we end up . . . down . . . and like grounded basket cases, we sit in pools of our deflated dreams.

Yet, even knowing better, we still sometimes set ourselves up to suffer sudden downdrafts of disappointment. Usually my earthward spiral comes from expecting too much from circumstances and people.

I remember as a young teenager being invited to the park one time for a day of swimming with the neighborhood kids. Even though it was a spontaneous event, my expectations were at their peak as I ran about the house to grab a bathing suit, sunglasses, and towel. I heard the knock on the door and anticipated some of my friends had come to get me. When I swung open the door, however, one of the kids hurriedly sputtered, "Sorry, we don't have any room left in the car." With that announcement, she ran to the vehicle, crammed herself in, and off they went on their merry way. I was devastated.

My mom tried to console me without success. I had gone from crushed to fuming, and I was using my fumes to pump up a megatude. Mom caught my attention, though, and defused my ballooning ˋtude when she said, "Patsy, it's possible the Lord was protecting you from some unforeseen thing. Perhaps you could have been hurt or drowned. We have to trust when things don't go our way that He's watching out for our best interests."

Since that time, my mom's insight has helped me accept a myriad of thwarted events as divinely provisional. Mom's explanation was my first introduction to God's sovereignty, which is an understanding that we have a Divine Director who superintends our every step—yesterday's steps and tomorrow's steps, as well as today's.

Embracing His perpetual care allows us to rest in the confidence that whatever happens, He's not surprised, He hasn't taken the day off, and He's busily at work even in the midst of our darkest nights . . . or our sunniest days while our friends are frolicking at the pool.

Les and I entered our marriage with wild expectations, causing us to take shifts sportin' a megatude. One of Les's assumptions was that I would know how to cook. Can you imagine? I remember his suggesting I make breakfast. I thought, *How ludicrous; we don't even own a toaster.* Les proposed I fix the toast in a skillet. I had never heard of such a thing, so he demonstrated several ways toast could be made on top of and in the oven. I was fascinated but still intimidated by the kitchen. As the years went by, it was my family who became intimidated when I headed toward the kitchen. I guess we could say I wasn't a natural with the culinary arts, although I did find out I was quite good at establishing an artful ambiance.

I love creating a pretty table and preparing an inviting atmosphere: lit fireplace, candle glow, soft music, lively table settings, flared linen napkins, and creative centerpieces. Then I send out for Kentucky Fried Chicken. I know, I know, the Colonel doesn't fit the aura of my efforts, but honestly, it's better than my meat loaf. Mine always seems to be doing the backstroke in a sea of grease (not Greece).

Speaking of stroke, my sister-in-law almost had one when she stopped by my home and noticed I had totally immersed my roast beef in water to bake it. I should have known that was wrong when it gurgled, "Help, I've fallen, and I can't get up!"

I don't think I was meant to cook, but I was meant to converse; not to bake but to blab; not to be a Galloping Gourmet but to have a chatty forte. Once Les was convinced my cooking skills would at best remain at their worst, he gave up his expectations and made reservations. What a relief for us both!

I expected when I married that Les would understand my monthly mood swings. But he thought three rocky weeks out of each month was more like an avalanche than a relationship. He complained just because I whined, "I'm only acting this way because it's the week before." Then the next week I would cry, "I'm only like this because it's the week of." And then, to be consistent, the following week I would assert, "You know I'm this way because it's the week after." That only left us 12 good weeks out of the year.

I finally had to realize Les had never had a menstrual cramp, birthed a baby, or had the blues, and I needed to let him off the understand-me hook. I also needed to obtain help for my erratic hormones and not sport a megatude because others didn't understand me when I didn't understand myself.

Having expectations can be healthy, like being pregnant with hope. But when we become married to our own way, not leaving room for people's imperfections and God's perfect plan, our hope is aborted and we're left grieving.

Expectations aren't wrong so long as we're prepared to shift gears quickly when life takes a twist. Otherwise, if we can't go with the flow, we end up twisted into so many stress-filled knots that we work ourselves into a mega-sized `tude.

A number of years ago, a hot air balloon landed in our field. The people aboard needed to make some adjustments to their aircraft, but because they made a premature landing, they had to call for drivers to pick them up. They were saddened to change their plan but optimistic that they would be back in the air soon. Perhaps that needs to be our flight plan as well: Fly high when we can (expect the best), land when we need to make adjustments (be prepared to live with change, disappointments, and repairs), and then take off on another day . . . up, up, and away!

25

Feud `Tude
(fyōōd´ tōōd) n.

Dictionary's definition:
Ongoing disruption.

Patsy's definition:
Them thar are fightin' words.

L IKE THE HATFIELDS and the McCoys, a lot of feud `tude-in' is goin' on in this here world. Seems as though we get so married to our own way of thinkin', we don't have room for nobody else's.

Take Les and me, for example. Les and I come from different schools of thought on many topics. Les comes from Bullwinkle's alma mater, What's a Matter U? I attended the notorious School of Hard Knocks. Do you get the picture? We have Hard Head duckin' down in a cornfield and Wise Guy hidin' in the holler, ready to take potshots at anybody (includin' each other) found steppin' on this here land of theirs.

Les and I are both strong-willed people who like being right. Don't get me wrong—I'm not advocating ornery behavior, I'm confessing it. Over the years, Les and I have worked on a more amiable atmosphere, with periodic success. But there are times when we wear each other out by being picky and thin-skinned.

The major issues of life don't seem to be as feud 'tude-in' for us as its constant, minor irritants. For instance, Les likes lots of lights on in our home, floodlight fashion, whereas I'm into the subtleties of candle glow. We seem to go from room to room, canceling out each other's lighting choices. I turn on the dining room lamps that I've strategically placed to add a soft ambiance, and Les walks in and flips on the 300-watt overhead, transforming the room into an interrogation booth. Yes, I want to see what I'm eating, but no, I don't want sunstroke while I'm eating it. Les has accused me of using low wattage to disguise my cooking. Yes. So what's his point? I say, "Whatever works." Besides, if I've already burned the chicken, why regrill it under a blazing chandelier? Anyway, Les and I aren't getting any younger, and like my chicken, we look better under the camouflage of flickering candles. I figure in a couple more years, we'll be eating our drumsticks in the dark.

Lights aren't our only feudin' ammo. There's also the mail. Since Lee is retired, he thinks he should be the Pony Express and get the mail every day. But you see, for the first 30 years of our marriage, that was a regular part of *my* day. So now we play mail roulette: Whoever gets his or her hand in the slot first wins the jackpot. If you visit us at noon, enter our porch at your own risk. Neighbors watch from a safe distance as Les and I scramble for position. The mailman has learned to approach our home cautiously in his attempt to remain an impartial participant. He tosses the mail from his saddlebag into our box and then gallops toward the safety of our next-door neighbor's porch.

Once inside our house, the mail-winner gives the loser all the bills, advertisements, and occupant flyers. Of course, that means the winner is often left empty-handed but still wearing a big smirk of victory.

Victory in our home is also won by who has possession of the newspaper. Actually, I don't mind that Les rises first in the morning and brings in the paper. I don't mind that he leaves it spread out all over the couch. I can even deal with the newspaper print permanently tattooed on our furniture. But beware if anyone has tampered with my crossword puzzle! That two-inch part of the newspaper is mine, mine, mine. Do not wrinkle or crumple it. Don't set your coffee cup on it. And whatever you do, don't even think about defiling it with an answer. Them that' are fightin' words, bub.

For years, some sadist at the newspaper printed the crossword puzzle in the same section as the sports, causing unnecessary strife between Les, the wannabe sportscaster, and me, the wannabe crossword queen. Gratefully, the newspaper repented and moved the crossword and the funnies to a more neutral section, bringing a greater measure of harmony to Les and me.

Added discord, though, can occur between us when we go out to eat—not over our newspaper but over the menu. Les likes to know what I'm going to have before I order. I prefer to order without discussing my decision with him or guests at our table. Don't ask me why, but I just don't want to reveal my choices until the waitress is ready to write them down. Now, isn't that silly?

I find my devotion to my little preferences often indicates the size and condition of my heart. When all is well in my world, I'm more pliable, more amiable, more malleable. But when my preferences become my rights, I tend to be resistant, demanding, and defensive. And if perchance my body is in hormonal havoc the week my preferences are infringed upon, honey, it's feudin' time.

I once threw a hissy fit when Les accidentally tossed out the newspaper before I removed my sacred crossword. You would have thought I had lost my wedding ring instead of a 25-cent, replaceable piece of paper. Besides, I should have been applauding his help in tidying up the house. (Something he had been taught real men don't do.)

Les's dad, Lawrence, was an alcoholic lumberjack who pulled out his own teeth and sewed up his own wounds. Now, that's tough. He had a definite line drawn regarding what he would or wouldn't do as a man. Basically, the way it worked was that if he didn't want to do something, he would make his wife and kids do it.

Les's mom, Lena, was an industrious woman who worked diligently to care for her six children and abusive husband. She chopped wood, built fires in the wood furnance, made her own bread, hung out mountainous loads of wash, and ironed endlessly, including pressing her boys' underwear.

From that background of clearly defined roles, Les then married me. My beliefs and experience were far different from his. I believe a man who helps around the house deserves to live there. I'm into team effort. Besides, two mules can do far more than one.

And one thing this mule doesn't do is iron underwear, though I do wear them (my own, of course). I did, however, light a fire once. I struck the match, and a spark ignited the fuzz that ran down the front of my flannel pajamas. It was quite exciting, but not an experience I cared to repeat. I have, contrary to popular belief, baked bread. It resulted in a loaf that weighed more than me and looked like an oversized hockey puck. Not an experience my family cared to repeat.

Les and I have both had to make adjustments to each other's idiosyncrasies, beliefs, and preferences over the years. And we've learned, in a general sense, that preferences aren't as important as people. Acknowledging and fulfilling our personal desires can certainly be healthy, but putting them ahead of kindness, thoughtfulness, and politeness can be selfish and counterproductive.

If we're gonna go to feudin', we need to 'bide by some guidelines. Number one: Let's fight fair (be kind, thoughtful, and polite). We need to get to the point, not get the person. Number two: Let's fight for what matters—not our rights but righteousness; not preferences but purity; not even beliefs but blamelessness.

Shucks, y'all, we need to lay down our feudin' 'tudes (most of 'em don't add up to a hill of beans anyhow) and instead celebrate our kinfolks and our company.

26

Platitude
(plat´ e tōod) n.

Dictionary's definition:
Trite remarks.

Patsy's definition:
Easy way out.

IT'S NOT BRIGHT to be trite. (Oops, I think I just broke my own rule.) Triteness and brightness are pictures of contrast. Brightness denotes illumination and savvy, whereas triteness suggests being in the dark and clueless. And that's where we seem to come from when we spout easy-isms.

For instance, if one more person tells me "When life hands you lemons, make lemonade," it's not a lemon I'm going to squeeze. When that phrase first started to circulate, I thought it was sweetly motivating. Now it has gone sour. Yes, I get the point, but repetitive cutesy is as annoying as Chia Pet commercials.

"No pain, no gain" is another saying that's beginning to wear thin. It's accurate but aggravating. I know it's costly to grow, but when I'm walking through the challenge of change with perspiration dripping off my furrowed brow, that's not the time to toss a glib quip my way. Trust me.

Can you imagine Noah hanging a sign on the end of his ark that taunted, "No boat, no float"? True as it was, under the circumstances, it would have lacked sensitivity. Or how about Joseph mocking his brothers with a sign dangling from his multi-colored cloak: "No coat, no gloat!" Joe was in enough trouble without spouting platitudes.

I realize our sayings aren't meant to be flippant, but like repeated wearings of even the finest garment, they eventually wear out, lose their initial impact, and become downright tacky. There comes a time to hang 'em up, air 'em out, and give 'em up.

I couldn't help but giggle (and wince), however, when I thought about Bible folks spouting some of our well-known sayings. Imagine big boy Goliath skipping out to meet young David and singing, "Sticks and stones may break my bones, but names will never hurt me." Goliath would have been right about the first part but wrong about names not being hurtful. For after his skirmish with David, Goliath was henceforth referred to as "dead." Following his conquest, David could have, in a vain moment, carved on his sling, "Little strokes fell great oaks," "The bigger they are, the harder they fall," or, tackier yet, "Dynamite comes in small packages."

What about these:

The serpent, as he struts in front of the forbidden tree, waves a placard that announces, "An apple a day keeps the doctor away." (Boo.)

Or picture Jesus calling to the drowning Peter, "Sink or swim!"

What about an engraved stone in front of Lot's wife's statue inscribed, "When it rains, it pours." How about "She wasn't worth her salt"? Or worse yet, "Keep a stiff upper lip."

Imagine Sarah, after Isaac's arrival, pounding this notice on Hagar's tent: "Two's company, three's a crowd." And Hagar's response to Sarah over the camp's loudspeaker: "Too soon old, too late smart."

How about Jonah proclaiming to Nineveh, "Shape up or ship out." Now, that would be the kettle calling the pot black.

Actually, all those comments are grounded in some truth—not sensitive or helpful, but accurate. I'm convinced that the knee-jerk response of a quick retort to life's hard questions is one of humanity's besetting sins. We've all been guilty, out of neglect, ignorance, or indifference, of giving a trite answer to someone in crisis. Often it's because we've either not experienced what that person is going through, forgotten our own neediness when we were in a dilemma, or are unwilling to (or can't) invest the time to help another struggler.

Life can be tough, unfair, confusing, and unexplainable. So there, I've said it. Whew, it's finally out. There's just a lot I don't understand about people and life, but especially about God. I feel safest when I understand what's happening in me, around me, and to me, but often life is a big, fat mystery. And I'm no detective.

I proved that when Les and I attended a mystery dinner with our friends David and Nancy. We ate our meals as a story unfolded around us. Performers portrayed characters involved in a crime, and we were supposed to guess who the criminal was. Only problem was, we didn't understand the play, much less figure out the crime or the guilty party. At first I was afraid I was the only one puzzled by the skit, but when we were supposed to vote on who the villain was, I realized everyone was as stumped as I. Yet we all hesitated to admit our confusion lest we be the solitary soul in the dark.

I find that true of life as well. None of us like to feel we don't "get it." Sometimes we feel safer and smarter when we give a quick reply rather than appear answerless. Our human tendency is to select comfort over vulnerability. But life's mysterious ways often force us to choose between being trite or admitting we're lost.

And as scary as admission can be, it's liberating. What a relief it is, when we're asked something beyond our experience or understanding, to be able to simply say, "I don't know"! The other person may initially be disappointed she didn't find the answer she was searching for, but at least we didn't offend her or mislead her. I'd rather hand out the brightness of honesty than a dim platitude any day. Wouldn't you?

When a friend gave birth to a severely learning-disabled child, person after person told her, "My, the Lord must really love you to trust you with this baby." I think those individuals believed that was a loving statement, but for this woman, in the throes of her shock, grief, and adjustment, it only increased her pain.

Perhaps what we need to do when we have no background in a situation is to say to the one suffering, "Tell me what I can say or do that will help you and not add to your pain." At least that way, the person knows we care enough to be involved and that we're being cautious not to complicate his or her plight with platitudes.

I have learned (the hard way, of course) even to be careful of saying, "I'll pray for you." That begins to sound empty when tossed around casually and constantly. It can be a way for us to detach from others and escape their set of difficult circumstances while maintaining our spirituality. A better way to approach people may be, "How can I pray for you?" That question draws us toward them instead of distancing us. And it says to others, "I'm serious about my prayer offer, and I'm willing to listen while you tell me your greatest need."

One of my favorite proverbs is "A word fitly spoken is like apples of gold in pictures of silver" (Prov. 25:11, KJV). That's what I want to offer to others with my words, a treasured investment of lasting value. The key word is *fitly*. Do our words fit the situation, and do they fit the hearer? Are our words meeting that person's needs? Are we arranging our words as carefully as an artist would if he were painting apples of gold in a setting of silver? Perhaps we should think of our hearer as a canvas, our words as brush strokes, and our interchange as our opportunity to create a masterpiece.

When my friend gave birth to her disabled child, many people extended platitudes. My friend learned she needed compassionate support far more than quick answers. People's advice didn't help like people's availability. Some knew to hold her and her husband and let them weep. And a few left healing brush strokes on the canvas of these parents' hearts when they said, "I can't imagine

how you must feel. If you need to talk, I'm available. I'll walk with you through this season. I love
you."

A platitude or a masterpiece—one is easy, the
other takes effort. It's our choice.

27

Magnitude
(mag´ ne tōōd) n.

Dictionary's definition:
To a large extent.

Patsy's definition:
Know-it-all.

WHEN I CHECKED into a hotel to speak for a woman's retreat one day, I was impressed with the beauty of the place. It was obviously a notch above the norm. My lovely room was equipped with lots of amenities . . . and a couple of unnecessities. Seems some sadistic designer decided to include in the bathroom furnishings a digital scale and, worse yet, an oversized magnifying mirror. At this stage of my life, making weight and wrinkle apparatuses available is not the way to brighten my day.

The magnifying mirror, mounted on an extra-long extension arm, reached out at me as if it were in a hurry for the two of us to share a good laugh. Actually, magnifying even a good thing can be, well, too much of a good thing. But there's something about magnifying our imperfections that can be down-right discouraging. Magnifiers have no mercy, they're unforgiving, and their memory for details is uncanny.

Oh, no, I think I've just described what happens to me when I make a big deal out of a small offense! If I harp on trivials until they become trials, I unmercifully magnify errors. And I'm unlikely to forget the details of just how the offense happened. Plus I can't see someone else's perspective—or present.

When Les handed me my fiftieth birthday presents, I was eager to discover what wonderful things he had chosen for me. My husband is thoughtful in his selections and pays close attention to what I delight in, so I knew my gifts would be special. I opened the first box, and it contained a Winnie the Pooh night-light. Being a Pooh fan, I thought it was adorable. Les insisted I plug it in and turn it on. So I did. The light was in the shape of Pooh pushing pots of honey in a wheelbarrow. The pots glowed warmly, enhancing the light's charm.

"What's that?" Les said as he pointed to a wad of plastic wrap taped to the wheelbarrow. I pulled the packet free, looked through the plastic, and saw replacement bulbs for the night-light.

"It's bulbs," I told him.

"Really?" he said with a doubtful air.

"Yes, really," I responded, feeling a twinge of annoyance at his tone.

"Well, it doesn't look like the right size to be bulbs," he stated flatly.

So I looked at the plastic more closely, and sure enough, I saw two replacement bulbs. "Well, that's what it is all right," I smugly assured him.

Then Les picked up the night-light, turned it over, and exposed a lightbulb much larger than the plastic wad I was holding. I began to think my assessment was wrong, and I defensively wondered why the big deal was being made about the bulbs anyway. So when Les challenged me again about the contents of the plastic, I wanted to shove him into the wheelbarrow.

To satisfy him, though, and hopefully to prove my point (my confidence was fading), I tried to open the wad of plastic, but it was secured tightly with Scotch tape. I no longer had the patience to mess with the packet (my `tude-ometer was on tilt), so I tossed it onto the counter and told him if he needed to see inside, he could open the packet himself. Which he promptly did. Inside was not a replacement bulb but a replacement ring. Les presented me with a breathtaking diamond *ring*. I never had a `tude dissolve so quickly, nor had I ever been more willing to admit my error.

After I settled down from the thrill of my gift, I was amazed to think that I had been so certain I saw replacement bulbs. I was convinced I was right, and even on close examination, I couldn't see beyond my original evaluation.

I wonder if that's how we become narrow-minded, jump to conclusions, and think ourselves into ruts. We become bound to our own small thoughts that are then magnified by our insecurity and our need to be right. And oh, how I love to be right!

"You really goofed with that one," I chided Les one time as I pointed toward the garage. "What were you thinking? No bluebird will nest in that box with it so close to the buildings, next to the circular drive, and only feet away from where we park. And besides that, it's too high."

A week later, a bluebird scout scoped out our grounds. Les had set up four bluebird locations to choose from, not counting the useless one on the garage. Because we had an ideal setting of open fields skirting the property, I wasn't surprised when the bluebird returned a short time later with his bride.

What did throw me, though, was that this featherhead chose the house of havoc attached to the garage. This bird was obviously not a member of the Audubon Society, nor had he read the same bird habitats book I had.

After several weeks of reminding me (that is, *gloating*) of his keen bird sense, Les took me out to the box to prove (flaunt) once again how discerning (smart) he had been. He lifted the top, and inside, the female bird sat breathlessly still. I was amazed she didn't attempt to fly away—that is, until I heard soft, little peeps. Then I realized she had babies tucked under her wings.

I oohed and cooed and ate every word I had cast in Les's direction regarding his bird savvy. The scene was so dear that I didn't even mind that I was the birdbrain. The picture of those chicks pressed next to their mother's heart has nested in my mind. It magnified for me the shepherd's song of security:

"He will cover you with His pinions, and under His wings you may seek refuge" (Ps.91:4).

When I press in close to the Lord, I feel safe even in my failures. But when I respond out of my own pridefulness, I'm quick to be defensive and unteachable and to overstate my situation. Then, instead of escaping into the safety of His shelter, I find myself tripping over my puffed-up pride.

I wonder if that's how Paul felt when he fell on his know-it-all face on his way to persecute the Christians. Blinded by the piercing light, Paul's course was diverted and his perspective changed forever. He leaned into the Savior, denounced his prideful ways, and began to magnify Jesus, saying, "He is the Son of God."

What a difference it makes when, instead of inflating ourselves or trying to exaggerate the faults of others, we exalt the Lord together! "O magnify the LORD with me, and let us exalt His name together" (Ps. 34:3).

28

Altitude
(al´ te tōōd) n.

Dictionary's definition:
Distance upward.

Patsy's definition:
View from our knees.

I'M NOT INTO heights. In fact, I'm a little wary of being five feet tall. With that in mind, imagine how I felt when Les and I bought "Big Bed." That's what we dubbed our stupendous bed after it was delivered to our home.

We purchased Big Bed at an expansive, warehouse-sized store. The vast rooms and vaulted ceilings there swallowed up the enormity of the bed, leading us to believe it could easily be tucked into our modest bedroom.

Les and I saw the bed at home for the first time when we had just flown in from a speaking engagement. We had made arrangements for it to be delivered and set up while we were away. When we walked down the hall toward the bedroom and took it in, we literally took two steps back in shock. Actually, I was appalled. Our bed looked more like a boat—no, make that a battleship. Ol' Ironsides had moored in my room. The iron frame, even with its airy cutout design, looked massive in our petite boudoir.

Heightening our growing dilemma was our giant mattress. We had selected a pillow-topped mattress for comfort, not considering the inches it would add to an already overstated predicament.

After moving the bed around, we finally discovered an angle that would allow us and the bed to be in the room at the same time. Now the challenge was for me to scale Big Bed. When I couldn't just fling myself up onto it, I tried running leaps. I would start in the bathroom and speed toward the bed in an attempt to catapult myself heavenward, only to fall short each time. While I wasn't successful at getting onto the bed, I did manage to entertain my husband and sons with my wild efforts.

Finally, my husband appeared at the doorway holding a step stool. I climbed up onto Big Bed, sat down, and started to giggle. I had never been that close to the ceiling (or Jesus) before. Two things immediately concerned me, though: One was nose bleeds; the other was the ceiling fan. I could just imagine sitting up in bed when the fan was on and getting the ride of my life and a Mohawk haircut at the same time.

Eventually, I adjusted to reaching up to make the bed, to the uphill climb to get into bed, and to the altitude after I arrived. Then I realized how much I enjoyed feeling so . . . so . . . *big.* It was as if I were queen and the rest of the room was my realm. That fantasy fizzled fast, though, when I tried, from my new throne, to give some edicts to my family. They laughed themselves silly.

I've noticed there's something about feeling like a big shot that drastically reduces us in size. The bigger I think I am, the smaller I seem to behave. I guess that's why the Lord warned us against haughtiness. In those moments when we've climbed to great heights, He knows we're susceptible to thinking more highly of ourselves than we should.

Some years ago, I spoke for a ladies' retreat. It was put on by a denomination I hadn't been exposed to before, but one I had nonetheless decided was not very spiritual. I was pleased to be invited and felt I would be able to give them spiritual direction. I knew they would benefit from my insights. Much to my amazement, however, I found them to be far more perceptive, insightful, and spiritual than myself. I wasn't the teacher that weekend; I was the student. I went into the group haughty; I left humbled.

Proverbs 11:2 says, "When pride comes, then comes dishonor, but with the humble is wisdom."

We shouldn't confuse confidence and pridefulness. Confidence comes from a healthy understanding of our worth and capability (see Rom. 12:3). Pridefulness comes from an exaggerated misunderstanding of our worth and capability. Confidence is peaceful; pridefulness is puffed up. Confidence gives credit; pridefulness *takes* credit. Confidence acknowledges supreme authority; pridefulness is its own authority.

I remember that as a teenager, I thought it would be wonderful to escape my parents' authority. Little did I realize what a protection their authority was for my naive and prideful heart. In that same manner, I've learned that being under the Lord's authority protects me—even from my haughty self. When I bend my willful knee before the Lord, He extends to me, like a loving parent, shelter and strength. "The name of the LORD is a strong tower; the righteous runs into it and is safe" (Prov. 18:10).

I ran to a tower once on a Boy Scout reservation, but it wasn't very strong, and neither was I. My friend Edith and I had taken a stroll down to the lake. We came to a towerlike structure with a seat on top for a lifeguard. I decided to scale it, and as I climbed, I informed Edith about some decisions I had made in regard to my future. She cautioned me against being so adamant about my tomorrows. She also wondered if I was sure I wanted to climb the rickety tower. "No problem for me," was my certain reply.

As I ascended onto the chair, I looked down for the first time. That was a mistake. I had more altitude than I knew how to handle. My heart started to do flip-flops, my stomach felt strangely unfamiliar, and a frozen fear descended on me.

Edith, aware of my predicament, began to talk to me gently and reassuringly. She then climbed partway up the ladder and offered her hand. I haltingly moved to the platform's edge and inched my wobbly leg down onto the first rung. Edith supported my foot with her hand to give me the courage to make my next shaky move. Gradually, I made it back down.

If you saw the tower, you would probably laugh at my terrified reaction, for it was fairly modest in size. But you couldn't have convinced my traumatized body or erratic emotions that I hadn't been perched atop the Eiffel Tower. Perhaps that's why Proverbs says "the righteous runs into it [the tower]" and not "on top of it."

On the walk back home that day, I released (again) the tight mental grip I held on my future. I remembered (again) I wasn't ultimately in charge. And I acknowledged (again) that only One should be high and lifted up, and only One can truly guard our lives.

Speaking of guarding, my friend Naomi learned she could neither guard nor control her husband's choices when he became involved with another woman. Naomi had believed her marriage was a model to be emulated. She and her husband had been untouched by hardships and appeared to be the "Cleavers" in their church and neighborhood. But even though she had been approachable, hurting people often failed to connect with her emotionally. Naomi didn't flaunt her family success but rather wore it smugly and mentally criticized others for not having a better grip on their relationships.

Her carefully ordered world fell apart, however, when she discovered her husband had been in a long-term affair. Naomi was devastated by her sense of betrayal. But equally difficult for her was giving up the perfect family picture she had so painstakingly painted.

Eventually, Naomi not only owned her imperfections and her family's, but also she and her husband worked through the betrayal and infidelity to experience deep relational healing. Now she's the first to confess her proud heart (feeling self-righteous) and judgmental spirit prior to the adultery. She knows her husband's behavior was sin, but she also realizes her attitude of superiority toward others had been wrong. Today, people are drawn to Naomi during times of crisis and find they experience empathy and acceptance in her presence.

To gain altitude, we often need an attitude adjustment. That seldom happens when we're strutting, but it usually occurs when we're kneeling. From that low position, when we are contrite before the Lord, He lifts us up.

"Humble yourselves, therefore, under the mighty hand of God, that He may exalt you at the proper time" (1 Pet. 5:6).

29

'Tude Carriers
(tōōd´ care ē erz) n.

Dictionary's definition:
Vessels of grace.

Patsy's definition:
Sportin' His Spirit.

A YOUNG GIRL CLIMBED into the seat next to me at an airport recently. She informed me her name was Victoria, and she had been named after a queen, but I could call her Tory. She studied me for a moment and then asked if I knew my name. How astute of her to realize a woman of my age might not have kept track of such weighty information!

I was immediately smitten by this bright-eyed youngster. She was definitely a 'tude carrier of the finest kind.

Tory regaled me with one story from her life after another. Yet only once did I detect a slightly contentious 'tude. That came when she mentioned a classmate, Theresa. Tory's brown eyes rolled from side to side even at the thought of this girl. It turned out Theresa had stolen two of Tory's boyfriends.

Then a small smile lit up Tory's face as she re lated that her mom had told her two words she should say to Theresa if she ever bothered Tory again. I wasn't sure it was safe to pursue this insight, but before I could decide, Tory clued me in. She said Theresa came back and tried to steal her best friend, and Tory told her to "bug off."

Trying to hold back a major snicker, I asked Tory is those words had worked.

"Yep," she said. "Theresa never bothered me again."

I couldn't help but think how simple life would be if we could rid ourselves once and for all of negative elements by simply saying, "Bug off." How about "Bug off in Jesus' name"? It's sort of a modern ver- sion of "Get thee behind me, Satan." Well, perhaps not.

It's so tempting, like Tory, to want to "give it" to someone who crosses us. But what are we giving them? Yep, our `tude. Sometimes it's tricky to tell if we're establishing a boundary or generating a `tude barrier. Boundaries help educate people in how their relationships with us can be amiable. Mean- while, feisty `tudes alienate others from us, pre- venting closeness.

It's gracious of the Lord to supplement our edu- cation by allowing us to be a part of each other's lives. I find my involvement with others often squeezes out `tudes I didn't even realize I had. I know someone else can't bring out of me something that isn't already there. (Phooey.) We have both negative and positive potential, and often that potential is revealed as we interact with others. This revelation, whether jolting or pleasing, presents us with a more accurate assessment of who we are, which then helps us decide who we want to become.

I passed a mirror the other day and glanced toward it, only to see an essence of my father on my face. It startled me, for I've always thought of myself as looking like my mom.

Even if I wanted to, I can't do a lot, short of surgery, to alter my physical appearance. But I can enhance my outer look by my inner attitudes. We're instructed by the apostle Paul to "have this attitude in yourselves which was also in Christ Jesus." Paul went on to define Jesus' attitude. The Lord "emptied Himself, taking the form of a bond-servant" (Phil. 2:5, 7). Jesus displayed a servi'tude.

A young child will one minute beg to help and the next minute plead to have. A sign of growth is when we increase our "help" 'tudes and decrease our "have" 'tudes. We learn to relinquish our right to call the shots and be in control so we can become more like Christ, to empty ourselves so He might fill us.

My secretary, Jill, remembers going one summer day to Lake Michigan with her husband, Greg, and some friends. The weather was bright, but the winds were brisk. The whitecaps were invitingly exciting. Greg and Jill waded out into the water, but within a short time, she felt intimidated by the threatening waves. She was now in over her head, and in a frantic move, she swam for a nearby buoy and clung to it.

Greg allowed the suddenly-fierce waters to push him back toward land. But Jill refused to let go of the buoy, even though the water was rapidly rising around her. Greg repeatedly yelled to Jill and begged her to let go and allow the waves to carry her to the beach. She persistently held on until she realized that if she didn't take the risk and release her grip, she would drown. In a terrifying moment, she thrust herself toward shore. The turbulent waves took her to safety.

That's how it feels at times to give up our ways and submit to the Lord's—scary and threatening. Yet that act of relinquishment will deliver us from clinging to our negative attitudes and pull us to the safety of His ways. And that brings us full circle, back to our opening chorus:

"Change my heart, O God
Make it ever true.
Change my heart, O God
May I be like you."

As we change, instead of sportin' a 'tude, we can sport His Spirit and become 'tude carriers of the finest kind.